W9-CKQ-559

Euclid Public Library
631 E. 222nd Street
Euclid, Ohio 44123
216-261-5300

THE DAY THE WORLD WAS SHOCKED

THE DAY THE WORLD WAS SHOCKED

THE *LUSITANIA* DISASTER AND ITS INFLUENCE ON THE COURSE OF WORLD WAR I

JOHN PROTASIO

CASEMATE

Philadelphia & Newbury

Published in the United States of America and Great Britain in 2011 by
CASEMATE PUBLISHERS
908 Darby Road, Havertown, PA 19083
and
17 Cheap Street, Newbury RG14 5DD

Copyright 2011 © John Protasio

ISBN 978-1-935149-45-3
Digital Edition: ISBN 978-1-61200-0480

Cataloging-in-publication data is available from the Library of Congress
and the British Library.

All rights reserved. No part of this book may be reproduced or transmitted in
any form or by any means, electronic or mechanical including photocopying,
recording or by any information storage and retrieval system, without
permission from the Publisher in writing.

10 9 8 7 6 5 4 3 2 1

Printed and bound in the United States of America.

For a complete list of Casemate titles please contact:

CASEMATE PUBLISHERS (US)
Telephone (610) 853-9131, Fax (610) 853-9146
E-mail: casemate@casematepublishing.com

CASEMATE PUBLISHERS (UK)
Telephone (01635) 231091, Fax (01635) 41619
E-mail: casemate-uk@casematepublishing.co.uk

CONTENTS

FOREWORD

The enemy submarine slowly and silently crept toward the British ship. Its captain intended to attack without warning, with the goal of sinking or at least disabling the vessel. Though the loss of that particular ship would not win the war, it could incite a wave of fear that would sweep into the hearts and minds of the British.

The time was the American Revolution. The submarine was the American *Turtle,* and the British vessel was HMS *Eagle.* The plan called for the *Turtle* to drill a hole in the bottom of the British warship, and secure an explosive to the hull. However, the drill failed to penetrate the bottom of the *Eagle,* and the *Turtle* had to leave its bomb afloat.[1] Thus the British frigate escaped the attack undamaged, with no casualties.

One hundred and thirty-nine years later, another submarine launched a surprise attack against a British ship. This time the attacking vessel was a German U-boat, and the British ship was a luxury passenger liner—the *Lusitania.* The date was May 7, 1915, the day the world was shocked...

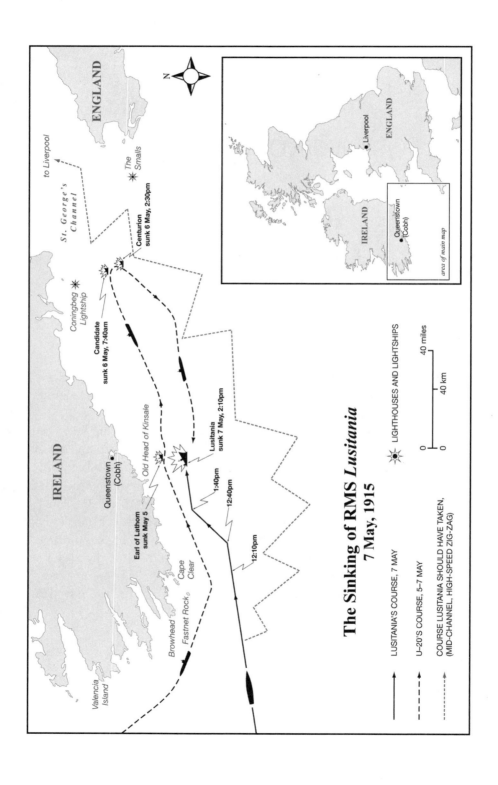

The Sinking of RMS *Lusitania*
7 May, 1915

LUSITANIA'S COURSE, 7 MAY

U–20'S COURSE, 5–7 MAY

COURSE LUSITANIA SHOULD HAVE TAKEN,
(MID-CHANNEL, HIGH-SPEED ZIG-ZAG)

☀ LIGHTHOUSES AND LIGHTSHIPS

0   40 miles

0   40 km

ENGLAND

N

to Liverpool

St. George's Channel

The Smalls

Centurion
sunk 6 May, 2:30pm

Coningbeg
Lightship

Candidate
sunk 6 May, 7:40am

IRELAND

Queenstown
(Cobh)

Old Head of Kinsale

Earl of Lathom
sunk May 5

Lusitania
sunk 7 May, 2:10pm

1:40pm

12:40pm

Valencia
Island

Browhead

Cape
Clear

Fastnet Rock

12:10pm

ENGLAND

Liverpool

IRELAND

Queenstown
(Cobh)

area of main map

CHAPTER 1
"...DO SO AT THEIR OWN RISK"

NOTICE!

TRAVELLERS intending to embark on the Atlantic voyage are reminded that a state of war exists between Germany and her allies and Great Britain and her allies; that the zone of war includes the water adjacent to the British Isles; that, in accordance with formal notice given by the Imperial German Government, vessels flying the flag of Great Britain, or of any of her allies, are liable to destruction in those waters and that travelers sailing in the war zone on ships of Great Britain or her allies do so at their own risk.

IMPERIAL GERMAN EMBASSY
Washington D.C. April 22, 1915[1]

This notice appeared in many of New York City's newspapers. At that time World War I was less than a year old, with all major Western powers involved except the United States of America.

The notice was placed in the shipping section by the German Ambassador to the United States, Count Johann von Bernstorff. He had received instructions from his government to publish the warning earlier in April, but thinking it "a grave mistake" he kept it in a drawer of his desk. When Berlin sent a second message ordering him to publish it, he only did so reluctantly.[2]

Many readers, however, were more interested in the advertisement next to the warning, which read:

CUNARD
EUROPE via LIVERPOOL
LUSITANIA
Fastest and Largest Steamer
Now in Atlantic Service Sails
SATURDAY, MAY 1, 10 A.M.[3]

That Saturday several hundred people, travelers and well-wishers, gathered at New York's Pier 54 at the foot of 11th Street. Though it rained that day, it wasn't enough to dampen the spirits of the travelers. Apparently, neither was the warning printed in the newspapers.

"As for submarines," declared Charles P. Sumner, the Cunard Line's agent in New York, "I have no fear of them whatsoever."[4] Others shared Sumner's feelings. "Another piece of German bluff," concluded Liverpool shippers.[5] The Washington correspondent of the London *Times* called it a piece of "impudent bluff." It was "an insolent attempt to prejudice British commerce," an "infantile effort to make Americans afraid of the non-existent."[6]

Alexander Campbell, general manager of the British distillery John Dewar and Sons, said, "I think it's a lot of tommyrot for any government to do such a thing and it is hard to believe the German Ambassador dictated the advertisement. The *Lusitania* can run away from any submarine the Germans have got and the British Admiralty will see the ship is looked after when she arrives in striking distance of the Irish coast."[7]

When queried by reporters about the German warning, the ship's captain, William Thomas Turner, shrugged, "I wonder what the Germans will do next. Well, it doesn't seem as if they scared many people from going on the ship, by the look of the pier and passenger list."[8]

Captain Turner was right. The *Lusitania* was to carry more passengers on this trip than on most previous voyages since the war broke out. When hostilities were present, the Cunarder typically traveled below her passenger capacity of 2,198;[9] on this voyage she would carry about 1,257. Approximately 290 were traveling in first class, 600 in second class and 367 in third class (steerage). Most of the passengers were British or Canadian. Some 317 were from neutral nations, of which 197 were American.[10]

By far the wealthiest passenger was Alfred Gwynne Vanderbilt, handsome, 37 years old and with assets reported at $70,000,000.[11] Vanderbilt obtained his wealth the easy way—he inherited it. A Yale graduate, he married Ellen (Elsie) French in 1901, but their relations became strained following allegations of adultery, and the couple divorced in 1908. A few years later he married a wealthy divorcee named Margaret Emerson McKim. Vanderbilt enjoyed the sporting life, and owned several automobiles and horses. His interest in horses led him to acquire shares in both the Metropolitan Horse Show, Ltd., of London, and in America's National Horse Show. He in fact was traveling to England to attend a meeting of an international breeders association and to review his property.[12]

People speculated about a skeleton or two in his closet. In 1909, a woman named Mary Agnes Ruiz committed suicide by shooting herself at her house in Grosvenor Street, London. A former actress, she had in 1903 married the wealthy Don Antonio A. Ruiz y Olivares, an attaché of the Cuban Legation in Washington. After three years, they separated and Mrs. Ruiz led a quiet but financially comfortable life in New York. When she was named as a correspondent in the 1908 divorce proceedings by Vanderbilt's first wife, Ruiz divorced her.[13] The following May she killed herself. Rumors circulated that her suicide was the result of dwindling visits from Vanderbilt. Results from the coroner's inquest, said to be riddled with perjury, were never made public "by means of the outlay of a large sum of money."[14] In 1909, the *New York Times* reported that British society considered Vanderbilt "beyond the pale."[15] However, the millionaire managed to survive the scandal.[16]

Another first-class passenger on this voyage was Elbert Hubbard, the wildly popular author of *A Message to Garcia*, which had sold more than 40 million copies. After a successful career in business, Hubbard became perhaps the most important proponent of the Arts and Crafts

Movement in America. Modeled on William Morris' Kelmscott Press, he founded the Roycroft Press to produce finely handcrafted books. He called himself "Fra Elbertus," and edited the monthly magazines *The Fra* and *The Philistine*. A community of several hundred artists and craftspeople producing pottery, furniture and other carefully handmade objects eventually grew out of the Hubbards' publishing endeavors.[17] He also wrote *Little Journeys*, monthly sketches of places he had visited in England and, eventually, biographical sketches of famous people.[18]

Like Vanderbilt, Hubbard was divorced and into his second marriage. Hubbard's first wife, Bertha, was a trustee of the local school in East Aurora, New York. As was customary, she invited the new teacher and suffragist Alice Moore to live with them. In 1894 Alice bore Hubbard a daughter, Miriam. In 1901 Bertha sued for divorce, and public knowledge of Hubbard's affair and illegitimate child created a storm of disapproval. Hubbard and Alice Moore married in 1904. In that day divorce was almost unheard of, making Hubbard the center of controversy.[19]

Hubbard became controversial again in 1913 when he was convicted of misusing the postal service by sending objectionable material—his magazine *The Philistine*—through the mails; on this count he was fined $100. This felony conviction prevented him from obtaining a passport, so he requested a pardon from President Wilson, which was granted a short time before the voyage on the *Lusitania*.[20]

Hubbard was eager to go to Europe now that war was on. Although he respected the German people for their science and music, Hubbard placed responsibility for the outbreak of hostilities squarely on the shoulders of the German Kaiser. Wilhelm II, Hubbard wrote, "... has a withered hand and running ear, a shrunken soul and mind reeking with egomania." The German emperor "is swollen, like a drowned pup, with pride that stinks," Hubbard concluded. The American editor was eager to see firsthand the havoc unleashed by the Kaiser, perhaps to justify his own strident views.[21]

He did not expect to be welcomed in Germany. Hubbard told a reporter that the Kaiser might want "to make me look like a piece of Swiss cheese," but in reality he took some satisfaction in courting death by way of a German submarine. "To be torpedoed would be a glorious way to peter out, but it would be a good advertisement."[22] As for the

Kaiser, he said, referring to one of the islands where Napoleon Bonaparte was exiled, "if he wanted to see me this time I'll wait until after the war and visit him at St. Helena."[23]

Hubbard wasn't the only American on the *Lusitania* anxious to see the war. Justus Forman, a 41-year-old writer, also traveled in first class. Forman had recently turned to writing plays, including *The Hyphen*, a controversial play which examined the loyalty of German-Americans in their adopted country. Now a special correspondent for the *New York Times*, he intended to go to France to report on the war.

The theater world was also represented by Charles Klein, a successful playwright whose hits included *The Lion and the Mouse*. It was his intention to introduce Justus Forman to some theater people in London.[24]

The internationally respected producer, 54-year-old Charles Frohman, boarded the *Lusitania* keenly anticipating his annual trip to Marlow, a quiet village he loved outside London.[25] Frohman had begun his career as a night clerk for the *New York Graphic* newspaper and at 17 entered theater management. In 1881 he bought the rights to the road productions of *Shenandoah*, and by 1915 had produced more than 500 plays,[26] with a payroll that included no fewer than 700 thespians. Among his shows were *Rosy Rapture, The Pride of the Beauty Chorus*, and *Peter Pan*. The last was too great a gamble for other producers, who dismissed the play as a waste of time. Much to his credit, Frohman saw its potential and risked producing it—on both sides of the Atlantic. Although his most recent and pioneering venture, *The Hyphen*, had failed commercially, he loved the work and had invited Justus Forman to join him on this trip.[27]

Frohman traveled first class on the *Lusitania*, but daily he lived a simple life, rarely patronizing expensive restaurants or hotels. "Charlie does things differently," a friend of his explained. He formed close friendships, never took a curtain call and lived privately.[28]

In the spring of 1915, Frohman owned some 60 theaters in Britain and the United States. He knew the risk involved in traveling aboard the *Lusitania,* as did his friend, the actor John Drew. Drew telegrammed Frohman, "I'll never forgive you if you get blown up by a submarine." To another friend, actor Paul Potter, Frohman was dismissive of the risk. "Aren't you afraid of the U-boats, C.F.?" asked Potter. "No, I'm only afraid of IOUs" the theater manager flippantly replied.[29]

Oliver Bernard, a theatrical designer, read the warning from the German Embassy in his newspaper while breakfasting at the Knickerbocker Hotel. Bernard was "not seriously perturbed nor quite sure that this warning was entirely another bluff to embarrass the United States Government and create further consternation in England." He believed that the presence of so many Americans on board, coupled with the speed of the liner, would reduce the likelihood of submarine attack to "zero."[30] He was going to England to enlist.

Certain British subjects were also traveling in first class. At 59, Welsh industrialist David Alfred Thomas had many investments in the New World, including the mining interests in Pennsylvania that he and his daughter had just inspected. He was also beginning a barge service on the Mississippi and expanding his Canadian railroad operations. Thomas had served 20 years in Parliament as a member of the Liberal Party, where he championed the causes of the poor and the working class.[31]

Accompanying Thomas was his daughter, Margaret Lady Mackworth. Margaret was brought up in the wealthy Thomas household where she listened to her father's daily accounts of business transactions. She eventually married Humphrey Mackworth, a neighbor and heir to a baronetcy. The marriage proved unhappy, and turned Margaret to social causes that included joining the Woman's Social and Political Union, an organization that pushed for women's suffrage. This led to her arrest in 1913 for burning Post Office mail and a sentence of one month in prison.[32] Margaret's hunger strike persuaded officials to release her after five days.

Another passenger was Sir Hugh Lane, an Anglo-Irish art collector responsible for founding Dublin's Municipal Gallery of Modern Art in 1908. An important collector of Impressionist art, he "persuaded leading artists of the day to donate a representative work to form the nucleus of the collection, as well as personally financing many acquisitions including a number of major Impressionist masterpieces."[33] Returning home with valuable paintings, Lane was cheerful and confident he would arrive home safely in spite of his poor health. He considered the submarine threat "too absurd for discussion."[34]

Sir Hugh wasn't the only one in poor health. Lieutenant Fred

Lassetter, an Australian on medical leave from his Scottish regiment, was returning to England after visiting relatives in Los Angeles.[35] His mother, Elizabeth, accompanied him.

Doris Maud Charles, soon to be married, was traveling with her father, John H. Charles, a book dealer in their home city of Toronto who had in his possession valuable manuscripts.[36] Doris was awed by the size of the *Lusitania* and said she felt "something new" in her life.[37]

Some of the passengers had war-related business. Among them was Madame Marie Depage, wife and colleague of Dr. Antoine Depage, a royal surgeon, head of the Belgian Red Cross, and, with Queen Elizabeth of Belgium, founder and director of the military Hospital l'Océan at De Panne in Flanders. After experiencing the shortage of medical supplies at the hospital in Flanders firsthand, Marie went alone to the United States to raise money for the Belgian Red Cross.[38] She intended to take an earlier ship home, the *Lapland*, but a last-minute speaking engagement prevented this, so she booked her return to Europe on the *Lusitania*. She had spoken to her audience of the horrors of war, a topic that had personal resonance since one of her sons was serving on the Western Front and another would soon report for duty.[39]

Another first-class passenger, George A. Kessler—a legendary wine merchant from New York—carried with him $2 million in stocks. In 1902, according to author Kolleen M. Guy in *When Champagne Became French*, Kessler, "Moët & Chandon's agent in the United States, created an enormous stir in both the American and European press when he managed to substitute a bottle of his firm's champagne for a bottle of German sparkling wine at the highly publicized launching of the German emperor's new yacht, the *Meteor*, in New York."[40] Thus began the tradition of christening ships with champagne. Four years later, "with touching concern for human suffering," he donated an entire boxcar of champagne to those affected by the San Francisco earthquake.[41]

Chicago businessman and brewery manufacturer, Charles A. Plamondon, wanted to establish a foothold in Europe before Prohibition dried up his business prospects in the U.S.[42] His wife, Mary, decided to accompany him on the trip, perhaps to celebrate their wedding anniversary on May 6th.[43] Charles E. Lauriat, Jr., also expected to do business in Europe. He worked for his family's bookselling firm, which had offices in Boston and London. This was his 23rd crossing, but his first on a liner as fast as the *Lusitania*.[44]

A number of children traveled on the *Lusitania*. Nursemaid Alice Lines cared for a three-month-old baby and three siblings aged year and a half, two and a half, and five. Four-year-old Cecil Richards was with his parents, older brother and 20-month-old sister. Eight-year-old Edith Williams, along with her five brothers and sisters, were accompanying their mother back to England after being deserted by their father.[45] One youngster, W.G.E. Meyers, could not really be considered a "boy." This 16-year-old Canadian expected to enlist in the Royal Navy once he arrived in England.

Two natives of Ireland, Florence and Julia Sullivan, traveled second class. Flor, thanks to Julia's childless employers who had virtually adopted her, worked as a bartender at New York's Stuyvesant Club, where he had regular contact with wealthy urbanites. Flor's father had requested that Flor and Julia come home to run the family farm, but the couple could never find the time. However, when Flor's father died and the family risked losing their farm, they decided to return to Ireland and claim their inheritance.[46]

Margaret Cox, another Irish woman traveling second class on the *Lusitania*, had been living in Winnipeg with her infant son Desmond. Since Desmond was weak and recovering from whooping cough, his mother thought it was the right time to return home.

A pair of newlyweds also boarded the liner. Harold and Lucy Taylor had planned to take a lesser ship until, as a wedding gift, a relative paid the difference for them to take the *Lusitania*. Lucy did not want people to know she'd just gotten married, but confetti dropping from her clothes revealed their secret.

In third class, Elizabeth Duckworth was making her way back home. She had worked in cotton weaving, but now, at 52, she found herself homesick and eager to return to England. Duckworth took a trolley to New London and from there a train to New York, where she boarded the Cunarder with her two straw suitcases. Her son-in-law had warned her that the voyage was too dangerous, but Duckworth stubbornly insisted on making the journey.[47]

Duckworth apparently wasn't deterred by the Germans' warning in the newspaper, but neither were many other passengers. As Charles

Lauriat later said, "I did not think any human being with a drop of red blood in his veins, called a man, could issue an order to sink a passenger steamer without at least giving the women and children a chance to get away."[48]

Others felt the Cunarder's speed would give them protection from U-boats. "We can outdistance any submarine afloat," Alfred Vanderbilt flatly declared.[49] This was an accurate statement; the *Lusitania* could easily run at 25 knots, compared to German submarines that could make 15 knots on the surface and only about 9 knots submerged. Other passengers agreed. "We heard rumors that the *Lusitania* was going to be sunk by the Germans, which we thought was the most ridiculous thing we ever heard," recalled a passenger. "We kind of laughed it off," said another. One passenger thought it was "sacrilegious" that the Germans would sink such a ship.[50]

The ship's master, Captain Turner, shared this view. "Do you think all these people would be booking passage on board the *Lusitania* if they thought she could be caught by a German submarine?" Turner told reporters, "Why, it's the best joke I've heard in many days, this talk of torpedoing!"[51]

On the surface, Turner seemed to have complete confidence in the *Lusitania's* safety, perhaps the outcome of long experience. He first went to sea at the age of 13, serving on the windjammer *White Star*, then sailed on the *Queen of Nations* with his father in command. He joined the Cunard Line in 1878 as third officer of the *Cherbourg*. One day the *Cherbourg* collided with a barque in foggy weather. The barque sank, drowning the pilot and four crewmembers, but Turner jumped into a boat and saved a man and a boy from the sinking ship. In 1885 he saved another life, and in so doing received the Shipwreck and Humane Society's Silver Medal for leaping into the icy water at Liverpool to rescue a boy who had fallen in.

Turner rose through the ranks of Cunard slowly. He won command of the *Aleppo* in 1903 and eventually received command of the *Lusitania* and then the *Aquitania*. With the illness of the regular captain of the *Lusitania*, David "Paddy" Dow, Turner was once again at the *Lusitania's* helm.[52]

Turner found problems with the number and quality of the crew. With the advent of World War I, many of the regular crewmembers went to serve in the Royal Navy; this meant that six of her boilers would make a wartime voyage cold. Fewer boilers reduced the Cunarder's top speed to only 21 knots—though still faster than any U-boat.

Because the submarine menace concerned all British vessels, Captain Turner received some instructions directly from the Admiralty. These were "suggestions" rather than orders, although officials at the Admiralty no doubt trusted they would be carried out to the letter. They instructed Turner to avoid land and steer a mid-channel course. He was to zigzag at top speed during a submarine alert, and maintain wireless silence when approaching the British Isles. One part of the Admiralty's instructions would prove significant to German apologists later: the instruction to ram enemy submarines if possible.

Shortly before sailing, Captain Turner was summoned to the British Consulate. Turner briskly made his way to the Consulate, believing that the sailing would be cancelled due to the German warning, or that sailing orders would be changed. Sir Courtenay Bennett greeted the Captain.

"Is something the matter, Sir Courtenay?" Turner asked, "Is it about the German warning?"

"Not really," Bennett answered, "We regard the warning as serious but, of course, it will not affect your sailing." The Consul informed Turner that his course would be the same as his last crossing, and gave the master mariner his code and wireless signals. Turner returned to his command satisfied that everything was under control; he would sail after all. The Captain decided that in spite of any concerns to the contrary, he would not let any lingering apprehension affect the passengers.[53]

Turner's officers also had to mask any personal worries about German threats. Staff Captain John Anderson had been with the company for a number of years. First Officer Arthur Jones was considered competent, as was Second Officer Hefford. One junior officer, Albert Bestic, had been brought up on sail and took pride in being a part of the *Lusitania's* crew. Other members of the crew felt fortunate to serve on the Cunarder. George Wynne and his father, Joseph, worked in the ship's galleys. Seventeen-year-old George had always wanted to serve on a luxury liner and came recommended by his friend Charles Westbury, the second cook.

Another young man who had long dreamed of serving on a luxury liner, Benjamin Holton, was a bellboy. He had once worked as a clerk in Liverpool and during lunch breaks would go to the piers to watch liners arrive and depart. Holton finally got his coveted job on the *Lusitania*. Later, he recalled a day when he and another boy went down to a storeroom and discovered rats scampering about, whereupon Holton took out his air rifle and began shooting at them. A seaman heard the shots and reported the two. For this stunt Holton and the other boy raked ashes in the stokehold for a while.[54]

Some seamen signed on at the last minute. Leslie Morton and his brother John had originally booked passage on the steamer *Naiad*, wanting to return home to England. Leslie had cabled his father requesting money for the tickets, but when the money arrived the brothers soon realized a better opportunity presented itself—being hired as deckhands for the *Lusitania*. They were approached by one of *Lusitania's* officers.

"What are you boys looking at?" he asked. They told him that they were planning to go on as passengers.

"What ship are you off?"

"Oh, we have just paid off a full-rigged ship and are coming home to take our examinations."

"I thought you looked like seamen. Why do you want to come home in *Lusitania* paying your fare? We have had ten of our deck hands run away this trip in New York, we suspect it is the threat of conscription coming in at home. They don't like the idea. I could use two boys like you."

Leslie Morton replied, "I think there could be more Sir. Some of our other shipmates have paid off."

"Well, be down here tomorrow morning with as many as you can get. We are sailing in forty-eight hours."

Morton and his brother returned to the *Naiad* and told their shipmates of the offer. In all, eight men from the *Naiad* joined the crew of the Cunarder.[55]

With her speed, *Lusitania* appeared to be destined for a safe crossing, since no ship faster than 15 knots had so far been sunk by a German submarine. Cunard officials made every effort to calm prospective passengers. When Charles Lauriat bought his ticket in Boston he was assured that "every precaution will be taken."[56] Similarly, when the ecclesiastical author Reverend Charles Cowley Clarke asked if there was any risk he was told, "No, none so far as I know. The Cunard Company is not likely to risk a ship of such enormous value if there was any danger."[57]

Some passengers received anonymous warnings. Alfred Vanderbilt was given a message that read, "Have it on definite authority that the *Lusitania* is to be torpedoed. You had better cancel passage immediately."[58] The note was simply signed "Morte" (death).[59] Charles Frohman received anonymous letters as well.

There were those who did cancel their passage. Edward B. Bowen, a wealthy shoe dealer, telephoned his travel agent and told him he wasn't going, later explaining he had a vague feeling that something was going to happen to the *Lusitania*. Al Woods and his friend Walter Moore also cancelled their trip, worried about the German threat. Woods was a theatrical manager and had reserved a stateroom next to Charles Klein. John McFadden, a millionaire from Philadelphia who had made his fortune trading cotton, had booked passage on the *Lusitania*, but cancelled it after having a premonition of disaster."[60]

On the pier men were handing out leaflets, cautioning people against sailing. One person who received a leaflet was Alice Lines, the family nurse to Surgeon-Major Frederic Warren Pearl and his wife, Amy Lea. Mrs. Pearl told Alice, "Take no notice, dear. It's just propaganda."[61]

While Cunard officials had every confidence the liner would not be torpedoed, there did exist the risk of sabotage. To minimize this danger, a purser and a Cunard agent screened each piece of passenger luggage, which slowed down the boarding.[62] The *Cameronia*, another passenger steamship, caused further delay. At the last minute she was taken over by the Admiralty, and 41 of her passengers had to be transferred to the *Lusitania* causing a two-hour delay.

The well-known feminist architect Theodate Pope was also aboard, on her way from Farmington, Connecticut to visit the British Society for Psychical Research, in the company of Edwin Friend, a member of the American society. She regretted that she didn't have an extra two hours with her mother, who had left the *Lusitania* when they called "all ashore."[63]

Oddly enough, the American passenger liner *New York* was scheduled to leave New York for Liverpool the same day as the *Lusitania*. She had vacant accommodations for 300 passengers, more than enough for all the Americans who had booked on the *Lusitania*. It needs to be understood that since the United States had formally declared herself to be neutral, the Germans at this time had no intention of sinking American ships. James Gerard, American ambassador to Germany, had wired the State Department on February 20, 1915, stating that the Germans had requested silhouettes and other data about American liners.[64] In hindsight, it appears obvious that the safer alternative would have been to book passage on the *New York* rather than the British liner, but as one passenger recalled, "no one believed that the *Lusitania* could sink."[65]

An interesting incident caused some stokers to jump ship. Dowie, a black cat and stoker mascot, had attempted on three occasions to flee. The day before the liner was scheduled to sail, the cat managed to run down a hawser and disappeared into the night. Some of the "black gang"—stokers—saw this as a bad omen, and followed Dowie's example.

While in New York harbor, the '"neutrality squad" watched over the *Lusitania* day and night to ensure that ships' agents adhered to the neutrality regulations set by President Wilson. Before departing, the Collector of the Port Dudley Field Malone conducted a final, thorough inspection of the ship.[66] They looked for guns or evidence of any attempt to mount guns. These people were also responsible for preventing any illegal merchandise from leaving port. Finding none, they gave the liner a clean bill of health.[67]

Thus at 12:30 p.m. on May 1, 1915, the great luxury liner *Lusitania* departed New York harbor. She carried a cargo that included furs, sheet brass, cheese, beef, copper, machinery and some two hundred barrels of oysters from Long Island Sound. Later, it was revealed that 4,200 cases of rifle ammunition (4.2 million rounds) and 1,250 cases of reportedly empty shrapnel shells were also stored below.[68]

Amid the crowds of onlookers at pier 54 that afternoon, several reporters took both still photos and motion pictures of the *Lusitania* as she sailed from New York on her 201st voyage. Certainly some wondered if it would be her last.

CHAPTER 2
RIVALRY ON
THE ATLANTIC

The *Lusitania's* origins went as far back as the early 19th century. Following the British capture of the American, square-rigged *White Oak* during the War of 1812, the ship was put up for auction in Halifax and bought by Samuel Cunard, a Nova Scotian born in 1787. He put the vessel on the Boston to Liverpool trade in 1813 with good accommodations for passengers, and in time the *White Oak* became profitable.[1] The British Admiralty soon provided Cunard with a contract for "sailing vessels on His Majesty's mails between Halifax and Newfoundland, Boston and Bermuda" at his own risk. Soon afterwards, Cunard had more than 40 vessels fulfilling this contract.[2]

His father Abraham retired shortly after the war, and Abraham Cunard & Son became S. Cunard and Company. Samuel tried his hand at whaling, but after three unsuccessful expeditions abandoned the idea. He then turned his attention to lumber, acquiring timber rights to a section of New Brunswick. He sent his brothers Joseph and Henry to establish the business, but in time Henry gave up on it and went into farming. Joseph stayed with it, and eventually built a successful lumber and shipbuilding empire under the banner Joseph Cunard and Company.[3]

Meanwhile Samuel expanded his shipping business. He obtained a contract with the East India Company and began transporting tea from

India to Nova Scotia. Cunard soon had one of the biggest teahouses in the world.

In 1829, two men by the names of Ross and Primrose wrote to Cunard urging him to consider building steamships. This was a bold idea in 1829, to which Cunard replied, "We have received your letter of the twenty-second instant. We are entirely unacquainted with the cost of a steamboat, and would not like to end up in a business of which we are quite ignorant. Must therefore decline taking part in one you propose getting up."[4]

Yet within a few months Samuel Cunard would reconsider: "Steamers properly built and manned might start and arrive at their destination with the punctuality of railway trains on land ... the day will surely come when an ocean steamer will be signaled from Citadel Hill every day in the year."[5]

Ten years later, in 1839, the British government put out a request for steamers to deliver mail between England, Halifax, and New York. Cunard, at the time ignorant of the request, travelled to London to seek backers to build a fleet of steamers. While there, he learned of the government request through social contacts; two of those contacts, James Melvill, former secretary of the East India Company, and William Parry, who had contacts with the Admiralty, offered their complete assistance.[6]

Parry tried to convince shipbuilders to build steamers, but wasn't able to generate much interest. Turning to Cunard, he suggested he bid on the mail route. The timing was right for Cunard and he went ahead with a bid, offering "to furnish steamboats of not less than 300 horsepower to convey the mails from a point in England to Halifax and back twice each month." He pledged to have the ships ready by May 1, 1840, for the subsidy of £55,000 per anum. The contract was awarded to Cunard.[7]

The people of Halifax were overjoyed by the news. "You have, sir," said one of them to Cunard, "on all occasions been anxious liberally to encourage and forward ... the prosperity of this your native land." Cunard replied, "Having embarked so largely in this enterprise I need not assure you that every exertion will be used on my part to carry into effect the intentions of the Government ... but did I require anything to stimulate me to renewed exertion it would have been the approbation of my fellow townsmen: the warm manner in which they have hailed this undertaking assures me of its success."[8]

Cunard set out to plan for the construction of the vessels, telling his agent in Glasgow, "I shall require one or two steamboats of 300 horsepower and about 800 tons. I shall want these vessels to be of the very best description, plain, and comfortable, not the least unnecessary expense for show. I prefer plain woodwork in the cabin, and it will save a large amount in cost."[9] Some friction soon developed. The shipbuilder in charge wanted changes to the vessels, which would cost an extra £2,000 for each ship. However, after a long talk, Cunard and the designer reached a compromise. The steamboats reached completion and once the vessels were afloat both mail and passengers were able to travel heedless of the wind.

The Cunard Line soon expanded its fleet, and through the years the ships became progressively larger and faster. The Line also employed only the best in personnel. As Mark Twain explained,

> The Cunard people would not take Noah himself as first mate till they had worked him up themselves all the lower grades and tried him ten years or such matter. They make every officer serve an apprenticeship under their eyes in their own ships before they advance him or trust him. ... It takes them about ten or fifteen years to manufacture a captain; but when they have got him manufactured to suit at last, they have full confidence in him. The only order they give the captain is this, brief and to the point: "Your ship is loaded, take her, speed is nothing; follow your own road, deliver her safe, bring her back safe—safety is all that is required."[10]

In time, the pressure to deliver passengers, mail and cargo on schedule compromised safety. Some captains, including those of the Cunard Line, would run at top speed in fog- and iceberg-infested waters. Later, during World War I, some captains chose to ignore the need for evasive maneuvers in order to avoid any extra fuel consumption. One observer noted that Samuel Cunard "thought in services when other people thought in ships." "Never in advance of the time," someone declared, "but never far behind them, never experimenting, but always ready to adopt any improvement thoroughly tested by others."[11]

When Samuel Cunard died, the Cunard Steamship Company was more willing to risk innovation. One of these innovations was installing electric lamps. In 1884, the *Armbria* was launched with this improvement, followed by the *Etruria* in 1885. Cunard official John Burns said at *Etruria's* launching, "The company which reduces the time in crossing the Atlantic ... will ensure success in the long run. There is no courage in entering upon great enterprises in prosperous time, but I have faith in the future, and confidence that the Cunard Company will hold its own upon the Atlantic."[12]

The Cunard Line faced many rivals in the 19th century. Among them was the Collins Line, an American shipping company. Given a generous subsidy from Congress, Collins built some of the finest passenger steamers of the day. The *Arctic*, built in 1850, was an especially popular transatlantic vessel. Passengers were spared the discomfort of cold weather by an elaborate system that distributed heat from the boilers to various parts of the ship. The grand saloon, filled with magnificent mirrors, carpets, armchairs, sofas and other luxuries, rivaled Cunard's ships. One passenger described the *Arctic* as "worthy of Neptune."

The *Arctic* was impressive in other ways. Measuring 284 feet from bow to stern and registered at 3,500 tons, the Collins liner had the distinction of being the second largest vessel in the world. The liner was also noted for her speed—she was a side-wheeler that could make 13 knots. In February 1852 the S.S. *Arctic* set an eastbound Atlantic crossing record by arriving in Liverpool from New York in just under 10 days.[13]

Unfortunately, on September 27, 1854, she encountered fog on her way to New York and at 12:15 in the afternoon the French steamer *Vesta* rammed into the *Arctic's* starboard side. The *Vesta* survived but she had fatally punctured the *Arctic* in several places below the waterline. Her captain, James Luce, attempted a dash toward land to beach his command, but the liner sank and 350 of the 435 people on board were lost, including every woman and child.[14] In 1856, just two years after the *Arctic* disaster, another Collins liner, the *Pacific*, vanished without a single survivor. Experts speculated that she had struck an iceberg off Newfoundland.[15]

Cunard's rivalry with the Collins Line came to an end soon afterward when Congress cut the latter's subsidy, leaving Collins unable to operate at a profit. In February of 1858, the last three Collins ships were sold at a fraction of their value.[16]

Other competing ships followed. A famous British vessel built in 1858, the *Great Eastern*, registered at an unheard of 19,000 tons, displaced 32,160 tons and measured nearly 700 feet long—the largest ship afloat at the time. She was the genius of Isambard Kingdom Brunel, a renowned Victorian engineer who spared nothing to make this ship the best in the world. The first double-hulled iron ship, the *Great Eastern* had a second hull 34 inches inside her outer hull, joined by a network of braces. She was divided into 16 watertight compartments by 15 transverse bulkheads. The liner also had two longitudinal bulkheads that gave her a total of 40 watertight compartments.[17] As maritime historian Walter Lord has noted, Brunel was cautious: "The *Great Eastern*'s bulkheads were carried 30 feet above the waterline; the Titanic's, only 10 feet."[18]

This system of safety paid off. On August 27, 1862, the *Great Eastern* experienced a serious accident. Heading for New York with 820 passengers onboard, she struck a rock, a collision that left her with a gash 82 feet long and 9 feet wide. As planned, she did not go down and was still able to limp to New York under her own power.[19]

By the late 19th century, the rivalry on the Atlantic had grown fierce. No fewer than 11 shipping lines competed for business, mostly for the immigration trade and the government mail subsidies. Thomas Ismay founded the White Star Line, with a view to operating ships on the Atlantic trade.[20] His company experienced several setbacks such as the loss of the *Atlantic* in 1873, but continued to compete aggressively with Cunard.

With this struggle for maritime supremacy, ships became faster and larger. The *Olympic* of the White Star Line measured 882½ feet in length and was registered at more than 46,000 tons; a triple screw, she could make 24 to 25 knots. She completed her maiden voyage in 1911 and was an instant success.[21]

In the first decade of the 20th century, a major development in transatlantic passenger service arose when the great financier J. P. Morgan began to form a trust company by buying up shipping companies engaged in the Atlantic trade. He devoted his energies to this task with the same ruthlessness he brought to railroads. One by one the "Morgan combine" absorbed the shipping companies of Great Britain and the United States into the International Mercantile Marine Company.[22] The combine incorporated the great White Star Line.

However, Morgan encountered problems with the German companies. Albert Ballin, chairman of the Hamburg-Amerika line, had responded positively to Morgan's offer for 51 percent of the company, but Kaiser Wilhelm II, concerned Germany would lose control of these large ships, which were built as "auxiliary cruisers," made it known he did not favor the transaction.[23] Morgan asked Ballin to speak with the Kaiser in 1902. During conversations he presented an agreement to buy a majority interest in the two largest German shipping companies, with assurances to Wilhelm that the operational independence of his country's shipping lines would remain intact.[24] The Kaiser read the agreement with interest and, in the end, gave his approval.[25]

This put the Cunard Line in a precarious situation. The chairman of the company, Lord Inverclyde, decided to resist Morgan. Though the Morgan combine offered a tempting £18 per share for 55 percent of the stock, Inverclyde felt that the proposal was inadequate. He applied to the British government for help to remain independent. This impressed the first lord of the Admiralty, Lord Selborne. He told Inverclyde that "when such vast issues are at stake a patriotic company is bound to keep its Government informed as you have hitherto done." Cunard's chairman insisted, however, that his shareholders wanted help soon.[26]

Some people suggested that forming an "anti-combine" to counter the Morgan shipping trust might be effective. Inverclyde was against this course of action, but was informed explicitly by Selborne that only three options remained: fight the Morgan combine with government assistance, join the combine, or join a British anti-combine.

Inverclyde told the British government that the Cunard Line faced "absorption or annihilation." "Frankly," he declared impatiently, "I think the time has come when you should say what you intend to do with regard to the Cunard Company and not continue on the present indefinite course." He bluntly told the government in London, "If you do not intend to make any arrangement with us but prefer to work with somebody else I would much rather that you would say so and let us know where we are." Inverclyde pointed out that Cunard shareholders were growing edgy and the company's directors needed to act soon.[27] Meanwhile, the British press grew increasingly hostile to the "Morgan threat." One newspaper, with the headline "License to Remain on Earth," attacked Morgan and accused him of trying to buy up Britain.

In the end the British government acted. It gave Cunard a £2,6000,000 loan at an interest rate of 2¾ percent, to be paid in 20 annual installments. The company also received £150,000 annually for maintenance, in addition to their mail subsidy. In return, Cunard was to remain an exclusively British concern and, in case of war, its ships would be at the government's disposal.[28] The Cunard Line would also build two vessels to serve as passenger liners in peacetime and act as auxiliary cruisers during war. They were to be named the *Mauretania* and the *Lusitania*.

CHAPTER 3
THE LUXURY LINER/
AUXILIARY CRUISER

The Cunard Line wanted the *Lusitania* and her sister ship the *Mauretania* to be among the best luxury liners in the world, but the two ships also had to meet Admiralty specifications as auxiliary cruisers. The shipbuilders they chose had to meet very exacting standards, and be equipped for the challenge. In the end, Cunard commissioned Swan, Hunter & Wigham Richardson, Ltd., to build the *Mauretania*, and awarded the contract for the *Lusitania* to John Brown & Company of Glasgow.

John Brown & Company, a Sheffield steel manufacturer founded in 1859, had acquired the highly respected J & G Thomson Shipbuilding and Engineering Company and its Clydebank shipyard in 1899. The shipyard's unique position at the mouth of the River Cart provided the ideal environment to build heavier, large-scale ships. John Brown then allied itself with the Norfolk Works of Thomas Firth & Sons, a company that specialized in turbine machinery. They later acquired a large interest in several armor and ordnance companies. As a result, by the turn of the 20th century John Brown was, in the words of *Engineering* magazine, "an organization so comprehensive that they can produce, complete for service, every type of warship and merchant vessel with all accessories."[1]

The steel and other metals used in the construction of the *Lusita-*

31

nia were produced by John Brown's Atlas Works in Sheffield, a company that occupied roughly 36 acres of land. The Works included some 43 furnaces burning an estimated "400 tons of coal and 100 tons of coke each day of the year." It boasted ten hydraulic presses, one of which wielded an incredible 10,000 tons of power. The organization had 94 traveling cranes, some with the capacity to move 150 tons, and its own system of locomotives.[2]

The Atlas Works increased considerably in size from the time of its founding in 1856 to the eventual construction of the *Lusitania*. The land area grew twelvefold. The budget increased from £30,000 to £3,000,000 annually, and the company increased its output from 5,000 to 1,000,000 tons per year by the early 20th century. The company's staff had expanded to about 20,000 workers by 1907.[3]

Brown & Co. constructed the *Lusitania* in their shipyard on the River Clyde near Glasgow, where since 1873 the firm had produced both commercial vessels and warships. The yard began with sloops of war, and ultimately made some of the biggest battleships and cruisers the world had known. *Engineering* magazine concluded that "the managers and staff have accumulated an experience which enables them to undertake naval work with the assurance of absolute success . . ."[4]

Initially the Cunard Line and its naval architect, Leonard Peskett, envisioned the new passenger liners with three funnels. However, since four smokestacks symbolized power and provided additional venting for exhaust, they added a fourth funnel to each ship. Other models were developed in the early stages of design and tested in the experimental tank at Clydebank shipyard. Careful study led to decisions about the proper dimensions for various parts of the ship.[5]

The Cunard Line turned its attention to the question of engines for the two new liners—whether to use reciprocating engines or turbine. The latter offered speed, but the economics of the relatively new turbine engine were uncertain. So the line appointed a committee of experts to consider the matter, including James Bain, Cunard's Marine Superintendent; Engineer Rear-Admiral H. J. Oram of the Royal Navy and others. After careful study, the committee recommended turbine engines, which had achieved considerable success on Cunard's *Carmania*, a liner that reached a speed of 20 knots.[6]

The turbine engine chosen was of the Parsons type, known for its immense size. The rotor-drum of the high-pressure turbine was 140 inches, with blades that ranged in size from 2½ to 22 inches. To accommodate them and fulfill Admiralty specifications, the main propelling and auxiliary machinery were situated in nine different watertight compartments.[7]

The number of propellers the new liners would need had yet to be decided. Most large passenger steamers around 1910 were twin-screw, a typical example being the *Lucania*, which wielded 30,000 horsepower. However, four propellers powered many destroyers in the Royal Navy. Since these ships performed well in sea trials, Cunard decided that the *Lusitania* and *Mauretania* would be quadruple-screw. The sterns would be designed with two inner screws forward of the rudder, and two additional propellers positioned about 70 feet to stern.

To achieve high speeds, the propellers had to turn at a rapid rate. Engineers had adopted high rotating speeds in smaller boats, and it was decided that the same must hold for the *Lusitania*. Thus, the screws would rotate at 185 revolutions or more per minute.

The new liner required a great deal of steel, so John Brown conducted tests to select the most suitable type. The *Lusitania*'s hull would undergo tremendous stress traveling through high seas; calculations showed that the hull plates could experience stress of 10 tons per square inch.[8] Furthermore, since the liner would serve as an auxiliary cruiser for the Royal Navy during times of war, the designers chose high-tensile steel an inch thick for the hull plates.[9]

The armor of this auxiliary cruiser represented the steady progress underway toward tougher plating for warships. John Brown had fabricated armor plating for the Royal Navy since 1853, pioneering the process of welding a succession of bars together in 1873 for the warship *Dreadnought*. Then the German company Krupp entered the field and developed a superior method to produce armor plating. John Brown & Co. followed suit.[10] They armored *Lusitania* with an alloy of iron and other metals. Atlas ran the plates through high temperatures in a furnace and then reheated them in such a manner as to make them extremely tough. Placed in "cementation" furnaces, the plates' surfaces would absorb additional carbon that charcoal liberated as it was heated. Sudden cooling hardened the carbon-enhanced surfaces to create harder, fatigue-resistant "carburized" armor plates.[11]

Finally, on June 7, 1906, the Cunard Line launched its great liner. Problems arose because the ship was nearly 800 feet long, and the River Cart only 610 feet wide. Since the *Lusitania* was built at a 40° angle to the river, the confluence of the Rivers Clyde and Cart had to be dredged and the corners cut away. The standing ways were built of oak logs 12 inches square and 6 feet wide, coated with Russian tallow and soft soap five-eighths of an inch thick. These preparations paid off, for after being christened by Dowager Lady Inverslyde, the liner reached her natural element in 86 seconds with no difficulty whatsoever.[12]

The *Lusitania* measured 785 feet from bow to stern, the largest ship built for the Cunard Line up to that time. It was more than twice the height of the Statue of Liberty, including her pedestal. Her breadth spanned an incredible 88 feet, and her depth, 60 feet 4 inches. The super liner's gross tonnage totaled 32,550 tons, nearly twice that of the *Great Eastern*. Each anchor weighed 10¼ tons, and was attached to a 3¾-inch diameter chain of 125 tons.

Everything about this liner was huge. Some four million rivets held *Lusitania* together, cumulatively weighing 500 tons. About 65,000 gallons of water per minute cooled her engines, and some 250 miles of cable supplied her electrical power.[13] The *Lusitania* generated a great deal of power, equipped with 25 cylindrical boilers heated by 192 furnaces. All told, she boasted 68,000 horsepower, surpassing all other ships afloat in 1906.[14]

The vessel produced and consumed a great deal of electricity. Generating stations abaft the engine room included four generating sets, each with the capacity of 375 kilowatts, and voltage ranging from 110 to 120. Parsons turbines, the prime movers, ran the dynamos at 1,200 revolutions per minute.[15] Water consumption ranged from 46.08 to 60.6 ponds per hour.[16]

The ship's galleys were among the finest afloat. The saloon kitchen and pantries extended across the breadth of the ship, and 126 feet fore and aft, with a main cooking range that had a hot plate covering more than 250 square feet. A half-dozen steam stockpots, a half-dozen steam ovens, and a half-dozen hot closets also equipped the galleys. All steam used for cooking was specially evaporated to remain absolutely clean.

Two different pieces of refrigerating machinery, of the silent, carbonic-anhydride type, served the liner. One preserved food for the crew and passengers while the other refrigerated only cargo. The refrigeration chambers had an interior capacity of about 13,000 cubic feet. An outside layer of soft cast steel encased and supported a liner of hard, close-grained cast iron.

Since the *Lusitania* burnt a great deal of coal, ash disposal presented a problem. The firemen gave careful attention to the firing, but it became especially difficult when the stokeholds were cluttered with ashes. To overcome this problem, eight See's ash ejectors were installed. The firemen would shovel the ashes into hoppers in the stokehold and the ejectors would then disperse the ashes 20 feet clear of the ship.[17]

Lifting mechanisms on the new ship included four deck cranes and four baggage and mail hoists. Constructed by Stothert and Pitt, Ltd., of Bath, the electric motors for the deck cranes could lift a full load at 100 feet per minute. The ship also provided the latest communication innovations. Graham's loud-speaking telephones enabled officers on the bridge to speak directly with the engine-room starting platform, the after bridge, the steering-gear compartment, the forecastle and the crow's nest. First-class suites included telephones their passengers could use to contact various services and other passengers. When in dock, they could even call friends on shore.[18]

The new ship performed well on her sea trials. Under the watchful eyes of Cunard officials and representatives from the Admiralty, she steamed at 26¼ knots in a measured mile. In a deep-sea trial of 1,200 nautical miles, her mean speed was 25.4 knots. The machinery worked throughout the long sea trials with "uninterrupted mechanical precision." The only major problem was that the torsion meter recorded the engines at 64,600 horsepower instead of 68,000, as designed.[19] Her stern also vibrated at high speed—not a mild vibration, but a violent shaking that made her stern unstable.[20] Extensively modifying the strength of the internal bracing seemed to solve the problem, and the ship was delivered.

The *Lusitania* set sail on her maiden voyage from Liverpool to New York on September 7, 1907, burning an incredible 1,090 tons of coal each day—though ten tons less than anticipated.[21] The liner set a record by crossing the Atlantic in five days and 54 minutes, and later broke this record when she arrived in New York in four days, 19 hours and 52 minutes.[22] In July of the following year, *Lusitania* became the first ship to cross the Atlantic Ocean with an average speed of more than 25 knots. In August 1911, for the first time on record, she made two complete round trips between Liverpool and New York in less than a month.

Besides speed, the Cunarder also offered comfort. "The *Lusitania* is not only a great step forward from the mechanical engineering standpoint," declared *Engineering* magazine, "but marks the highest conception of artistic furnishing and internal decoration"[23] Cunard commissioned James Millar, a respected Glasgow architect, to design the liner's interior spaces, for which he chose a light, airy color scheme that became a draw for passengers.[24]

The First Class Dining Saloon accommodated about 500 passengers. To facilitate seatings, two saloons were constructed, one on the Upper Deck and another on the deck above, both around a central dome and all in the white and gold reminiscent of the French king Louis XVI. The lower saloon measured 86 feet by 86 feet. The upper was somewhat smaller, 62 feet square, but was more intimate and overlooked the main dining area. The saloon's dome rose 30 feet, with ornate plasterwork and four artistically conceived floral panels.

The First Class Smoking Room, located on the after end of the Boat Deck, also echoed the 18th century with its Italian walnut paneling. "The fireplace," noted *Engineering*, "is a striking feature of this room."[25] The room was well ventilated to prevent the accumulation of tobacco smoke, and offered a perpetually stocked buffet and bar. The First Class Lounge and Music Room was located near the entrance hall on the Boat Deck. Done in late Georgian style, this 68- by 52-foot room had furniture built of mahogany and satin wood. A green marble fireplace 14 feet high anchored each end of the room. The Writing Room and Library, situated near the grand hall, measured 44 by 52 feet, and Millar decorated these in the Adam style of the late 18th century. Above cream-colored wainscoting, framed panels in grey and cream silk brocade softened the acoustics.

Of course, the second-class passengers had to settle for somewhat less, but they, too, traveled in style. Second class had a drawing room, a smoking room and a lounge, with the drawing room and lounge designed in the Georgian style. Third-class passengers lived better than their counterparts on most ships. The forward end of the liner from the lower to the forecastle decks, which included a 79- by 60-foot dining room with a piano, belonged to third class.

As a transatlantic ocean liner, the *Lusitania* carried a large complement of workers and thousands of passengers. She had accommodations for 552 first-, 460 second- and 1,186 third-class passengers for a total of 2,198. Her full crew consisted of 827, giving the liner a potential for 3,025 people aboard.

The *Lusitania* also had a dual role. During times of peace she served the Cunard Line as a luxury liner and delivered mail for the British government, but in wartime, the Royal Navy could require that she act as an auxiliary cruiser. Thus the steering gear and motive gear were placed below the waterline to protect them from enemy shellfire. Her design included a capacity for emplacing 12 six-inch guns with a velocity of 3,000 feet per second, and a muzzle energy of 6,000 foot-tons.[26] This auxiliary cruiser, concluded *Scientific America,* "would be capable of putting up a stiff fight against any protected cruiser."[27] The *Lusitania* probably would not have been an effective warship due to her consumption of more than 1,000 tons of coal per day. However, she could have been an excellent troop transport or hospital ship, much as the *Mauretania* became during World War I.

Shortly after the *Lusitania* entered service, the *Mauretania* upstaged her. Although sister ships, the *Mauretania* quickly captured the love and interest of the public, though it is difficult to say why. The admiring author Theodore Dreiser had this to say about the *Mauretania*:

> There were several things about this great ship that were unique. It was a beautiful thing all told—its long cherry-wood, paneled halls in the first-class section, its heavy porcelain baths, its dainty staterooms fitted with lamps, bureaus, writing-desks, washstands, closets and the like. I liked the idea of dressing for dinner and seeing everything quite stately and formal. The little be-buttoned call-boys in their tight-fitting blue suits amused me. And the bugler who bugled for dinner! That was a most musical sound he made, trilling the various quarters gaily, as much as to say, 'This is a very joyous event, ladies and gentlemen; we are all happy; come, come, it is a delightful feast.'[28]

Another *Mauretania* enthusiast, Franklin Delano Roosevelt, wrote,

When she was born in 1907 the *Mauretania* was the largest thing ever put together by man. . . . [she] always fascinated me with her graceful, yacht like lines, her four enormous black-topped red funnels, and her appearance of power and good breeding... Yet, not for one minute did I ever fail to realize that if there ever was a ship which possessed the thing called 'soul,' the *Mauretania* did... Every ship has a soul, but the *Mauretania* had one you could talk to. At times she could be wayward and contrary as a thoroughbred. To no other ship belonged that trick of hers—that thrust and dip and dive into the seas and through them, which would wreck the rails of the Monkey Island with solid sea, or playfully spatter salt water on the Captain's boiled shirt as he took a turn on the bridge before going down to dinner. At other times, she would do everything her Master wanted her to, with a right good will. As Captain Rostron once said to me, she had the manners and deportment of a great lady and behaved herself as such.[29]

Other shipping companies began to build ships to compete with these twin Cunard liners. The White Star Line completed the *Olympic* in 1911. One-and-a-half times the size of the *Lusitania* but not as fast, she boasted luxuries that attracted American millionaires. The following year the *Olympic*'s sister ship, the *Titanic*, entered service.

Then tragedy struck when the *Titanic* hit an iceberg on her maiden voyage from England, and she sank two hours and forty minutes later. The magnitude of this disaster was starkly appalling. More than 1,500 people perished in the icy water of the Atlantic on April 14–15, 1912. The sinking brought into harsh relief questions about the modern ocean liner's safety.

The Cunard Line insisted that the *Lusitania* and *Mauretania* were safe, having been built as auxiliary cruisers for the Royal Navy. They stressed the fact that each liner had a double skin (two layers of steel) throughout the hull, which "is 5 feet in depth." *Scientific America* boldly went on, "There are nine decks in all, and the hull is divided into 175 separate water-tight compartments, which, surely establishes the claim that she is unsinkable by any ordinary disaster."[30]

Yet the designers of the *Lusitania* overlooked a few critical points. For instance, the coal bunkers needed to be closed by stokers during an emergency. If disaster were to strike, the black gang might panic and abandon their posts before closing the doors. With open bunkers, the ship would lose buoyancy and stability.

There were other problems. If the ship listed seven degrees or more, water would rush into any open porthole on *Lusitania's* F Deck. To overcome this problem, the bridge had a control panel to close off this area. The crew understood that anyone trapped there could escape by means of a manual override system. However, no explanation on how to use this system was given to any of the passengers. Consequently, if disaster struck and this area were closed off without crewmwmbers nearby, passengers in the vicinity would be trapped and unable to reach safety.

The loss of the *Titanic* in 1912 led to many reforms designed to make transatlantic travel safer. One reform concerned the number and handling of lifeboats. Under the old law, any vessel of 10,000 tons or more was required to carry a minimum of 16 boats. Clearly this was too few for the number of people aboard ships such as the *Titanic* or the *Lusitania*, so the newly revised law required, unequivocally, enough lifeboats for everyone. To conform to this new regulation, Cunard installed several lifeboats alongside those already in the davits. But this meant the crew had to lower the boats in the davits, haul up the ropes, attach them to other lifeboats, and lower again. This would use valuable time in an emergency. Furthermore, the new regulations called for boat drills. The Cunard Line cooperated, but in such a perfunctory manner as to make this regulation meaningless.

Despite these flaws, the *Lusitania* provided more safety than most liners of her day, and indeed, she crossed the Atlantic Ocean more than 200 times without mishap. Yet how safe would this luxurious ocean liner remain if she were to encounter a true predator?

CHAPTER 4

THE GREAT NAVAL RACE

As the 20th century dawned, Great Britain was the unchallenged naval power of the world. This was about to change, for Germany was initiating a great naval buildup, signaled by the Second Fleet Act of 1900, which sought to make the German fleet unsurpassed among the major powers. Rear Admiral Alfred von Tirpitz, secretary of state for the Imperial Navy office, instigated and fueled this ambitious program.[1]

Tirpitz's goal was two-fold: he wanted to unite Germany domestically and he wanted to expand German resources and influence abroad. Business, he believed, would support his naval program because of the jobs and shipbuilding contracts it would create. The latter part of the 19th century saw a slump in the world economy, and the recession that followed did not spare Germany. The promise of a set number of ships to be constructed and an enlarged German fleet to be maintained gave incentive for the German business community to support Tirpitz's policies.[2]

Germany's growing navy captured the imagination of the country's public, due in large part to the multi-faceted propaganda machine Tirpitz directed at gaining support for a naval buildup.[3] Not only did Tirpitz personally engage the interest of opinion leaders like the "Iron Chancellor" Otto von Bismarck, he instituted "a 'Section for News and General Parliamentary Affairs'... to establish close relations with the press, arrange publications of suitable articles, and create a favorable climate in German public opinion for a powerful fleet."[4] "Unless Germany owns a strong fleet," one magazine editorialized, "she will be without colonies by the end of the twentieth century." Without colonies, "she will suffocate in her small territory or else be crushed by the great world powers."[5]

The large navy would also distract workers from domestic problems. Near the turn of the 20th century, many in the German business establishment felt that workers were growing increasingly restless and would eventually revolt; by keeping them well fed, they reasoned, laborers would remain docile and pliant. In order to do this, Tirpitz asserted, the country would have to move further into the global economy, and sustain the ability to defend German territories overseas. This would require a large and powerful navy.

It was in this atmosphere that Tirpitz persuaded the Reichstag to pass a series of naval bills which called for the construction of new ships and the replacement of old ships during a fixed period of time. As much as possible, Tirpitz wanted control of the naval program to be firmly in the hands of the Kaiser rather than an elected parliament. The bill the Reichstag ultimately approved in 1898 pleased the Admiral. The Germans would build three battleships a year and replace old battleships and cruisers every 25 years. This would fulfill Tirpitz's goal by 1923. If the Reichstag could be persuaded to replace the ships every 20 years, the goal would be achieved by 1918.[6]

The time was ripe for Tirpitz's request. Captain Alfred T. Mahan, a retired American naval officer and respected naval historian, had written *The Influence of Sea Power On History*. This book convinced many people—in Europe and English-speaking countries—that a nation's future depended on a large navy.[7] Mahan argued that constant international competition led to the rise and fall of nations, a theory that found favor in the Kaiser's circle.

"Mahanism" also found support throughout Germany, as many Germans saw history as a periodic redistribution of power—essentially, that every so often a great war would destroy the existing world power and create a new one. In 1899, Chancellor Bernhard von Bülow stated, "It has been said, gentlemen, that in every century there will be a great conflict, a major liquidation [of some empire] in order to reallocate influence, power, and territorial possessions on the globe. Are we just about to witness another redistribution of the earth?"[8]

Of these empires, Great Britain was Germany's chief economic rival and the target of its expanded navy.[9] Britain possessed the largest fleet in the world. She also stood in the way of Germany's legitimate expansion since Germany could not claim new overseas colonies without Britain's approval. Therefore, Tirpitz believed, a powerful German navy would force concessions from Great Britain. With 60 battleships on the North Sea, Germany could "respond to a British attack and thus shift the balance of power virtually in one afternoon . . ."[10] Germany would then be free to acquire overseas colonies and markets.

The people and the government of Great Britain viewed the German naval buildup with alarm. The First Lord of the Admiralty, Sir Walter Kerr, responded that, "If any great naval power took action as regards to shipbuilding which would materially disturb the existing balance of naval power, this country would have to reconsider its naval program."[11] Another prominent government official in London declared that Germany was "our worst enemy and our greatest threat."[12]

On October 21, 1904, Admiral Sir John Fisher was appointed First Sea Lord. He supervised the buildup of the Royal Navy's ships and personnel, and overhauled the recruitment procedure to add men to the ranks. "Jacky" Fisher convened a committee to arrive at the revolutionary design of HMS *Dreadnought*, a warship powered by steam turbines capable of at least 21 knots, armed with ten 12-inch guns. He pushed for the construction of additional battleships and armored cruisers of the same fast, all-big-gun type, the former since referred to as "dreadnoughts" after the 1904 prototype. Fisher became Tirpitz's great opponent.

Both nations pursued a buildup of warships, especially dreadnought battleships. In the end Britain won the naval race in large part due to her superior shipbuilding industry, but also to her large stock of older ships which performed valuable functions in remote locations around the globe.[13] By the time war broke out, the Royal Navy had 21 of the latest dreadnoughts to Germany's 13. The gap between the number of German and British cruisers and destroyers was not as pronounced, but the British Navy had an edge in these types of warship as well.

Yet, as later events proved, the advantage of quality lay with the

Germans. Admiral Sir John Jellicoe, commander-in-chief of the Grand Fleet during World War I, harbored no illusions about German ships. "My knowledge of the German navy, which is considerable, left me under no delusion as to its character. I had made it my business to keep myself very full acquainted with German progress...[T]ouch on many occasions with the German Fleet had convinced me that in *matériel* the Germans were ahead of us . . ."[14] Jellicoe also warned that it was "highly dangerous to consider that our ships as a whole are superior or even equal fighting machines"[15]

German cruisers were faster than their British counterparts, and had the added advantage of being well equipped to lay mines of excellent design. The British, by contrast, lacked mines at the outbreak of the war, and when they acquired them, discovered they had serious design flaws.[16] Fast, big German destroyers out-numbered similar British ships in European waters 96 to 76.[17]

Although the Royal Navy enjoyed a larger number of modern capital ships, the ships were not without their defects. British armored belts were not as thick or extensive as their German counterparts, and flaws in the basic design of some dreadnoughts caused problems. Jellicoe's flagship, the *Iron Duke*, originally had six-inch guns placed so low that gun ports had to be unshipped to prevent the sea from washing them away in rough weather. A similar problem with casemate flooding existed with the *Queen Elizabeth*-class battleships and the battle cruiser *Tiger*.[18]

The ships of the Royal Navy also suffered frequent breakdowns. During the first year of the war, five battleships had to have their condensers replaced, and in January 1915, four battleships and one battle cruiser were out of service. Additionally, the explosive lyddite used in British shells proved highly unstable. In 1916, two ships blew up in harbor, probably victims of their own ammunition.[19]

Because both German and British admirals consistently put their faith in surface ships, especially battleships, they overlooked one type of warship prior to 1914: the submarine, only a few of which were commissioned prior to the Great War. Britain had a numerical edge, but German submarines delivered superior quality.

A Dutchman, Cornelis van Drebbel, built the first known practical submersible and operated it in 1624.[20] A leather-covered, 12-oar rowboat, he reinforced it with iron against water pressure to a depth of 15 feet. This submersible operated in the Thames. In 1747, another decked-over rowboat appeared in the Thames with the first ballast "tanks," leather bags with their necks inserted in the bottom of the boat. To submerge, the operator allowed water to enter the tanks. To surface, water was squeezed out of the bags.

The submarine *Turtle* made its mark during the American Revolution. Built in 1775 by American inventor David Bushnell, this walnut-shaped submersible measured 7 feet tall and 5½ feet wide. Bushnell designed it to be operated by one man and capable of submerging 20 feet for up to half an hour.[21] To sink the British ship *Eagle*, the *Turtle* would need to come alongside and fasten a 150-pound bomb to the *Eagle*'s keel with a screw. As military historian Thomas Parrish put it, operating the *Turtle* "would have tested the dexterity of a trained octopus."[22] Bushnell himself was not up to the task, so he deferred to his brother, Ezra, who had some familiarity with the submarine. Ezra's poor health led to the plan's postponement. In the end a sergeant in the Continental Army, Ezra Lee, qualified for the task. On September 6, 1776, Lee set out for the attack, but unfortunately for the Americans, he could not drill a hole into the bottom of the *Eagle*. The attack failed.

In 1801, American Robert Fulton demonstrated the copper-hulled *Nautilus,* the first fish-shaped submersible that employed a screw to push rather than pull the vessel. This submarine included sails for surface propulsion and enough compressed air for a four-man crew for three hours.[23] In spite of its successful trials on the Seine River in Paris and at Brest, the French Admiralty declined to invest in this new technology.[24]

In the 1850s the Danes were at war with the German states, and the Danish Navy blockaded German ports. Seeing an opportunity, a Bavarian soldier named Wilhelm Bauer devised a plan to utilize submarines. With public support he built the *Brandtaucher* (*Fire Diver*), a submarine specially designed to attack the Danish ships. Disaster struck when the hull plates sprang a leak and the ship sank to the bottom where it became embedded in mud. Bauer persuaded his men to let the water flow in, equalizing the pressure inside and outside the submarine so that the hatch could be opened. This accomplished, the crew fled their doomed vessel. Wilhelm Bauer did not give up. In 1856 he built the

Seeteufel (*Sea Devil*) for Russia during the Crimean War, an improved 52-foot submarine with a rescue device.[25]

The Confederates attempted to use submarines during the American Civil War, and on February 17, 1864, the first successful submarine attack took place. The *H.L. Hunley*, a converted steam boiler with a complement of nine men, carried out the plan. This 40-foot Confederate submarine employed a crankshaft turned by eight men that rotated a propeller. A 90-pound explosive charge was attached to a spar from the submarine's bow, and it succeeded in sinking the Union steam sloop *Housatonic* while anchored off Charleston, South Carolina. But the *Hunley* sank as well, killing all nine members of its crew.[26]

Europeans continued to investigate the submarine's potential. Early in the 1880s, George Garrett, an English clergyman, and Thorsten Nordenfeldt, a Swedish inventor, built the first practical submarines. The *Nordenfeldt III*, their best, could submerge to a depth of 50 feet for a range of 14 miles. A steam engine powered the vessel on the surface and was shut down to dive. *Nordenfeldt III* also had twin torpedo tubes. In 1889, an officer in the Spanish Navy, Don Isaac Peral, designed a more advanced submarine. Named after himself, Peral's ship was entirely electrical and made of steel, capable of 10 knots on the surface and eight knots submerged. This submarine resembled, in many respects, the submarines developed in 1914.

By the end of the 19th century, the United States had become more involved in the development of submarines. John Philip Holland built America's best-known practical submarine, the *Holland*. A gasoline engine powered her on the surface and a battery-driven motor did so when submerged; she could fire 18-inch torpedoes from a single torpedo tube.[27] Assistant Secretary of the Navy Theodore Roosevelt encouraged the Navy to buy *Holland* after he witnessed her sea trials in 1898, but it was not until 1900 that she was formally commissioned and six more submarines of her type ordered.[28]

However, it was Simon Lake who, in 1894, launched the first practical submarine in the rivers of New Jersey. In 1895 the Lake Submarine Company began to build his first steel vessel, *Argonaut I*. His submarines had the first bow and stern diving plates for depth control, and in 1897 he patented the "even-keel" submarine. He developed the periscope and virtually eliminated the magnetic effect of a metal surround on the submarine's compass. In 1898, the *Argonaut* completed a thousand-mile cruise—above and beneath the surface of the ocean—up the Atlantic coast.[29]

Yet despite these strides, the submarine was relegated to a minor position in naval development prior to 1914. Not until the Great War would the utility of the submarine be proven.

CHAPTER 5
ARMAGEDDON

In the summer of 1914 the peaceful world awoke to the cataclysmic outbreak of the First World War.

On June 28, Archduke Franz Ferdinand, heir-apparent to the Austro-Hungarian throne, and his wife, Sophie, Duchess of Hohenberg, traveled to Sarajevo to inspect army maneuvers. Considering the bitter atmosphere in the multi-ethnic Balkans at this time, his visit could be seen as a reckless gesture, but the Archduke openly sympathized with the Slavs. While there, Gavrilo Princip, a 19-year-old member of "Young Bosnia," shot and killed the crown prince and his wife. Princip belonged to a team of assassins funded and organized by the "Black Hand," a secret Serbian society that included government and army professionals opposed to rule by the Austro-Hungarian Empire.[1]

For several years prior to the assassination, this organization had provoked trouble with the Austro-Hungarian government. Anti-Austrian propaganda poured out of Serbia along with acts of terrorism. Although government officials in Vienna and Budapest disliked the Archduke, they saw his assassination as a pretext for the Empire to move against Serbia. Kaiser Wilhelm II and Imperial Chancellor Theobald von Bethmann-Hollweg both promised the Austrians they would support any action they took. This has been referred to by historians as the "blank check."[2]

Confident of German backing, the Austro-Hungarian government sent Serbia a stern ultimatum. It demanded a formal apology, full cooperation in an investigation of the murders, punishment of the guilty parties, suppression of all newspapers and organizations hostile to the Empire, and an end to all propaganda against Austria-Hungary. They designed the ultimatum to be rejected, but Serbia agreed to some of the demands and temporized on others. Serbia responded in this way because she, too, had a "blank check"—from Russia. She knew she could count on the Tsar's support in the event of war.[3]

Vienna was now determined to go to war. On July 28, 1914, one month after the assassination in Sarajevo, Austria-Hungary declared war on Serbia. Russia reacted by ordering mobilization along her borders, including the German-Russian border. Berlin, believing that fast mobilization would ensure success, delivered an ultimatum to Russia, and on August 1, mobilized its own army and declared war on Russia. France on that same day began mobilization. Two days later, when Belgium refused to permit the German Imperial Army to cross its territory to reach France, Germany declared war on both Belgium and France. On August 3, units of the German Army crossed into Belgium. This led Britain to declare war on Germany. With some encouragement from Britain, Japan saw her opportunity and declared war on Germany. The spark had ignited a world war.

It is difficult to assess the guilt of the countries involved. Forces in Serbia clearly provoked Austria-Hungary, yet, in hindsight, she overreacted to the provocation. The incident "was of a kind that a confident Great Power could have ignored or dealt with less drastically," wrote historians Peter Gay and R.K. Webb.[4] Indeed, the declining Austro-Hungarian Empire was not a "confident" great power, but Russia's poor mobilization policies contributed to the problem as well. Much blame, then and since, has been directed toward German statesmen for the "blank check" supporting Austria-Hungary against Serbia. Yet the fear of encirclement by hostile countries, both exaggerated and self-fulfilling, along with the inept statecraft in Berlin, made dangerously impulsive action possible.

The two sides grew in number. The German, Austro-Hungarian and Ottoman Empires, known as the Central Powers, added Bulgaria to their forces in 1915. The Triple Entente, or "Allies"—Great Britain,

France and Russia—gained Italy's support in the spring of 1915, and Rumania joined them late in 1916.

The United States remained neutral. Though Americans monitored with keen interest the developments in Europe, they were divided on the issue. On one side, many sympathized with the Central Powers since a large number of Americans were German immigrants or of German descent. But millions of anti-British Irish-Americans were also sympathetic to the Germans, if by default.[5] A significant number of Swedish-Americans, because of good relations between Sweden and Germany and poor relations with Russia, favored the Central Powers.

On the other side of the fence, many Americans of British descent favored the democratic principles of the Allies. Some British-owned American newspapers displayed a natural bias toward the Allies. Ultimately, the great majority of Americans may simply have wanted to stay out of the conflict.

President Woodrow Wilson addressed the nation shortly after war broke out. "Every man who really loves America." he enjoined, "will act and speak in the true spirit of neutrality, which is the spirit of impartiality and fairness and friendliness to all concerned." He warned:

> It will be easy to excite passion and difficult to allay it. Those responsible for exciting it will assume a heavy responsibility, a responsibility for no less a thing than that the people of the United States, whose love of their country and whose loyalty to its Government should unite them as Americans all, bound in honor to this first of her and her interest, may be divided in camps of hostile opinions, hot against each other, involved in the war itself in impulse and opinion if not in action.[6]

Colonel Edward House, a close advisor to Wilson, wrote, "Your address on Neutrality is one of the finest things you have ever done, and it has met with universal approbation."[7] But House, disturbed by the conflict, continued, "The saddest feature of the situation to me is that there is no good outcome to look forward to. If the Allies win, it means largely the domination of Russia on the Continent of Europe, and if Germany wins, it means the unspeakable tyranny of militarism of generations to come."[8]

Many Americans agreed with this pessimistic view, but Europeans shared a different state of mind. The people of Germany, Austria, Britain, France and Russia were in high spirits, with crowds cheering in the capitals of Europe.

Germany completed the mobilization of her army first. For some years prior to 1914, the Germans had in place a war plan, the Schlieffen Plan, created to deal with a war on two fronts involving France and Russia. Based on the assumption that Russia would take weeks to mobilize, the Germans planned instantly to deploy the bulk of their forces to invade France through neutral Belgium and by sweeping with their right along the Channel coast, encircle the French Army.[9] After defeating the French army and capturing Paris, Germany would rapidly move forces to defend their border with Russia via their network of east-west railways. The Imperial German general staff overlooked two things: that the British might intervene following an invasion of Belgium, and that Russia might mobilize her army quickly.

At first, the venture went well for the Germans as their juggernaut forged across Belgium and northern France, but unexpected events arose. Contrary to predictions, the Imperial Russian Army quickly swept westward almost unopposed, forcing Germany to allocate more troops to the east. In the Battle of Tannenberg, a resounding German victory repelled the Russian Army. But the drain of troops weakened the German spearhead in France, and a combined French and British Army stopped the Germans outside Paris at the Battle of the Marne. With the German advance brought to a halt, the western front locked in a stalemate. The opposing armies dug trenches and settled down for a longer war than either had anticipated. Massive attacks by both sides continued during the next four years, only to fail with massive casualties. For three years, the lines moved no more than ten miles.[10]

The war at sea unfolded differently. Here the British enjoyed numerical superiority in battleships, yet the Royal Navy suffered setbacks during the opening months of the war. On September 22, 1914, three obsolete cruisers, the *Aboukir*, the *Hogue* and the *Cressy*, succumbed one after another to a German submarine, the *U-9*. Of the nearly 2,300 men on board the ships, more than 1,400 were lost. A single U-boat with the expenditure of six torpedoes proved that the submarine had come of age.[11]

Six weeks later the British suffered another defeat. Rear-Admiral Sir Christopher Craddock, in command of a squadron of the Royal Navy, was in pursuit of Vice-Admiral Count Maximilian von Spee's Far East Squadron.[12] The two forces converged off Coronel, Chile, resulting in disaster for the British. With Craddock aboard, the flagship *Good Hope* sank from shellfire and an internal explosion, and the German squadron then fired on the damaged *Monmouth* until she too fell beneath the waves. The British lost both aged but heavy cruisers along with nearly 1,600 men, while the Germans, by contrast, did not lose a single ship and counted only two men slightly wounded.[13]

The spell of Trafalgar was broken. The Royal Navy burned under its first major naval defeat in more than a century. Across Britain rang the cry, "Avenge Coronel." First Lord of the Admiralty Winston Churchill dispatched the battle cruisers *Invincible* and *Inflexible* and three light cruisers to the South Atlantic to join the remnants of Craddock's squadron. They met at Port Stanley in East Falkland Island to recoal on December 7, 1914.

By a twist of fate, Rear-Admiral von Spee arrived at Stanley the next day intending to raid the British colony. The result was the Battle of the Falklands. The British, with superior speed and firepower, destroyed the German Far East Squadron. Commanded by Vice-Admiral Sir Doveton Sturdee, the British sank every ship in von Spee's squadron except the *Dresden,* which was cornered and scuttled the following year.[14]

For the most part, the war at sea during the first year of conflict was much less spectacular and involved blockade duty by the Royal Navy. Geographically, blockading Germany presented no special challenges for a navy with superior numbers. As a result, few ships entered or left German ports, leading to starvation and malnutrition in a nation that depended on food from overseas. Estimates vary, but official statistics place the number of casualties from starvation until the armistice was signed above 750,000.[15]

The blockade conducted by the British was illegal. According to international law, a belligerent nation blockading an enemy must be close to port. However, given that modern guns could destroy British warships, the British intercepted ships in international waters. This angered many Americans.

The Germans retaliated by using submarines. While their surface fleet remained bottled up in harbor, their *Unterseeboote*—U-boats— could slip past the blockade and wreak havoc on British merchant ships. The British responded by instructing their merchant captains to evade and resist, to zigzag and, if possible, to ram submarines. Some British merchant ships even carried guns. Soon it became clear to the Germans that the best tactic was to remain submerged and fire torpedoes without warning. This too violated international law, but the Germans argued that technological advances made these laws obsolete, just as the British argued for their use of the long-range blockade.

The first merchant ship lost to a submarine in World War I was the S.S. *Glitra*. On October 20, 1914, a few months after war broke out, the German *U-17* warned the *Glitra* to stop. After a search of the vessel, the crew was ordered into lifeboats and the Germans sank the ship. The Germans would be less gentlemanly in future attacks.[16]

Some British captains hoisted American flags in order to fool the enemy. From a periscope view this might work, and the *Lusitania* was a case in point. Her regular captain, David "Paddy" Dow, flew the American flag, but it's doubtful that his ruse worked—the United States at this time had no four-funnel passenger liner the size of the *Lusitania*. Probably Dow did it to assuage the worry of his passengers.

Washington immediately issued a protest against British ships flying American flags. Sooner or later, Washington argued, the Germans would realize the game and sink all ships with American flags. This would not help the British and it would hurt the Americans, since some of their own ships could be torpedoed.

Then on March 28, 1915, came an event that threw a charge into diplomatic relations. The British *Falaba*, one day out of Liverpool and steaming for West Africa, was sunk by the German *U-28* commanded by Kapitänleutnant Georg-Günther Freiherr von Forstner. The U-boat surfaced some three miles from *Falaba* and ordered her, by use of flags, to "stop and abandon ship." The British steamer ignored the warning and attempted to flee at full speed, but the German submarine caught up and signaled, "Stop or I fire." The *Falaba* stopped and the U-boat came within about 100 yards of its victim. German and British accounts disagree on the amount of time the Germans waited for the *Falaba* to abandon ship; the Germans claimed 23 minutes elapsed, while the

British insisted it was only seven. The ship's wireless signaled for help, and, according to the Germans, the British crew also sent up distress rockets. Von Forstner decided he could wait no longer and fired.

The torpedo struck *Falaba* in the vicinity of the engine room. Some of her boilers exploded and the ship sank in eight minutes. Of the 242 persons aboard, 104 perished, including the first American causality of World War I, Leon Thrasher, a young mining engineer returning to his work on the Gold Coast.[17]

There was an official investigation into the matter. The man heading the British Board of Trade inquiry was Lord Mersey,[18] who later presided over the *Lusitania* hearings. Mersey blasted the Germans, claiming they should have given the people on board "a reasonable opportunity" to get to the lifeboats. Mersey concluded that "the Captain of the submarine desired and designed not merely to sink the ship, but in doing so also to sacrifice the lives of the passengers and crew."[19]

President Wilson remained silent during this episode. He had declared that he would hold Germany to "strict accountability" with regard to submarine warfare, but the *Falaba* was British, and many of the facts remained unclear. Furthermore, according to international law—of which Wilson was a strong proponent—the submarine was within its rights to sink a fleeing ship, which the *Falaba* was.

The situation grew worse. On April 29, 1915, about a month after the *Falaba* incident, a German airplane bombed an American oil tanker, the *Cushing*, off the coast of the Netherlands. The plane dropped three bombs, one of which hit the *Cushing*, causing slight damage but no injuries. The oil tanker flew the American flag, but had no flag painted on the deck for aviators to see.[20] Berlin stated that it was a case of mistaken identity and that no deliberate attempt was made to attack an American ships. The U.S. Naval attaché in Germany was informed by the Imperial German Navy that the attack was "an unfortunate, unintentional accident" that it "very much regretted."[21]

Two days later, on May 1, 1915, the very day *Lusitania* left New York on her final voyage, another incident occurred. The American oil tanker *Gulflight* was attacked by a German submarine. The tanker's captain had asked a British patrol craft where to obtain a pilot for Rouen, France. The patrol's crew informed him that none was available, and directed him to follow them into port. En route, the *Gulflight* encountered a U-boat that noticed the escort. The German commander fired a torpedo and then, too late, detected the American flag on the *Gulflight*. The tanker suffered severe damage, two of her crew drowned and the captain died of a heart attack.[22] Berlin expressed its "regret" at the "unfortunate accident." They offered to pay "full recompense" for any damage incurred.[23]

These pre-*Lusitania* attacks, of course, had many differences between them. The *Falaba* was a British ship, while the *Cushing* and the *Gulflight* were American. A German airplane attacked the neutral *Cushing*, a clear violation of international law. The same judgment cannot be applied to the *Falaba* or the *Gulflight*. The former tried to flee and the latter was under escort; both could be sunk without warning. Later, as we shall see, Wilson would include all three of these attacks in his first response to the *Lusitania* disaster.

These pre-*Lusitania* attacks revealed the ferocity of the world war at sea as well as the growing ruthlessness of both sides to gain advantage. The *Lusitania*, by this time, was steaming toward the war zone.

CHAPTER 6

A "LAURIAT CROSSING"

O n May 1, 1915 the *Lusitania* glided out of her pier in New York City to begin her voyage east to Liverpool. Within a few minutes, she passed the Statue of Liberty and Staten Island. The morning rain ceased and sun broke through the clouds. The beginning of the journey was routine.

A short time later, passenger Oliver Bernard, the theatrical designer, "got a glimpse of the dogs of war" as he witnessed two British warships, one of them the camouflaged liner *Carmania*, patrolling outside U.S. waters. Bernard noted that the *Carmania* was "armed with teeth."[1]

The following day the *Lusitania* encountered fog, and the lookouts were ordered to stay alert while the foghorn was blown at intervals. This area of the North Atlantic was notorious for its deadly mists. In 1898 the French liner *La Bourgogne* had rammed the iron-hulled schooner *Cromartyshire,* completely shearing off the schooner's bow.[2] *La Bourgogne* foundered in less than an hour with the loss of more than 500 lives,[3] even though *Cromartyshire* jettisoned its cargo to rescue survivors. In 1909, the White Star Liner *Republic* was hit amidships by the Lloyd Italiano passenger ship *Florida,* the former sinking with the loss of six lives. Forty-seven years later, the *Andrea Doria* would collide with the eastbound Swedish liner *Stockholm.*

In the fog Captain Turner anxiously paced the bridge, but once it had lifted he ordered an increase in speed and the *Lusitania* continued on to Liverpool. She traveled 501 miles on her first day from New York, but from then on made fewer than 500 nautical miles a day. From Thursday to Friday she covered only 484 miles.

This surprised Charles Lauriat, the Boston book dealer. He had never sailed on the *Lusitania* before but knew her reputation for speed, and fully expected that the ship "would put on steam" when they approached the Irish coast. He was confident enough to buy the high number in the pool for Friday, at 499 miles.[4] The voyage seemed to him uneventful—it was, in his words, "quite a 'Lauriat Crossing'; fine weather, smooth sea, and after the first few hours of Sunday (May 2) there had been no fog."[5] Lauriat had booked passage on the "Lucy" specifically to get to his company's office in England quickly, and the liner's relatively poor showing in speed disappointed him.

Lauriat had crossed the Atlantic 22 times. On this particular wartime voyage he noticed a few changes from the peacetime crossings. At night the shades in the saloon were "closely drawn." Lauriat also learned that his bedroom steward left notes for the night watchman informing him which ports were open when the steward went off duty.[6]

During the voyage many of the passengers, from different areas, countries and professions, got together to socialize. As Lauriat later explained, they "formed those acquaintances such as one does on an ocean crossing. Each evening in the smoking room, the pool for the following day's run was auctioned, and that always makes for informality and companionship."[7]

But not all of the passengers socialized. For one, Alfred Gwynne Vanderbilt spent much of the voyage in his cabin, perhaps in dread of encountering gossip about the tragic end of his rumored mistress, Mary Ruiz. In any event, he usually dined in his own quarters, served by his valet. At one party, the wine merchant George Kessler asked the millionaire if he would again do the four-in-hand run (a sport involving vehicles drawn by four horses) from London to Brighton. "No," Vanderbilt replied, "there'll be no coaching for me this year. I'm sorry, but to drive coach in these times is out of the question."[8] Vanderbilt talked about old times with his friend Thomas Slidell, recalling the day in 1907 when they watched the *Lusitania* on her maiden voyage from Vanderbilt's yacht. During this voyage, however, the tycoon told Slidell of his willingness to offer a fleet of wagons to the Red Cross with himself as driver, for he felt he was not doing enough for humanitarian causes.[9]

Vanderbilt wasn't the only first-class passenger who spent most of his time in his cabin. Charles Frohman kept busy studying new play scripts and devouring sweets during this time he described as a "dessert orgy." The producer was impressed with the gift his friend, the actress Maude Adams, had given him for the voyage—a basket shaped like a ship filled with flowers and fruit. Frohman sent a thank-you note that read, "The little ship you sent me is more wonderful than the big one that takes me away from you."[10]

Frohman also wrote a farewell note to his friend Charles Dillingham, the theater manager with whom he shared a country house. Included in the note, oddly enough, was a drawing of a liner being chased by a submarine.[11] Frohman was distressed about cuts in the prices of theater seats on Broadway, as some theater managers sold seats below the prices printed on the tickets. At one point he summoned the ship's physician, J.F. McDermott, to his cabin. "This is not one of my good days," he told the doctor.[12]

Unlike Vanderbilt and Frohman, Elbert and Alice Hubbard were out and about, and could often be seen at the Captain's table in the dining saloon. The musicians would play some of Hubbard's favorite tunes, such as "Memories," "The Curse of an Aching Heart" and "Can't Hear Me Calling Caroline."

While the *Lusitania* steamed on through the mid-Atlantic, the Toronto reporter Ernest Cowper interviewed Hubbard. He asked the editor of *Philistine* if he were afraid of U-boats. "Now, you know they will never torpedo the *Lusitania*," Hubbard answered. When Cowper asked how he came to this conclusion, Hubbard replied that the Germans would not be so foolish. What about the newspaper warning, countered Cowper, to which Hubbard responded, "If I was going to slug you as you came round the corner, would I advertise it in the newspapers?"[13] Nevertheless, Hubbard did consider the possibility of a submarine attack, confiding it to a journal of his voyage experience, *Lusitania Diary*, which he intended to cable to his readers in America from London.

If Hubbard showed no outward hint of apprehension, Charles Sumner, Cunard's New York manager, more openly concerned himself about panic among certain passengers. The *New York Tribune* reported that telegrams had been sent to first-class passengers, warning them of the danger of sailing on the *Lusitania*. Sumner sent Captain Turner a wireless message that read, "Ask Vanderbilt Frohman Klein whether they received telegrams warning against sailing or threatening if so secure them and return us an answer." Turner replied, "No one received telegrams of nature mentioned." This must have brought the New York manager a great sense of relief.[14]

Among those on board who took the warnings seriously was Albert L. Hopkins, the president of the Newport News Shipbuilding and Drydock Company. Travelling to England on shipyard business, he hoped with the construction of future vessels to assist in overcoming the general submarine threat that Britain faced. As might be expected there were also adventurous spirits on board, including Commander J. Foster Stackhouse, who was planning the International Oceanographic Expedition to Antarctica for 1916.

David Alfred Thomas, less bothered by the risk of traveling, concerned himself instead with his daughter's puzzling depression. In spite of traveling first class on a fabulous liner, Margaret felt morose, a condition she tried to hide from her father. Leaving the thrill of New York behind only to return to a loveless marriage back in England disheartened her. Yet the shipboard friendship she developed with Dr. Howard Fisher and his sister-in-law Dorothy Conner, who were on their way to start a field hospital in France, lifted Margaret's spirits somewhat. Lady Mackworth and her father had met them at lunch, and in a short time formed a valuable friendship. They decided to dine together for the balance of the voyage.

During meals, the four would discuss the possibility of being torpedoed, a possibility that actually excited Conner. At one point Dorothy interjected, "I can't help hoping that we get some sort of thrill going up the Channel."[15] Dr. Fisher believed the possibility of being torpedoed certainly existed. He took passage on the *Lusitania* only to save time, and if they struck a mine they would "have more chance of staying up." If torpedoed, he was confident they would still have enough time to abandon ship.[16]

The Cunard Line was well aware that the submarine threat disturbed some passengers. To ease their fears, Cunard placed British government leaflets throughout the ship. Written with a propagandistic slant, the leaflets absolved Britain of starting the war while placing blame for the conflict squarely on Germany.

As passengers speculated about potential threats, rumors circulated that the *Lusitania* was armed with guns. To see if this were so, Michael Byrne, a first-class passenger, carefully inspected the liner from bow to stern, examining every deck above the waterline. In the end he found no trace of guns.[17]

George Kessler's worries extended beyond than guns and torpedoes. He worried that his business would suffer if American prohibitionists got their way and passed a law that prohibited the sale of alcohol. Until now he'd managed to accumulate a fortune from importing wine, which made it possible to indulge himself and his friends in an extravagant lifestyle. Once he transformed the courtyard of the Savoy Hotel into a little replica of Venice by flooding it with water and serving his guests on a gondola. Another time he turned the winter garden of the Savoy into a replica of the North Pole with icebergs of silver tissue and fields of plastic snow.[18]

In third class, George Hook, a widower, traveled with his young children, Elsie and Frank. George had worked at a metal plant in Toronto but felt he might make out better in his native England. Originally his plans were to travel second class, but when he learned that his housekeeper Annie Marsh and her family would be traveling steerage, he decided to stay with them and benefit from their company. The Hooks became acquainted with another returning immigrant, John Welsh. Welsh dined with the Hook family during the Atlantic crossing, accompanied by a young woman he'd met onboard named Gerda Neilson. It was no secret that Neilson and Welsh were developing a romantic attachment to one another.[19]

More passengers from Canada were on board. Among them was 15-year-old William Holt, the son of Sir Herbert Samuel Holt, a fabulously wealthy Canadian banker. Fearing a German invasion, his parents had brought him back to Canada from his school in Britain, but now that this possibility seemed remote, they consented to let their son return to school at Marlborough.

A large number of other children from the north were onboard as well. Lady Mackworth "noticed this with some surprise," and concluded that the families of Canadians serving in the war were crossing the Atlantic to join them.[20] Many of these youngsters clearly enjoyed themselves. The children in first class had their own dining room and playroom side-by-side amidships on C Deck, watched over by a stewardess. Another stewardess attended the second-class children, who were provided with a large playpen.

Among the children onboard were the Crompton's. Paul Crompton and his wife had brought their six offspring, ranging in age from five months to 14 years, as well as their governess, Dorothy Allen. Crompton, an associate of Cunard chairman Alfred Booth, was traveling on business. In the Hodge family, eight-year-old William and six-year-old Dean accompanied their father, William Sr., on his way to France to take charge of the Baldwin Locomotive Works.

Some passengers who had originally intended to travel steerage upgraded to second class, taking advantage of the ticket price reduced from $70 to $50. Walter Mitchell and his wife Jeanette, with their baby, changed to second class for the voyage to see their parents in Ireland.

On the second day of the voyage the ship held its usual Sunday service, led by Captain Turner. He conducted it by reciting the English Baptist General Confessions and asking the Almighty to bless the royal family and all those at sea. A few hymns were sung. It was a simple and unaffected service, which for some had a significant impact. When one immigrant arrived in the United States on a Cunard liner, he listed his religious preference as "Cunarder."

In certain respects Captain Turner could not be considered an ideal choice to command a luxury liner, as he had unpolished personal manners and could at times be surly. The line desired that the captain of a ship such as the *Lusitania* be tactful and socialize with the passengers, especially those from first class. Turner felt awkward in this role, yet he had some sterling qualities desirable in an officer. He had ample courage and had proved himself a superb navigator. He knew how to handle men both above and below his station. It was on the bridge—and not at the captain's table—where Turner felt most accomplished.

The Cunard Line must have thought highly of Turner, or they wouldn't have given him a command such as the *Lusitania*. Until then Turner had performed impeccably for Cunard, having set records crossing the Atlantic while in command of both the *Lusitania* and the *Mau-*

retania. After *Aquitania*'s maiden voyage, he docked his ship in 18 minutes, a record for a vessel that size.[21] It was no wonder that Turner earned £1,000 (about $5,000) a year, considerably more than most master mariners at the time.[22] But that was while peace still prevailed.

Now it was wartime, and the situation was suddenly different. The Admiralty's suggestion that he zigzag his route would cause the liner to consume more coal. What would Alfred Booth, Cunard's chairman, think of this waste? The talk of menacing submarines was nonsense, he thought. Submarines might threaten small, plodding cargo ships, but not his command; the *Lusitania* was simply too fast. Some captains such as Turner, accustomed to independent command, were having difficulty adjusting to the new circumstances of war. They resented the interference of anyone telling them how to run their ships.

It took years for an officer in the Cunard Line to rise to command. Officers in the Merchant Service generally started out as apprentices in their mid-teens. After spending about three years "learning the ropes," they took an examination that allowed them to serve at a rank no higher than second officer. After serving as an officer for 18 months, they could sit for their mate's certificate, which would allow them to serve as a first officer. After an additional 18 months, they could take the test for their master's certificate. As an additional feather in their caps, some men took the more thorough exam for an extra master's certificate. All officers in the Cunard Line, including Turner, held an extra master's certificate.

By the early 20th century, life had improved for officers in the Merchant Service. Instead of wind-driven wooden ships, these men now sailed in steam-powered, steel-hulled vessels. Since they traveled much faster they could be home with their families more often, but repeated voyages still taxed a man's stamina. "If ever there was a kill or cure," remarked Charles Lightoller, the second officer of the ill-fated *Titanic*, "it was a Western Ocean mail boat in winter time."[23]

It took far more than navigational skills to run a ship like the *Lusitania*. Equally important was the engineering staff, which provided the power to run the liner. Chief Engineer Archibald Bryce, now 54, had served the Cunard Line for 32 years. He and his staff took on the critical job of keeping the engines running and the electrical power serviceable for the crew and passengers. The Bryce family had a long tradition at sea, including Archibald's father, who had been an engineer on a Cunard paddle steamer in the 1840s. Being appointed chief engineer of the *Lusitania* was no small accomplishment; the Cunard Line must have held him in very high regard. Some of the engineers serving under Bryce, however, were "green," like 22-year-old Walter Scott Quarrie. Hired on as a ventilation engineer, this was his first voyage.

Part of Bryce's job involved overseeing the stokers. These men would work shirtless, shoveling coal into the furnaces. Around the clock, alternating shifts of the "black gang" fed the fires. Life was far from bucolic for these men, but at least this generation of stokers had the advantages of better ventilation and accommodations. Nevertheless, the stokers' lot was hardly enviable, and the constant heat could cause tempers to flair. One chilling story told of an engineer who mysteriously disappeared, and speculation was that he was killed by a mad shovel-wielding stoker. The body, it was assumed, was conveniently cremated in one of the furnaces.[24]

The navigational officers were kept busy during the voyage. Junior Third Officer Albert Bestic (whom Captain Turner called "Bissett") had many duties, including watching the bridge and writing up logbooks and meteorological forms. Every so often a passenger would want his or her trunk brought up from the baggage room, and Bestic would supervise its transfer from belowdecks to the owner.

Occasionally Bestic would be interrupted by strange requests. On Wednesday, May 5, he was enjoying a game of bridge with some other officers when Captain Turner's messenger came in with a piece of rope tied in a peculiar fashion. The Captain wanted another rope tied the same way. Chief Officer Piper could not identify the knot, but Bestic recognized it as a Turk's head, a knot used in sailing ships for decorative purposes. Piper assigned Bestic the task of duplicating the knot for the Captain, and they returned it to Turner with the wardroom's compliments.[25]

Other seamen, during the seven days the *Lusitania* steamed toward Liverpool, washed the decks and the lifeboats. One day, Seaman Leslie Morton was assigned the job of putting an eye splice—a permanent loop in the end of a rope—in an eight-stranded wire hawser on the foredeck. A crowd of passengers gathered to watch the complicated procedure with keen interest. Morton grinned to himself as the passengers breathed "ooo's" and "aaahs."[26]

On May 6 Morton, lying on his back painting a lifeboat, heard footsteps. He peered out and saw Lady Allan's two daughters running up to him.

"What are you doing, sailor?" they asked.

"I'm painting the lifeboat," Morton answered.

"May we help?"

"I don't think this is a job for little girls," replied Morton.

But the older girl ignored him. She took up a paintbrush, began painting, and in the process got paint on her dress. Just then Morton heard the sound of heavier footsteps. He glanced out and saw the boatswain approaching. The girls promptly dropped the brushes and ran, and Morton, not wishing to face the boatswain, slid outboard and over the side onto the next deck.[27]

The *Lusitania* was more than a ship—she was a hotel. A total of 306 men and women labored in the victualling department, including cooks, bakers, bellhops, stewards and those who set the breakfast tables. Purser James McCubin, who had been in the business for 35 years, supervised them.

The ship's physician, Dr. J.F. McDermott, was a substitute on this voyage for the *Lusitania*'s regular doctor who was ill. McDermott was largely preoccupied by a recent outbreak of typhus fever in New York City that might have infected some of the passengers. To his relief, he found no cases aboard the ship.

The ship's five-musician band had previously found work though the individual shipping lines, until C.W. & F.N. Black entered the scene. They were a Liverpool talent agency that promised to deliver music more cheaply, an attractive incentive to any organization. Eventually, all the Atlantic lines signed contracts to hire only through the Blacks, which meant ships' musicians had to work for lower wages than before. The Amalgamated Musicians Union protested, but was not strong enough to improve the situation.[28]

On Tuesday, May 4, 1915, the *Lusitania*'s crew conducted a lifeboat drill. They used only one boat, No. 14 on the port side. An officer gave an order and a handful of men donned lifejackets and climbed into the boat. The officer gave another order and the men got out of the boat. Thus satisfied, the officer dismissed the crew. It was, in the words of one passenger, "a pitiable exhibition."[29] Oliver Bernard witnessed the boat drill. He concluded that these "sanguinary drills" meant the "possibilities of submarine attack were to be regarded as extremely remote." Still, he couldn't help but wonder what would happen if all the boats had to be lowered about 50 feet to the ocean's surface fully loaded.[30]

The token drill caught the attention of other passengers as well. George Kessler spoke to Purser McCubbin about it, who suggested he talk to the captain. Kessler did just that, but Turner showed little interest. Why not, Kessler proposed, have a boat drill where everyone participated—after all, this voyage had merited a specific warning from the German Embassy.

"A torpedo can't get the *Lusitania*. She runs too fast," the captain replied. Kessler pressed the point, but Turner insisted it wasn't within his authority to counter Cunard's policy. The grim lessons of the *Titanic* disaster three years earlier had apparently gone unlearned by Turner and Cunard.[31]

Passenger Ian Holbourn, like Kessler, felt concern about the lifeboat drill. Holbourn was a lecturer returning home from his third tour of the United States, traveling second class. An avid yachtsman,[32] he urged his fellow passengers at least to try on their lifejackets, but without any luck; no one took him seriously. Holbourn also spoke to the captain about the uselessness of the lifeboat drills, but Turner's only reply was that he'd speak to the chief officer about it. Holbourn concluded that Turner had just dodged the issue, and did not intend to do much of anything about it.

Turner wasn't the only one to object to Holbourn's proddings. A man approached Holbourn and told him he was sent by certain male passengers to persuade him to stop talking about the life-saving equipment, because it "will frighten the lady passengers." Holbourn referred to this group as the "Ostrich Club."[33]

Holbourn spent his spare time working on a book tentatively titled *The Philosophy of Beauty*, which he hoped to get published sometime that year. He also managed to befriend the 12-year-old Avis Dolphin, who was travelling to school in England. Because she suffered from what was termed "neuralgia," a nurse was required to bring food to her cabin, though she flatly refused to eat it. On Wednesday her nurse suggested that she go to the second-class lounge to lie down. She did this, and was approached by Holbourn, who asked, "Are you quite comfortable, my girl?"

"Yes, thank you," she replied.

"I don't think it's possible that you really are," said Holbourn. He went and got her a pillow wrapped in a shawl.

"There you are. Now you'll feel more comfortable." The professor offered to get her some fruit and tea, but Avis declined. Turning to her nurse, Holbourn suggested they go on deck and get some fresh air. As they settled into their deck chairs, Holbourn told Avis that he was the laird of Foula, his summer home on a Shetland island with about 150 "subjects." He said he'd make her an honorary subject. And with this little scenario to preoccupy her thoughts, Avis began to improve.

Early in the voyage, the architect Theodate Pope came across the German newspaper warning while she was reading the latest issue of the *Sun*. "This means of course that they intend to get us," she said to Edwin Friend, her traveling companion. She chose to believe a friendly convoy would be waiting for them when they reached the war zone. Nevertheless, to be on the safe side she told Friend and her maid, Emily Robinson, to meet on the Boat Deck in the event of a disaster. Within a few days Pope had lost some of her apprehension. She and Friend sat on adjacent deck chairs with the latter translating Bergson's *Matiene et Memoire* for her as he read. Friend impressed her; he seemed "endowed richly in heart and mind."

Pope now had a small space of time in which to reflect on her life. Although a successful architect, she had turned to psychic research when her father had died two years earlier. She and Friend were going to meet with Sir Oliver Lodge and like-minded believers at the British Society of Psychical Research, to generate support for a new magazine on psychical phenomena. Friend, secretary of the Society for Psychic Research in New York, was to be its editor.[34]

Seaman Leslie Morton occasionally overheard the normal chatter of passengers, but never detected any discussion about being torpedoed. Personally, he "pooh-poohed" the notion of being sunk.[35] Other passengers belittled the risk of a submarine attack, too. As F.J. Gauntlett remarked, "From the day we sailed we complacently spoke of the possibilities of the German menace, but no one believed it. So we scorned the idea of being torpedoed."[36]

Charles Lauriat, however, was taking no chances. He decided to leave his papers and other valuables in his cabin instead of locking them up in the purser's safe, thinking that in the event of an emergency they could more easily be retrieved. He considered the danger of theft to be "negligible." Lauriat also kept a box of matches in his cabin in the event of a power failure.[37]

A few passengers felt somewhat alarmed by the danger. While strolling on deck with her mother and siblings, Edith Williams was struck by the strangeness of her mother's words: she said that if the ship were torpedoed she hoped they'd all drown together, to be saved together. This sentiment puzzled the nine-year-old Edith.[38]

As the liner made her 201st voyage, John Welsh warmed up to his new friend Gerda Nielson. They would meet in a corner of the third-class lounge, and at night take a stroll on deck. Welsh had earned a tidy sum as an engineer in Honolulu; he was now prepared to settle down and start a family. Although the couple had known each other for only a few days, the chemistry seemed perfect.[39]

Elizabeth Duckworth spent much of her time on this voyage socializing with her roommates, Mrs. Alice Scott and her son Arthur. Alice, though more than 20 years younger than Elizabeth, also had a British upbringing. The three shared a cabin in steerage and got along splendidly.[40]

Some passengers were in poor health. Besides young Avis Dolphin, Sir Hugh Lane, returning home after giving testimony in a New York lawsuit, felt unwell. He wondered if his solicitor had completed the changes to his will so that his collection of Impressionist paintings would return to Dublin. Despite this concern, he still joined Lady Allan for bridge in the smoking room.

Scenic designer Oliver Bernard reprimanded the steward who changed his dinner table to suit another passenger. Bernard bitterly asked, "Will you condescend to inform me why the genius of marine engineers, shipbuilders and financiers who have built this ship must be depreciated because you think some passengers are entitled to more attention than others?"[41] Leslie Mason and her new husband Stewart[42] had been entrusted to Bernard's care for their wedding trip. Leslie's father, a Boston industrialist and playwright who had employed Bernard, had asked him to "Keep an eye on my little girl, please!"[43]

Julia Sullivan took advantage of the *Lusitania's* swimming pool. Dressed in her swimming costume from Florida, she would dive into the pool and gracefully swim from end to end, pleased to see that her swimming surpassed that of most other women aboard. Second-class passenger Archibald Donald spent much of his time on deck, mostly to avoid the cramped quarters that he shared with three others. Donald, a Canadian working for Truscon Steel Company, was en route to Edinburgh University for officer's training. Donald liked to play bridge. He and his companions usually started at ten o'clock in the morning, paused in the afternoon to socialize with women, and then returned to their game until late into the night. Julia Sullivan and her husband Flor formed a friendship with Patrick Callan, a stockman from Chicago. Together the three would observe men playing poker in the first-class smoking room, whereupon Julia realized, shrewdly, that some players were evidently cardsharps.

Professional gamblers frequented luxury ocean liners such as the *Lusitania*. These men would win large sums of money from wagers with first-class passengers, and though the steamship lines knew of the presence of cardsharps on board, they did not forbid gambling. The lines took no action for many reasons, but primarily because they were reluctant to interfere with the freedom of their passengers. Instead, the Atlantic shipping companies would issue warnings such as the following from the White Star Line:

SPECIAL NOTICE

The attention of the Managers has been called to the fact that certain persons, believed to be professional Gamblers, are in the habit of traveling to and fro in Atlantic steamships. In bringing this to the knowledge of Travelers the Manager, while not wishing in the slightest degree to interfere with the freedom of action of Patrons of the White Star Line, desire to invite their assistance in discouraging Games of Chance, as being likely to afford these individuals special opportunities for taking unfair advantage of others.[44]

A few men of the cloth also made this voyage, among them Father Basil Maturin, a Roman Catholic chaplain at Oxford University. And, as in any large group of people, some aboard were in a tragic phase of life, such as 60-year-old Martha Ann Whyatt, whose husband had recently died. As a widow she had decided to return to her native England.[45] Still others were journeying to Europe to serve in the war. Second-class passengers Dr. Daniel Moore and his roommate numbered among a "party of surgeons who had volunteered their services to the British War Office."[46] Another passenger going to Britain to enlist, Lt. Robert Matthews, had moved to Canada before the war and joined its 60th Rifles. He left his wife following a crumbled marriage, and was traveling with his mistress, Annie. Matthews hoped to obtain a commission in the Royal Army.[47]

During the final days of the voyage, Purser McCubbin had developed friendly ties with Flor and Julia Sullivan. McCubbin invited them to his table in the second-class dining room, where he joked that there was enough food to give every passenger four square meals a day. Later the purser brought the Sullivans to the first-class dining saloon, and in order to escape anyone's notice, carefully sat them in a remote corner. McCubbin assumed he could get away with this, or maybe he didn't care this late in the game—he was scheduled to retire at the end of this voyage. The 60-year-old purser had bought a farm 20 miles from London, on which he planned to happily retire. McCubbin, like Turner, was highly regarded by the Cunard Line. To be a purser one had to be both a good administrator and tactful with passengers. These were qualities McCubbin possessed, and serving as purser on the *Lusitania* was a fine way to end a career.[48]

A concert scheduled on the last night of the voyage included a group of singers from second class. McCubbin, known to have a flair for the flute, was asked to join in, and he agreed. During the concert Captain Turner spoke, thanking the passengers for sailing on the *Lusitania*, and acknowledging that there had been warnings of submarines. "But of course there is no cause for alarm," he assured them, "We shall be arriving at Liverpool early on Saturday morning."

"Are we in any danger, Captain?" a man asked.

"In wartime there is always danger," he answered, "but I must repeat there is no cause for alarm." Turner then requested that all smokers refrain from lighting their cigars on the open deck.[49]

In another part of the ship George Kessler entertained his guests with cocktails. Among them were the elderly Canadian woman Georgina Morell, Fred Gauntlett, Theodate Pope, Edwin Friend, Isaac Lehmann and Charles Lauriat. Alfred Vanderbilt decided to go to the dining saloon that Thursday. On his way he was handed a Marconigram, delivered via the ship's Marconi wireless set, from his friend May Barwell, saying that she looked forward to his arrival in England. This lifted Vanderbilt's spirits considerably.

Charles Lauriat, who had been in a hurry to get to England, was by this time becoming suspicious of the liner's slow progress. The advertisement had boasted of the *Lusitania*'s speed, yet for the past six days she had been traveling below par. Lauriat could only assume that the captain planned to fire up the boilers for an extra burst of speed on the last day. Oliver Bernard also questioned the ship's speed. This was his 12th voyage across the Atlantic, his second on the *Lusitania,* and he considered this a "rather disappointing" trip. The liner was by no means living up to her reputation.[50]

The report from the ship's engineer, Bryce, made the question of speed clear to Captain Turner. With its present volume of steam, the ship could make 21 knots. If the six cold boilers were fired up, they could easily give her 25 knots. But Turner decided against having Bryce recall the off-duty stokers the next day. Twenty-one knots seemed sufficiently fast to him.[51]

Before the war, passengers on ships like the *Lusitania* kept abreast of the latest news, sports and stock prices by radio; wireless had been on ships for years now. People at sea could contact loved ones, friends and business associates by sending and receiving "Marconigrams," messages sent via radio. Wireless was also important for navigation. Ship's captains kept up to date on weather and iceberg reports, and in the event of a disaster such as had befallen the *Republic* or the *Titanic,* wireless could be used to transmit distress messages. During World War I, it could also alert shipmasters of submarine activity.

The men handling the *Lusitania*'s wireless were Robert Leith and David McCormick. Though employed by Marconi Marine, with a pay rate ranging from $20 to $30 a month, they were under the authority of the ship's captain. Since a major war was in progress, the captain ordered Leith and McCormick to send no passenger messages, which could possibly be intercepted by the Germans—the ship was to observe radio silence as much as possible. At one point her wireless picked up a message from the Admiralty reading, "Questor," to ask which edition of the Merchant Vessel Code the *Lusitania* had. The ship's men signaled back "Westrona," which meant they used the first edition.[52]

On May 6, six days out of New York, the *Lusitania* picked up a warning from the Admiralty: "To all British ships. Take Liverpool pilot at bar and avoid headlands. Pass harbor at full speed. Steer mid-channel course. Submarines off Fastnet."[53]

Though many passengers were aware of the submarine peril, they assumed their arrival in Liverpool would be a safe one. Some, such as Lady Mackworth, thought "an attempt would be made in the Irish Sea during our last night," but the liner experienced no unusual events.[54] Charles Lauriat expected the ship to dock safely, for he strongly wanted to believe that Turner would give the vessel extra speed on Friday. That would be a grand end to another "Lauriat Crossing."[55]

CHAPTER 7
OLD HEAD OF KINSALE

On Friday, May 7, 1915, the *Lusitania* was seven days out of New York and scheduled to dock in Liverpool within a matter of hours. The ocean liner met with no major problems until a severe fog enveloped her that morning. Captain Turner reduced speed and ordered the foghorn sounded. At short intervals, the foghorn's wail rippled through the air.

The sound worried the powerful industrialist David Thomas. While breakfasting with his daughter, Lady Mackworth, he complained, "That wretched foghorn gives our whereabouts away."[1] Later at lunch in an effort to cheer him up, his daughter reminded him they would soon be home. But Thomas couldn't be distracted and repeated his concern: "I would be more pleased, my dear, if I believed that wretched siren hasn't given our whereabouts away."[2]

Passenger Harold Boulton, keenly aware of the foghorn, noticed the liner was traveling at a slower speed and called it to the attention of a steward. The steward assured him that the speed had been reduced because of the fog, but also pointed out that slowing down preserved coal that might be needed for a build-up of speed if a submarine were spotted.[3]

Within a few hours the fog lifted and clear visibility for several miles returned. The foghorn ceased, which must have relieved Thomas. In the first-class dining saloon, James Brooks drank his coffee, annoyed that the ship was traveling so slowly. He also noticed that the chains remained attached to the lifeboats, a fact that could hinder their use in an emergency.

Charles Lauriat awoke that morning at his usual eight o'clock. He bathed, but realizing he was still tired, asked his steward to rouse him if he didn't wake by noon. Thus assured, Lauriat returned to his bed to gain a few extra hours of sleep.[4] At noon he was awakened by the steward. The book dealer dressed and went on deck for a stroll before lunch, noticing that it was a beautiful day. A light breeze played across the deck, and with the lifting of the fog, he saw the sun and a smooth sea.[5]

Lauriat's thoughts turned to U-boats. He concluded that if the Germans were serious about their threats, they would at least wait for a better opportunity—in these conditions a submarine's periscope could easily be seen. But his thoughts shifted when he realized the Irish coast was visible. This meant the liner was following its usual course, though slowly. Lauriat, however, knew enough not to bother an officer with questions of safety since they were "told to discreetly hold their tongues."[6]

At noon the *Lusitania* approached Cape Clear off southern Ireland. The ship's clocks, put one hour and 40 minutes ahead of Greenwich time, meant that it wouldn't be long before they reached Liverpool. During lunch Oliver Bernard discussed with a woman passenger their lifeboat preferences in the event of a submarine attack. Bernard voiced the opinion that a life raft was preferable. He also mentioned to Theodate Pope that the change he received from a steward would be something to hold onto "in the event of an explosion."[7]

In the second-class dining hall, Charlotte Pye encountered passengers who were visibly upset. After breakfast she went up on deck and met clergyman H.L. Gwyer, who informed her that they were now in a danger zone.

"Will it be safe for us?" she nervously asked.

"Well," answered Gwyer, "I suppose something may happen so I've decided to stay on deck tonight."[8]

John Welsh, the engineer returning to England, and Gerda Neilson had just finished lunch and were headed for the third-class lounge. Jack had greatly impressed Gerda with his personality and his stories of fighting in the Boer War; the couple had already agreed to marry. Erstwhile neuralgia-sufferer Avis Dolphin sat on the Promenade Deck with Ian Holbourn, who was explaining to her the workings of the ship. The professor also told her more about the Shetland Islands and the ponies and seabirds that inhabited the area.[9] Mary Maycock, in anticipation of disembarking and seeing Yorkshire again, packed her luggage. She then went to the second-class library to write a letter to her brothers in New York.

At 11:20 a.m., the Admiralty flashed another warning: "Submarines active in southern part of Irish Channel. Last heard of 20 miles south of Coningbeg Light Vessel. Make certain *Lusitania* gets this."[10] And then, several minutes after noon, Captain Turner received yet another wireless warning: "Submarine five miles south of Cape Clear proceeding west when sighted at 10 a.m."[11]

A submarine was indeed active. The *U-20*, under the command of Kapitänleutnant Walther Schwieger, had departed from the German naval base at Emden a day before the *Lusitania* left New York. Upon reaching the Atlantic, she took position off the southern coast of Ireland. Schwieger's orders read:

Large English troop transports expected starting from Liverpool, Dartmouth. Get to stations on fastest possible route around Scotland. Hold as long as supplies permit. Submarines to attack transport ships, merchant ships and warships.[12]

The U-boat he commanded was a far cry from the mammoth submarines of today, yet it was greatly superior to the underwater vessels of the past. Commissioned in 1913, the *U-20* displaced 650 tons running on the surface, or 837 tons submerged. Two eight-cylinder diesel engines—capable of 15 knots—powered her on the surface; submerged, two electric motors could push her to nine knots. The *U-20* carried an 8.8-centimeter deck gun[13] and seven torpedoes similar to the Whitehead torpedo, developed by an English inventor of that name. They were 12 to 16 feet in length and each weighed about a ton. Air driven, these torpedoes could travel up to 40 knots the first 1,000 yards, with a warhead of 290 pounds of trotyl explosive.[14]

Schwieger was a cool and efficient U-boat commander. Thirty years old, he had joined the German Navy at 18, and at 27 won command of the *U-14*. He now commanded one of the best submarines in the world, and his men respected him. One officer who served under him described him as "the soul of kindness toward the officers and men under him. His temperament was joyous and his talk full of gaiety and pointed wit. He had the gifts to command both respect and liking and was a general favorite in the German Navy."[15]

Under Schwieger, the *U-20* experienced many perilous adventures as well as some festive occasions. On Christmas Eve, 1914, the first Christmas of the war, *U-20* had patrolled the North Sea looking for enemy warships. Though ordered to sink enemy ships, "the enemy was at home celebrating Christmas as a Christian should, because never a sign of British craft did we see."[16] After a long day of watching a calm sea, the captain ordered the submarine to dive until it rested on the ocean floor. "And now," cried Commander Schwieger, "we can celebrate Christmas." A wreath hung at one end of the sailors' mess and served as a Christmas tree (though without lighted candles due to the risk of fire). Dressed in their leather submarine suits, the officers and men ate a dinner of canned foods together, followed by many toasts and a little after-dinner speech by Schwieger. Then they listened attentively to the ship's "orchestra," three crewmembers with violin, mandolin and "the inevitable nautical accordion."[17]

There were other lighthearted moments on the *U-20*. One day "when we became positively desperate for a decent bite to eat," the ship happened to capture a large quantity of butter, which lifted spirits considerably. For several days "we piled butter on our hard tack and thought it was delicious." But soon the sailors began to yearn for something wonderful to fry *in* the butter. As one crewmember later recalled:

> Off the French coast the periscope showed a fleet of fishing boats busy at their nets. It was dangerous for a U-boat to show its conning tower in those waters—but we were desperate men. The fishermen saw a submarine pop suddenly into their midst. From the stories that were told of the U-boats, they expected to be massacred at once. They laughed and cheered and got very busy when they discovered that all the U-boat wanted was some fresh fish. We crammed our boat with fish, fine big fellows—

bonitos—with a pinkish meat. . . . And now there was fresh fish, fried in butter, grilled in butter, all that we could eat. We took a comfortable station, submerged, so that we might not be disturbed, and you can bet that jaws worked until they were tired.[18]

Not all experiences on the *U-20* were convivial. One day the submarine got itself entangled in a net and sank to a depth of 100 feet—luckily for the crew no bombs were attached. As Schwieger ordered the engines reversed to wiggle free, the sound of destroyer propellers became audible. (It was still early in the war and destroyers had not yet been armed with depth charges.) Despite the fact that the submarine freed itself and raced away, the destroyers remained in close pursuit—the enemy ships seemed able to track the submarine no matter how evasive. Schwieger could not fathom why, and the uncertainty raised tensions aboard the U-boat. When night came, the *U-20* finally managed to speed away from the destroyers. She surfaced and the crew immediately saw why the enemy destroyers could follow them: a cable had become fast to the submarine, and it dragged a buoy.[19]

Now, on Sunday, May 2, 1915, the submarine was patrolling the Irish coast. Suddenly the officer on watch, Lieutenant Raimund Weisbach, observed enemy destroyers approaching. The crew quickly closed the hatches and submerged. Fortunately for Schwieger the British ships passed overhead, and the *U-20* remained undetected. The German crew knew full well their level of vulnerability to gunfire or ramming.[20] Schwieger had already missed many opportunities to sink Allied merchant ships. Earlier in the mission he had come across a fast-moving White Star liner (possibly the *Arabic*), but the steamer's superior speed allowed it to get away.

Later, on Wednesday, May 5, the *U-20* encountered the *Earl of Lathom*, a sailing ship that could not outrun the U-boat. Schwieger came alongside the full-rigged vessel and demanded that the captain present her papers and abandon ship. The captain and his crew of five came across in a lifeboat. The papers revealed that the schooner carried a cargo of food. Schwieger ordered his gun crew to open fire, and the *Earl of Lathom* sank.[21]

The next day the *U-20* came upon a small steamer, the *Candidate* of the Harrison Line. This ship was bound for the West Indies with a cargo of food and hardware. Schwieger ordered his gunner to open fire, and a shell struck the steamer's funnel. The *Candidate*'s captain ordered his helmsman to turn to avoid a torpedo, but after the Germans directed their gunfire to the steamer's bridge, the master realized they could not escape. He reluctantly stopped the engines and ordered the crew to abandon ship.

The *Candidate*'s crew lowered four lifeboats. One was swamped as it hit the water but the other three rowed successfully away from the ship. Satisfied that the crew was safe, Schwieger fired a torpedo at the derelict. It struck near the engine room and exploded, but the *Candidate* remained afloat. Determined to sink her, Schwieger moved closer to the British steamer and fired with his deck gun at her waterline. This time the *Candidate* sank slowly to the bottom.

Just then a naval trawler came on the scene—the *Lawrenny Castle,* armed, but with a gun smaller than the German submarine's. The crew in the *Candidate*'s lifeboats hoped to see a duel, but to their chagrin, the *Lawrenny Castle* hurried away before it could be hit. Another naval trawler, the *Lord Allendale,* eventually picked up the shipwrecked British sailors.[22]

Later that day, the *U-20* spotted the *Centurion,* a British steamer of the Harrison Line bound for South Africa. Without giving the conventional warning to abandon ship, the U-boat fired a torpedo and the *Centurion* sank, although with no loss of life.[23]

As these instances show, Schwieger occasionally gave the conventional warning to abandon ship as required by international law, but at other times he torpedoed without warning. U-boat commanders had no way of knowing whether or not their prey had guns; furthermore, when U-boats surfaced to deliver a warning, they ran the risk of being rammed. This had happened to some German submarine commanders earlier in the war when they had attempted to give a warning, but were rammed or shot at in response.

The details of these recent U-boat attacks were unknown to Captain Turner. He had been warned by the Admiralty of submarine activity off the coast of Ireland, yet he seemed to underestimate the danger of an attack. Nevertheless he did take certain precautions. He ordered that lifeboats be swung out. He also had the doors of watertight bulkheads closed, and posted additional lookouts with instructions to be on the alert for submarines.

Aboard the *Lusitania* a rumor circulated that a submarine had been sighted that morning. According to the story, a U-boat "with four towers" surfaced a few hundred yards from the liner on her portside and then dived again. This was, however, a false alarm.[24] Stories like these were the topic of bewildered conversation in the dining saloons. One passenger was overheard ordering ice cream, and while waiting for the steward to get him a spoon joked that it would be a shame if the ship were torpedoed before he could finish his dessert. This prompted somewhat nervous chuckles among the rest of the diners.[25]

By 1:30 p.m. that Friday, the *Lusitania's* lookouts sighted Old Head of Kinsale, a stab of land off County Cork on Ireland's east coast. First Officer Percy Hefford and Junior Third Officer Albert Bestic had come onto the bridge. When Bestic saw the lighthouse of Old Head of Kinsale, he knew he'd soon have to supervise the unloading of the mail.

Several problems confronted Captain Turner that afternoon. If he continued at full speed, he would arrive off Liverpool harbor before the tide, forcing the *Lusitania* to circle outside the harbor for several hours. This possibility caused him to reduce speed. To make certain of his position, Turner began to conduct a four-point bearing, a long and tedious procedure. In so doing he violated his instructions to "keep mid-channel course" and to "reduce the chance of a successful surprise attack by zigzagging."[26]

Seaman Leslie Morton went on deck to put on his sweater and gear, preparing himself for lookout duty at two o'clock. He reported at the starboard side of the bow. "I was keeping a keen eye on my job as extra lookout," he later explained.[27]

Meanwhile, some of the passengers continued to enjoy the comforts of "Lucy" before she docked. One of them was Florence Padley, seated in a deck chair absorbing the sun. Oliver Bernard, the pithy scenic designer on his way home to enlist, also enjoyed the fine weather as he walked the promenade.[28] He mistakenly thought the ship had stopped, only to realize she was just moving very slowly. He crossed in front of the bridge to starboard, and then went aft to the Veranda Café, deep in thought, when he was interrupted by what he took to be a porpoise sighting.[29]

James Brooks, a businessman from Connecticut traveling to Europe to woo new clients, strolled on deck. For him this was a pleasant way to end a voyage. Julia and Flor Sullivan watched their native Ireland through binoculars loaned to them by Purser McCubbin.[30] Robert Rankin, the mining engineer, stood on deck talking with two other passengers.

Charles Lauriat had been eating lunch with Lothrop Withington, the renowned genealogist from Boston. "We had a jolly time together," he later said. The two made plans to see each other in London, since Withington lived near Lauriat's London office.[31] After lunch, Lauriat went topside. There he met Elbert and Alice Hubbard on the port side, and they struck up a conversation.[32] All the relaxed socializing was of no concern to Seaman Leslie Morton, standing lookout on the starboard forecastle head. Morton was told to watch for periscopes and torpedoes, but so far had seen nothing of the sort.[33]

Meanwhile, aboard the *U-20*, Captain Schwieger waited for prey south of the entrance to the Bristol Channel. Since sinking the *Centurion*, his mission had been hampered by dense fog. Schwieger had decided not to advance to Liverpool as assigned, in order to avoid British patrols and conserve fuel. His U-boat cruised the surface recharging its batteries and replenishing its oxygen supply; once "two-fifths of the fuel oil was used up," he would be forced to return home.[34] But the U-boat captain was determined to make one last kill on this voyage.

Then he saw a target: "Ahead and to the starboard four funnels and two masts of a steamer with course perpendicular to us come into sight. . . . Ship is made out to be large passenger steamer."[35] Schwieger acted quickly. He dove the U-boat to eleven meters below the surface and set a course for the unknown steamer.

The German submarine came within 700 meters of the steamer. From his periscope, Schwieger saw his intended victim. To his pilot, a man named Lanz, he described her as a four-funnel, 30,000-odd-ton passenger liner. From his familiarity with *Jane's Fighting Ships* and the *Naval Annual*, Lanz was able to identify the ship as either the *Lusitania* or her sister ship, the *Mauretania*. Both Cunarders were known auxiliary cruisers for the British Navy.

Schwieger had three options. He could let the liner go, but the liner itself could later be used as a troop transport, and this could be the Germans' last chance to sink her. He could surface and give the usual warning, but this might prove foolhardy since the liner was undoubtedly faster than his own ship—she could escape, or worse yet, ram the submarine. Finally, he could fire a torpedo without warning. He was in a good position to do so.

After careful thought, Schwieger made a fateful decision—he would torpedo the ship. Thus at 2:10 p.m. on Friday, May 7, 1915, he gave the order. He instructed the wheelman controlling the torpedo to arm it and prepare for release. Then he ordered, "Fire!"

The torpedo left the tube and raced toward its target. "Clear bow shot from 700 meters range (G-torpedo three meters depth adjustment) cutting angle 90 degrees. Estimate speed twenty-two sea miles," Schwieger recorded in his log. Then he waited.[36]

CHAPTER 8
EIGHTEEN LETHAL MINUTES

The torpedo traveled straight for the *Lusitania* at a speed of 40 knots. It left a trail of telltale bubbles as it streaked through the water. The journey to its target would take only a few seconds.

On the starboard forecastle head, Seaman Leslie Morton, first to see its foaming trail, shouted through a megaphone, "Torpedo coming on the starboard side!" Without waiting a second for acknowledgement, Morton rushed below to find his sleeping brother, a fellow crewmemer.[1]

High in the crow's nest, starboard lookout Thomas Quinn also spotted the torpedo's wake coming in behind the foremast. Immediately he shouted it to the attention of the bridge.

Seated comfortably in a deck chair, Florence Padley heard someone say they saw a porpoise.[2]

Michael Byrne also mistook the torpedo for a porpoise, but when he didn't see the usual curved leap, he looked more closely. Byrne thought he saw a submarine below the surface. He recalled from his earlier search that the *Lusitania* had no large guns.

James Brooks watched as something came straight for the ship. It resembled not a porpoise but rather the outline of a torpedo.

Oscar Grab, talking with some other passengers, saw one of them suddenly point out to sea and exclaim, "What is that over there?" Grab looked and saw what appeared to be a stick projecting out of the water—and in the next instant recognized it as a torpedo coming straight at the *Lusitania*. To him the wake looked like the white foam following a motorboat. Watching the torpedo's impact, Grab shouted, "I knew it would happen!"[3]

Joseph Myers had been relaxing in the Palm Lounge. Along with Frank Kellett he walked to starboard where he caught sight of a periscope in the water about 700 yards away. Myers looked more closely, and made out the *U-20's* submerged hull and conning tower. He grabbed Kellett's arm and shouted, "Look, there's a submarine!"[4] Myers then breathed, "My God…we are lost!"

Charles Hill, London executive of the British-American Tobacco Company,[5] stood near the rail talking with the *Lusitania's* Chief Steward Jones when he exclaimed, "Good God, Mr. Hill, here comes a torpedo!"[6] Hill saw the periscope, and in the next instant noticed a disturbance in the water. The men watched and waited, hoping the torpedo would only cross the *Lusitania's* bow.

Oliver Bernard, like Florence Padley, had come on deck after dining when he saw what he thought was a periscope, and a few seconds later detected a "long white streak of foam" making its way to the starboard side. The foam was like "frothy fizzing in water."[7] "Is that a torpedo?" someone near Bernard asked. Realizing that it was, he covered his eyes, corked his ears and waited.

Robert Rankin, the mining engineer, looked out from the deck while he was talking with other passengers when suddenly he saw the periscope. Then he saw something else: "That looks like a torpedo!" he exclaimed.

W.G.E. Meyers, the 16-year-old on his way to join the Royal Navy, was enjoying a game of quoits with two other boys on the Upper Deck. One boy glanced over his shoulder and shouted, "There's a torpedo coming straight at us!" Meyers rushed to the railing and saw a streak of bubbles coming in his direction.[8]

The torpedo exploded as it struck the liner on the starboard side, near the bridge and the foremost funnel. The *Lusitania* shook violently amidst a tremendous roar. As the explosion tore a hole in the ship's side, about "220 square feet of the *Lusitania's* outer hull plating . . . vanished in the blast."[9] A split second later a second explosion rocked the huge liner with more violence than the first. "Debris, dust and water were thrown up in a dense column through the entire superstructure of the vessel" near the bridge.[10]

Through the *U-20*'s periscope, Schwieger observed an "unusually great detonation with large cloud of smoke and debris shot above funnels. In addition to torpedo, a second explosion must have taken place. (Boiler, coal or powder?) Bridge and part of the ship where the torpedo hit are torn apart, and fire follows. The ship stops and very quickly leans over to the starboard, at the same time sinking at bow. It looks as though it would capsize in a short time."[11]

Aboard the liner, Seaman Leslie Morton ran down to the forecastle to see his brother, John. He heard "a tremendous explosion," followed immediately by a second one, and saw water, debris, and steam shoot up in to the air. The young seaman met up with his brother who asked, "What the Hell are you doing with the ship, Gertie?"

"We've been torpedoed," Morton shot back. "We have to get to our stations." The two brothers hurried off to their posts.[12] On the Boat Deck, Morton encountered a great deal of excitement. Passengers and crew were milling about, saying "Surely she cannot sink. Not the *Lusitania*?" or words to that effect. But the young sailor could tell the ship was sinking by the feel of the deck under his feet.[13]

Flor and Julia Sullivan, looking at the Irish coast through binoculars, hoped that Piper's Hill would come in to view. Suddenly Julia was shaken by "the most dreadful explosion the world has ever heard." The force of the explosion made the liner shake with such violence she seemed to be lifted out of the water. Julia grabbed her husband to keep from falling.[14]

First Officer Arthur Jones and Acting Senior Third Officer John Lewis were having lunch when the torpedo struck. To Lewis it sounded like a report from a heavy gun, two or three miles away. A few seconds later he heard the second explosion, a tremendous clap of thunder. Immediately both officers realized what had happened, jumped to their feet and ran to their posts.

To Captain Turner the sound was like the "rattling of a Maxim gun."

First Senior Engineer Robert Duncan was abaft the engineer's quarters when he heard an explosion. Duncan heard a second explosion that he assumed was closer, for a piece of a nearby thermo tank flew off and dropped at his feet. The engineer quickly proceeded to assist nearby passengers with their life belts.[15]

Samuel Knox, finishing his lunch, felt "a heavy concussion." The shipbuilding executive became aware that the ship had suddenly developed a list to the starboard, "which rapidly increased."[16] Seated with Knox were other shipbuilders, Frederic.J. Gauntlett and Albert L. Hopkins. When Gauntlett heard the explosion, he "knew at once what had happened."[17]

Young William McMillan Adams was in the first-class lounge reading a novel when he heard the explosion, which shook the liner "from stem to stern." He rushed to the companionway when he heard a second explosion that sounded like the mast had fallen down.

Josephine Brandell had just finished collecting money for the orchestra when the first blast went off. Someone at her table shouted, "They've done it!" Other passengers in the dining room rose from their chairs. As glass fell from the windows and portholes, the orchestra somehow continued playing "The Blue Danube" in a futile effort to calm the passengers.

Surgeon Major Warren Pearl was concerned for his children. Making his way to the deck, he discovered that the family's nurses and three of his children were missing. He finally located them below as one of the nurses, Alice Lines, tied a shawl around his infant daughter, Audrey. Lines then took Audrey and five-year-old Stuart to the deck "as quick as possible," discovering in the process the extreme difficulty of taking children upstairs in a listing ship.

Stanley Lines was having lunch with his wife, Ethel, when he heard the initial explosion. He promptly took her to the Boat Deck—already tilting noticeably—and put her into one of the lifeboats. The crew safely lowered it away.

Dr. Ralph Mecredy was on deck when the explosion came; a moment later he heard a second roar. Immediately he heard cries from those onboard that the ship had been torpedoed.[18]

Seated at a table in the second-class dining saloon, Archibald Donald heard the shattering of glass. It sounded to him as though someone had fallen through a glass house. The lights flickered off, and Avis Dolphin heard diners scramble to their feet. Her first thought was, "What a shame I'm going to miss dessert." Ian Holbourn called out to her, "Stay where you are!"

Margaret Cox was eating a pork chop cooked in breadcrumbs when she felt as though the roof were about to collapse on her. She picked up her baby Desmond and made her way through the throngs of people to her steward, who was closing portholes.

"Tell me what to do," she pleaded. "Whatever you say I'll do it."

"Get up the stairs," he told her. "Get up as quickly as you can."[19]

G.B. Lane was on B Deck when the torpedo struck. "I hardly realized what it meant when the big ship seemed to stagger," he recalled.[20] Lieutenant Fred Lassetter was with his mother Elizabeth when the torpedo struck. His mother considered going back to her cabin to retrieve her jewelry, but the severe list of the ship made this idea a foolish one. Elsie Hook, on the stairway leading to the third-class dining room, suddenly felt the ship shake. She quickly turned and ran to the deck where she found her father and brother Frank running toward her.

Theodate Pope was on the Promenade Deck with her companion, Edwin Friend. "How could the officers ever see a periscope there?" asked Pope. In the next instant they heard an explosion. To Pope it seemed like an arrow entering the canvas and straw of a target, only a thousand times louder. Water and debris hurled by them. Friend struck his fist in his hand and blurted, "By Jove, they've got us!"[21]

Mothers were naturally frightened for their children. Nora Bretherton was on her way to her cabin to put her son Paul to bed when she heard the huge initial blast. She wasn't sure which way to go, but after a moment's reflection she ran back to B Deck and got her baby Elizabeth out of the playpen.[22]

First-class saloon waiter Robert Wiemann was serving his last few diners when the torpedo struck. He detected a sharp list to the starboard, as wall fixtures fell and tables and chairs slid across the room. Wiemann and his customers quickly left the dining room. At one point he assisted a woman up the stairs, exclaiming "Take your time, she's not going down!" The waiter privately believed the ship would sink. Wiemann made his way to the Promenade Deck where he saw people rushing to the stern. He decided to follow them since he knew there were life belts in a locker at the foot of the stairs near his cabin.[23]

Elizabeth Duckworth was walking with Alice Scott and her son Arthur when she felt a "terrible crash." The ship shuddered as if mortally wounded.[24] To Robert Timmis, a cotton dealer from Texas, the explosion was a "penetrating thrust."

Mabel Docherty was in the dining saloon when the torpedo struck. She took her baby and headed for the Boat Deck when she suddenly remembered she had money in her trunk. Sensibly, she realized there was no time to rescue it.

Charles Lauriat was on deck talking with Elbert and Alice Hubbard. Hubbard was engaged in his usual jokes about being an unwelcome visitor to the Germans, when suddenly Lauriat heard "a heavy, rather muffled sound," and felt the liner "tremble for a moment." Immediately after this Lauriat heard a second report, which sounded different from the first; he thought perhaps a boiler had burst.[25]

Lady Mackworth and her father, D.A. Thomas, stepped into an elevator on D Deck when the torpedo struck. According to Thomas they didn't think "very much of it at the time." Nevertheless, they went on deck to discover what was afoot.[26]

Young W.G.E. Meyers heard an "awful explosion" while he was with his friends; immediately afterward flying wood splinters and water showered them. Meyers went below to get his life belt and en route came across a woman who was "frenzied with fear." The sixteen-year-old managed to calm the woman and lead her to a boat.[27] Mrs. C. Stewart heard the explosion while sitting with her eight-month-old baby in her cabin. She grabbed the child and went topside, where a man shouted to her "Come on with the baby!" and found places for both in a lifeboat.[28]

Down below in the galleys, several butchers were at work when suddenly they heard the roar of the torpedo hit. Some of them ran to the freight elevator but were trapped when it jammed between floors. George Wynne and his father, Joseph, along with several butchers, bakers and stewards rushed up to the Boat Deck.[29]

Dr. Daniel Moore was eating lunch when he heard a "muffled, drum-like sound" from the bow. He quickly ran to his cabin to fetch a life belt, but on the way encountered a stewardess who was handing them out. Moore helped fasten one on her, and then tied one on himself. The torpedo struck while the sisters Agnes and Evelyn Wilde were having lunch. Quickly they rushed on deck where they clung to each other "determined not to be separated," Agnes recalled, "even if we went to the bottom." Crewmembers saw the two and quickly assisted them into a boat.[30] As 49-year-old Belle Naish tried to make her way to

D Deck, she found herself engulfed by a swarm of passengers coming out of the companionway. Fearing that the crowd would push her over the railing, she fought her way through the human mass. She finally reached the cabin where her husband, Theodore, readied their life jackets. The couple helped each other until the jackets were secure.

Oliver Bernard ran to the port side of the Veranda Café where he found his friend, Leslie Lindsey Mason. Bernard could tell she was terrified. "It's all right now," he reassured her, "we'll go ashore directly, so don't worry."

"Where's my husband?" Mrs. Mason asked repeatedly. Bernard, sensing her growing panic, seized her by the shoulders and shook her. "Pull yourself together and listen to what I'm saying now. Stay right here, don't move from this spot, and your husband will find you here, surely, as they will be lowering the boats from this side. Do you hear?" She nodded. Bernard then told her, "If you go running 'round this town of a ship, you'll never meet at all understand? Now stay here whatever you do, and I'll find some life belts in case we need them."

Bernard went below to look for life belts. The list caused him to stumble several times, and since the lights were out, he had difficulty finding the corridor in darkness. He finally reached his cabin and grabbed a life belt. He returned to the Veranda Café but found Mrs. Mason gone. A frantic woman accosted him, coming up to him and asking aggressively, "Where did you get that? Where did you get that?" And Bernard allowed her to snatch the life belt from his hands.[31]

Mabel Henshaw had just laid her tiny baby Constance down to sleep and was on her way upstairs when she felt the ship shake. She rushed back to her cabin and hastily dressed the infant. She was about to return to the stairs when she suddenly remembered that the woman in the next cabin had an 18-month-old child. She couldn't locate the mother, and considered taking the other baby, too. In the end, Henshaw could not carry both children at once and had to leave the toddler to his fate. She was overwhelmed by the situation, and her own daughter required her full attention.[32]

Two young women traveling back to Ireland in second class, May Barrett and Kittie McDonnell, had just finished their lunch when, according to Barrett, they heard the sound of big dishes smashing, followed by a louder explosion. The two went on deck and saw the crew lowering the boats.[33] Florence Padley hurried to the elevator, where she saw it "go down in a rush." Realizing that her cabin was too far below, she instead went up the stairs toward the Boat Deck. Padley hurried so fast that she lost a shoe.[34]

James Brooks immediately turned toward the wireless shack after the torpedo struck and was knocked down by falling debris and water. The steam nearly suffocated the Connecticut businessman. Fortunately for Brooks, the wind blew the steam in the opposite direction and he was able to regain his breath. He then quickly got to his feet and ran down the port side to the Boat Deck, making his way to the smoking room. Finding it empty, he went over to the starboard side where he witnessed several stokers rushing from below.

Harold Taylor ran into his third-class cabin and told his bride, Lucy, "Well, that's it. We've been hit."

"Hit?" she asked.

"Yeah. We've been torpedoed."

The two dashed out of their cabin and climbed the stairs to the Boat Deck.

In the dining saloon, F.J. Gauntlett realized that the ship was listing "perceptibly." He shouted to his friends to close the portholes and then went to his cabin for a life belt. On the way topside he was assured by members of the crew that there was no cause for alarm, yet Gauntlett was perfectly aware that the ship was sinking gradually deeper.[35]

Captain Turner, from the port side of the lower bridge, heard Second Officer Hefford call out, "There is a torpedo coming, sir!" Turner rushed to starboard. By the time he reached the starboard bridge wing, he could see the torpedo coming and the explosion shook his ship wildly.

Turner acted quickly. He checked the clinometer, a device used to measure the ship's stability. To his horror it showed the liner already had a 15° list to starboard—the situation was undeniably precarious. Turner ordered that the lifeboats be lowered down to the rails, but some members of the crew had already begun lowering occupied boats.[36] The list prevented any boats from being lowered on the port side.

Senior Second Engineer Andrew Cockburn was on C Deck above the engine room when he heard a deafening explosion and witnessed a flash of light. He then rushed to F Deck to check bulkhead doors and procured himself a lifebelt. Just as he reached the engine room, the lights suddenly went out and he was left in darkness. The rising coal dust made breathing difficult. Cockburn heard incoming water from somewhere forward, and by now believed the damage was in the numbers one and two boiler rooms. The engineer suspected that a boiler had exploded. His suspicions were correct; there was severe damage in number-one boiler room. Water rushed in like a tidal wave, knocking trimmers and firemen off their feet and inducing chaos.

Trimmer Tom Lawson was running through the passageway in the boiler room when he heard the lead fireman Albert Martin shout, "Everyone follow me!" Martin was making for the forward starboard ventilator, hoping that the men could make it out in time. Lawson began to follow Martin when he felt frigid water rushing in on him. Fortunately, Martin, Lawson and four others managed to climb the ladder to the Boat Deck.[37]

Seawater also cascaded into boiler room number two at an alarming rate, sweeping several men off their feet. The flood carried stoker Leslie Plummer past the boilers and pinned him against a bulkhead. Water washed Eugene McDermott and William Mallin toward a ventilating shaft, and McDermott managed to reach the shaft ladder and climb to the deck. Mallin, Plummer and everyone else in number-two boiler room, however, did not escape.[38]

Thomas Madden thought the explosion took place near the forward starboard boiler, but water poured into his own boiler room on the port side. Terrified of being scalded to death, he ran to the watertight door only to discover it closed; he banged on it helplessly. Madden rushed to the escape ladder but was knocked down by the incoming water, and as he gulped in the cold water the lights went out. Through it all, Madden managed to climb up the ladder to safety.

The damage below caused the steam pressure to drop drastically, from 150 pounds per square inch to just 50 pounds. The engines stopped. With the intake of water from the ship's forward motion, the list to starboard continued to increase.

The crew of the *Lusitania* had by this time sprung into action. Marconi Operator Robert Leith rushed from the second-class dining saloon when the torpedo struck, and made his way to the wireless room. There Leith quickly relayed an SOS followed by, "Come at

ONCE—BIG LIST, 10 MILES SOUTH OF OLD HEAD OF KINSALE," adding the ship's call letters, MSU.[39] For several minutes Leith tapped out the distress message. As the power grew weaker, he resorted to the emergency dynamo in the wireless shack.

Chief Steward John Jones did his best for the passengers and crew. He told "everybody, stewards and passengers, to get their life jackets on and come on deck." Many of the stewards under his authority were furiously clearing their cabins and assisting passengers with their life jackets.[40] Stewardess Marian Bird kept a remarkably cool head. She told a group of women passengers "to keep calm, get their life jackets as quickly as they could, and get on deck." She remained below in third class until she was certain that everyone under her care had gone on deck. The darkness caused by the power failure made this a difficult task.[41]

Junior Third Officer Albert Bestic was on his way to the baggage room when the *Lusitania* was attacked. He quickly ran topside and reported to his emergency station, lifeboat 10, on the port side. When Staff Captain John Anderson arrived he ordered Bestic to "Go to the bridge and tell them they are to trim her with the port tank." It was the Staff Captain's idea to correct the ship's stability by adding the weight of seawater to the port side to counteract the list to starboard. Bestic ran to the bridge and informed Second Officer Hefford of Anderson's order. The Junior Third Officer quickly returned to his boat station where he perceived that the ship had righted itself somewhat.[42]

Meanwhile Captain Turner climbed to the navigation bridge to judge whether lifeboats could be lowered. From there he saw the ship was still moving forward, which put a strain on the bulkheads and made it impossible to lower the boats. Turner headed the ship toward the land, and ordered her "full speed astern, to take the way off her."[43] He summoned the Staff Captain Anderson and ordered him not to lower any of the lifeboats until the ship stopped. Turner took Anderson's advice and ordered the port side ballast tanks to be flooded, but unfortunately the crew stationed at the flooding valves had already abandoned their posts. The list to starboard continued to increase. All hopes of saving his ship were now gone.

Turner ordered Second Officer Hefford below to the forecastle to close the watertight doors. As he left to carry out this order, Hefford told Quartermaster Johnston, "Keep your eye on the indicator on the compass and the spirit level and sing out if she goes any further!"[44] Johnston kept his eyes glued to the instrument, which registered a 15° list to starboard. Johnston feared the ship would capsize; the indicator gradually showed that the list was increasing.

Chief Officer Piper reported to Captain Turner, "I'm going down to the fo'csl [forecastle] to help Hefford with the hatches—she seems to be sinking fast by the bow! Perhaps we can slow her a bit!"[45]

Meanwhile Charles Hill made his way to the cabin of his friend, Beatrice Witherbee, and her four-year-old son, Arthur, but he could not find them. Hill went to his own cabin to fetch his dispatch case and overcoat. His steward helped him put on a life jacket and advised Hill to leave for the Boat Deck. Paul Crompton and his wife were deeply concerned for the safety of their six children. The confusion on the sinking, heavily listing ship made locating them and then keeping them together a formidable challenge even with the children's nurse.

Charles Lauriat recommended to the Hubbards that they return to their cabin for their life jackets, but Elbert and Alice decided to remain where they were. "If you don't care to come," Lauriat suggested, "stay here and I will get them for you."[46]

Chief Third Class Steward John Griffith discovered a strange brown smoke he had never encountered before when he went to his cabin for a life jacket and his pistol. The smoke appeared to be coming from the cabin's internal windows that opened onto the number-two funnel casing. Griffith then went below, directing passengers under his care to the Boat Deck. After this he went to see whether the Main Deck had been evacuated, and was shocked to see "one green mass of water" coming straight for him. He ran up the stairs just before "the wall of water" reached him.[47]

On the upper Promenade Deck, Charles Frohman was talking with shipboard friends when the first blast occurred. "This is going to be a close call," Frohman remarked. The actress Rita Jolivet arrived from below with only one life jacket. When George Vernon asked about others, the British captain Alick Scott told him, "Stay here! I'll fetch some life jackets." "Why not stay where your are, Captain Scott?" Frohman asked, "We shall have more chance by staying here than rushing off to the boats." But Scott wasn't persuaded and soon returned with life jackets, all of which he gave away.[48]

In the confusion of getting from the galley to the Boat Deck, George Wynne and his father Joseph, who had gone to find life jackets, got separated. At one point a crewmember ran past Wynne shouting, "Get out! We're lost!" Wynne continued on to the Boat Deck, still unable to find his father.

In the second-class dining room, Archie Donald watched his fellow diners jump from their seats after the explosion. A few seconds later the lights went out, filling those in the room with panic. Reverend Gwyer tapped Donald on the shoulder, saying, "Let us quieten the people."

Gwyer and Donald moved to the entrance of the saloon and urged the others to remain calm—everything will be all right, they insisted. Their efforts helped; the diners walked more calmly from the room. According to Donald they behaved like a "regiment of soldiers." One woman fainted as she came to the entrance. Her husband took her by the shoulders while Donald held her by the feet and they carried her up the stairs, which tilted dangerously from the list.[49] Once outside the dining saloon, Donald saw several stokers and cooks rushing from their posts. As he listened to the sound of tumbling lifeboats, he saw terror on the faces of the crew.

Fireman McDermott was at his lifeboat, number 18, when he decided to go to his quarters for a life jacket. The darkness complicated this task, but he was able to make his way to the third-class promenade. A passenger seized him and begged, "Will you look after my mother and sister? Take them to a saloon." McDermott led the two women into the third-class saloon, told them to wait there and went back on deck.[50]

Passenger Herbert Ehrhardt tried his best to be useful. He knew that portholes were still left open, permitting water to rush in. Along with his roommate and some of the stewards, he closed all the portholes he could find and then went to his cabin. He made his way down the darkened corridor to his room, only to discover that someone had already taken his life jacket. Ehrhardt calmly made his way topside and joined the people waiting for lifeboats to be lowered. One little girl told him that her brother was missing. Ehrhardt agreed to find him, which he did, and returned the boy to his family. Afterwards he reflected that he was lucky to be without dependents at a time like this; he did, however, say a prayer for his fiancée and his mother.[51]

Professor Holbourn took it upon himself to look after his young friend, Avis Dolphin. They went to his cabin to get life belts, but finding them proved difficult due to the chaotic disarray of his cabin and the ship's list. He fastened one on Avis and they went back on deck, where they met Hilda Ellis and Sarah Smith, the nurses traveling with Avis. As Miss Smith had no life jacket Holbourn offered his, but she refused, saying that he should keep it for the sake of his wife and children. Holbourn reluctantly tied it on himself and took Avis and her friends to a lifeboat. After saying goodbye to his friend, he continued to offer life belts to children. Finally he went forward, where he dove off the sinking ship, swimming for his life.[52]

Dr. Mecredy noticed people making a rush for the lifeboats. He weighed the possibilities and after watching the perilous lowering of one lifeboat decided he had a better chance if he dived off the ship. He fled to his cabin, stripped off his coat and vest, and donned a life belt. The doctor then returned to the Boat Deck only to discover it flooded; the ship was sinking rapidly.[53] Mecredy chose to follow others who slid down the log line—constructed of rough wire after the first section of rope—to the water. Two stokers were close behind, and as Macredy's descent accelerated, the skin was stripped from his hands. He then dropped into the water.

Archie Donald watched as a fireman, who had been standing by the rail, suddenly demonstrated impressive skill in diving overboard. Donald questioned the propriety of such a display at a time like this, but then he heard a boat tumbling into the water. Donald noticed Norman Stone by the railing, removing his wife's clothes in order to fasten a life belt on her. Stone then tore the canvas covering off a collapsible boat with Donald's help.

Donald went to the starboard side where he assisted in loading a boat with women and children. A group of panic-stricken stokers also tried to board, but Donald and the other men kept them off. "The women must be put in first!" he shouted. Unfortunately, the lifeboat's forward end was lowered faster than the aft and everyone aboard plunged into the ocean. Donald turned to see Elbert Hubbard and his wife Alice holding hands, and overheard them refuse to be assisted into a lifeboat.

The *Lusitania* was still making headway. Staff Captain Anderson ordered, "Will the gentlemen kindly assist me in getting the women and children out of the boats and on the upper decks?" Harold Boulton and another passenger helped Anderson empty a boat, but as he glanced forward, Boulton noticed the ship's bows dipping below the water and said grimly, "This ship is going to sink."[54]

James Brooks heard Captain Turner shout, "Lower no more boats! Everything is going to be all right!" Brooks was confronted by a seaman who was waving a revolver in the air and refusing to let him board a boat. "Who in the hell is trying to?" Brooks replied. Brooks noticed a number of women desperately hanging onto the railing, too frightened to get into a lifeboat. "Come on ladies, I'll help you," he told them. Brooks held one arm on the davit and with the other grabbed each woman until they were safely in the boat.[55]

Others were flagrantly disobeying the orders of Anderson and Turner. William Adams observed people climbing aboard lifeboats on the portside, which he knew couldn't be lowered. Newspaperman Ernest Cowper kept a level head, and assisted six-year-old Helen Smith into a lifeboat. Olive North was asked by another woman to come to her cabin so they could die together. "No," she replied, "I will make a fight for my life."[56]

Charles Lauriat went down to his cabin in search of life jackets. It was dark, but by lighting matches—the very matches he'd stashed away for an emergency—he was able to locate a jacket. Returning to the Boat Deck, Lauriat found an atmosphere of total confusion. People milled about without purpose. "If the passengers, when they first came on deck, had found that the officer and the crew of each lifeboat were at their station, waiting or taking orders from the bridge," he later lamented, "it would have inspired confidence and saved the immediate confusion; but there was no such discipline."[57]

Lauriat went fore and aft among the passengers. He assisted them in putting their life jackets on properly, after finding that many had been put on incorrectly. When he neared the bridge, Lauriat overheard a woman ask Turner, "Captain, what do you wish us to do?"

"Stay right where you are, madam," Turner assured her. "She's alright."

"Where did you get your information?" the woman inquired.

The *Lusitania* arriving in New York City on her maiden voyage in September of 1907. She set a speed record on this voyage.
Photo courtesy of the Library of Congress

On May 1, 1915 the *Lusitania* departed from New York City on her final voyage. Prior to sailing, Dudley Field Malone, the collector of the port, and his "neutrality squad" examined the liner and found no guns mounted or unmounted. *Photo courtesy of the National Archives*

Left: Captain William Thomas Turner, captain of the *Lusitania* during her last voyage. Turner did not follow all of the instructions given to him by the Admiralty. *Photo courtesy of the National Archives*

Below: A stern view of the *Lusitania*. *Photo courtesy of the Library of Congress*

Right: First class passenger Elbert Hubbard. Hubbard said, "To be torpedoed would be a good advertisement." *Photo courtesy of the Library of Congress*

Below: U-20, the submarine that sank the *Lusitania*, ended its career in 1916 after running aground west of Jutland. *Photo courtesy of the Library of Congress*

Above: Dr. Carl Foss after his rescue. *Photo courtesy of the Library of Congress*

Left: A survivor of the *Lusitania* in Queenstown. *Photo courtesy of the Library of Congress*

Above: Alfred Vanderbilt, first class passenger on the *Lusitania*. Vanderbilt booked passage on the *Titanic* but cancelled at the last minute. Vanderbilt died attempting to save children on the *Lusitania*.
Photo courtesy of the Library of Congress

Right: J. Lane with another survivor.
Photo courtesy of the Library of Congress

Above: James Gerard, American ambassador to Germany at the time of the *Lusitania* incident. *Photo courtesy of the Library of Congress*

Left: William Jennings Bryan, Secretary of State at the time of the *Lusitania* incident. Bryan resigned because he thought that President Wilson was too stern in his protest to Germany. *Photo courtesy of the Library of Congress*

The White Star liner *Arabic* that was torpedoed a few weeks after the *Lusitania* with the loss of 44 people, two of them Americans. The American government's protest resulted in the Germans promising not to sink passenger liners. *Photo courtesy of the Library of Congress*

Robert Lansing, who replaced Bryan as Secretary of State. Lansing was pro-British. *Photo courtesy of the Library of Congress*

WHEN YOU FIRE REMEMBER THIS

ENLIST IN THE NAVY

Two years after the sinking of the *Lusitania* the United States declared
war on Germany. Numerous recruiting posters featured the lost liner.
Photo courtesy of the Library of Congress

"From the engine room," was the reply.[58]

This may have satisfied some, but Lauriat knew better. He believed the *Lusitania* would remain afloat for only a few more minutes, and decided it was time to retrieve some of his personal possessions—if the ship was going to sink, Lauriat thought, he might as well save what he could.[59]

He went to his cabin, and encountered an Italian family on B Deck on his return. The family was comprised of an elderly woman, whom Lauriat took to be the grandmother, with a mother and her three children. They pleaded for Lauriat's help in Italian, a language he didn't understand. So he did as much as he could—he placed life jackets on them all, and continued on. As he turned to look back he saw the family sitting on deck waiting for instructions. It was "one of the most pathetic things I remember. One felt so helpless," Lauriat later recalled.[60]

Martin Mannion was nearly alone in the second-class smoking saloon. Everyone else had fled after the torpedo struck. Mannion walked up the tilting room to the bar as the bartender untied his apron. "Let's die 'game' anyway," Mannion suggested. "You go to hell!" the bartender shouted, and then jumped over the bar and rushed out of the smoking room. Mannion shrugged and rooted around in the wreckage until he found an unbroken bottle of ale.[61]

Meanwhile Robert Timmis tried to calm a group of steerage passengers he thought were Russian. His only means of communication was to hold up his hand, nod his head and tell them, "All right, all right."[62]

About 700 meters away, Kapitänleutnant Schwieger recorded in his logbook, "There is great confusion on board. Boats are cleared and many of them lowered into the water . . ."[63] The confusion to which Schwieger alluded involved the lifeboats. The *Lusitania* carried 48 boats, of which 22 were the conventional wooden type suspended from davits, while the remaining 26 were "collapsible" boats situated on deck. This meant the crew first had to lower 22 conventional lifeboats, haul the ropes back up, attach ropes to the assembled collapsibles, and then lower once more. This procedure hampered the crew from clearing the ship in the few minutes available.

More serious conditions governed the portside boats. Staff Captain Anderson and Junior Third Officer Bestic attempted to restore some order to lifeboats 2 to 14. When Bestic arrived on the port side, some boats already carried a full complement of passengers. Because of the severe list to starboard, boats could not easily clear the side of the ship. The "moment the tension was released on the snubbing chain, the lifeboat, already heavy with passengers, would swing inward." He ordered the few seamen on deck and willing volunteers to push boats out to clear the ship's side. In the confusion, someone prematurely knocked out the pin from the snubbing chain on boat number two. The boat instantly crashed inward, crushing passengers and those waiting on deck, and then slid in the direction of the list and the sinking bow, pushing passengers before it until they were pinned against superstructure of the bridge. Several other lifeboats on the port side met a similar fate, each crushing or injuring anyone in its path.[64]

The men did manage to push lifeboat 12 outward so that it cleared the side, but the stern dropped too quickly in lowering the boat and nearly all aboard were thrown into the sea. The lifeboat then came loose and dropped onto them. Lifeboat 14 was being lowered when the bow of the *Lusitania* hit bottom. With the sudden impact, the men on the davits lost control, and number 14 boat dropped with an even keel onto the wreckage of number 12. Some occupants managed to climb back on board boat 14. With help the ship's barber rowed it away from the sinking liner, but it was so severely damaged that eventually it sank under their feet.

Isaac Jackson and several other passengers boarded a boat, and after waiting for instructions, an officer told them to get off and informed them that they would be in no danger if they waited on deck. Jackson and the others vacated the boat, then stood on deck talking while they anxiously awaited further instructions.[65]

Ogden and Mary Hammond were on the "high side" of the ship when a petty officer told Mrs. Hammond to get into a lifeboat. She initially refused because it would mean being parted from her husband, but as they watched the boat being filled, it occurred to the couple that there was still room for them both, so they climbed in. Disastrously, the boat came loose and tumbled down; Hammond survived, but his wife was lost.

When the torpedo struck, A. J. Mitchell was in his stateroom. He immediately ran out and found himself assisting Mrs. Ellen Hogg and her two children into a boat. He then got into a boat himself, despite an order being circulated that no boats were to be lowered on the port side.[66] Joseph Myers and Frank Kellett, after assisting a woman and her son into a lifeboat, entered the boat themselves. A steward then told them, "Everybody out of the lifeboats. We are hard aground and we are not going to sink." Believing this, Myers and Kellett climbed out.

Kittie McDonnell and May Barrett were about to leave the Boat Deck in search of life belts when a man standing nearby suggested they remain where they were, as he would get the belts for them. The man returned with two life belts and fastened them on the two women, but the increasing list caused them to loose their footing and they were thrown down. They managed to crawl to the edge of the deck where they saw a rope suspended to one of the lifeboats. The two muttered a few words of prayer, then jumped overboard. Barrett reached for the rope but missed and landed in the water, losing contact with McDonnell.[67]

Allen Loney, a retired businessman from New York who supported volunteer ambulances for Britain, placed his 15-year-old daughter, Virginia Bruce, and her mother, Catherine, into a lifeboat and watched their departure. The boat fell, tumbling its passengers into the water. Catherine never surfaced, but Virginia, a strong swimmer, got herself clear. She looked back to see her father quietly standing next to Alfred Vanderbilt as water neared the deck, each ignoring the single lifebelt between them.[68]

Avis Dolphin took her place in a lifeboat as Professor Holbourn kissed her and asked her to say goodbye to his family. The lifeboat capsized when two men jumped into it. While she attempted to climb onto the capsized lifeboat she saw a raft nearby. Avis managed to swim to the raft and was hauled aboard.

Isaac Lehmann had just watched in disgust as a lifeboat fell headlong into the sea with everyone on board. He rushed down the deck to the grand entrance and to his stateroom on D Deck. Someone had already taken his life jacket, but he grabbed his revolver, which he thought would "come in handy in case there was anybody not doing the proper thing." "I don't know whatever possessed me," he later said. He then made his way to B Deck where he encountered his steward. He told the steward to get him a life jacket, and the steward complied, helping Lehmann to secure it. Lehmann walked out on deck and met up with Dr. McDermott and Purser McCubin, who told him not to worry—that the ship was not going to sink.

Ignoring the two, Lehmann made his way up to the port side of A Deck where he saw number 18 boat with 30 or 40 people aboard. He asked the seamen standing by why this boat was not being launched; he knew perfectly well that the liner was settling down by the bow, and that "there was no chance that the *Lusitania* would not sink." "Who has got charge of this boat?" Lehmann demanded. A sailor with an ax in his hand answered that the Captain had given orders not to lower any boats. "To hell with the Captain!" he barked. "Don't you see the boat is sinking? And the first man that disobeys my orders to launch the boat I shoot to kill!" Lehmann pulled out his revolver and men moved to obey the order.

Fearfully, the sailor knocked out the snubbing pin. The ship at that moment gave a tremendous lurch and the lifeboat swung violently inward, crushing passengers waiting on the collapsibles and the deck and severely injuring Lehmann's leg. To add to his horror, the crew lost control of the lifeboat as it was finally being lowered, and the occupants were all thrown into the sea.[69]

The situation on the starboard side was only marginally better. With the exception of lifeboat 5, which was destroyed by falling water and debris, the boats remained undamaged. The list did not present the same problem, since this was the "low side." Supervised by First Officer Jones, the crew launched lifeboats 9 and 11 safely with a handful of passengers and crew in each. Number 13 made its way carrying about 60 people. With Jones in command, boat number 15 pulled away from the *Lusitania* with more than 80 aboard. When he spotted boat number 1 drifting empty, Jones transferred some of his people into it. Boat number 19 tipped out 12 passengers while being lowered, but it reached the water safely.

William Brown viewed with alarm the crew's struggle with the lifeboats. "I came to the conclusion that a life belt was the thing for me." He hurried down to his stateroom, found a life belt and returned to the Boat Deck. He then climbed down a rope and into the water, and swam away from the sinking ship.[70] Oscar Grab decided while watching the lifeboats that his only chance at survival was to avoid them completely, and he dove overboard.

Seaman Leslie Morton lost sight of his brother during the confusion, but found him next to a lifeboat. He and his brother lowered the boat, after which the two jumped in. Morton's brother tried to push off from the liner with a boat hook, as Leslie pushed off at the stern of the lifeboat. Their efforts were complicated by passengers hanging onto bits of rope still secured to the side of the ship. As the *Lusitania* heeled over, part of her Boat Deck hooked onto the lifeboat. "The time for heroics was obviously past," Morton recalled. His brother shouted, "I'm going over the side, Gertie." "So am I," replied Morton. The two brothers waved at one another and dove from the lifeboat.[71]

Seaman Leo Thompson was trying to lower boat number 17, but the crush of people threatened to push him over the side, and the noisy turmoil made communication impossible. He braced himself by putting his feet against the davit and his back against one of the collapsible boats, but the bow of boat number 17 dropped into the water and the lifeboat capsized.

Husband and wife Flor and Julia Sullivan debated whether to board a lifeboat. Flor joined their friend Pat Callan in a boat, but Julia refused to join them. Flor, who could not swim, left the boat and gave her their money saying, "You'll need this by and by." Julia, a strong swimmer, suggested they jump from the ship instead and he could hold onto her.[72] Steerage passenger H.A. Smethurst and his wife rushed to the lifeboats, and Mrs. Smethurst boarded. She called out for him to join her but he refused, saying it was women and children first. Smethurst put on a life belt and slipped into the water.[73]

Elizabeth Duckworth, Alice Scott and young Arthur Scott were walking on deck when the torpedo struck and shook the ship "from stem to stern." The trio suddenly lost their mental balance and rushed up the forward mast's rigging. An officer saw them and ordered them down off the rigging, assuring them that there would be a lifeboat ready for them in time. Duckworth descended and told Arthur to slide down the rope ladder, where she would catch him. The young boy hesitated at first, but gathered up enough courage to slide down. Unfortunately Elizabeth failed to catch the boy and he fell to the deck, where he remained motionless. Though she feared Arthur was dead, he soon regained consciousness.[74]

The three quickly made their way to a boat, where they were told there was only room for young Arthur. "All right, get him in," Duckworth replied. She rushed to another boat, which was also full. Anxiously scanning her options, she eyed a boat at the end of the ship on the starboard side. Rushing toward it she fell, but fortunately an officer helped her to her feet and took her to an available boat. Along with Alice Scott, she stepped into the boat. She then noticed that the crew was visibly struggling to lower it. Impatient and fearful, Duckworth decided to forgo her place in the boat and climbed out onto the sloping deck. The boat was lowered with Alice Scott still aboard when suddenly it plunged into the water. Duckworth watched in horror as everyone, including Alice, drowned.[75]

Theodate Pope and Edwin Friend witnessed the chaos unfolding, certain that the *Lusitania* would sink. They looked for a good place to jump, but feared accidentally falling on one of the lifeboats. They made their way to a Boat Deck ladder, walking close, "each with an arm around the other's waist. We passed Mme. Depage; her eyes were wide and startled, but brave." Friend noticed a lifeboat being filled and suggested that Pope board, but she refused. Friend "would not take a place in one as long as there were still women aboard and, as I would not leave him, we pushed our way towards the stern, which was now uphill work, as the bow was sinking so rapidly." Emily Robinson met them, as arranged. Theodate put her hand on the maid's shoulder and cried, "Oh Robinson." "Life belts!" Friend cut in. They found lifebelts in a nearby stateroom and Friend "tied them on us in hard knots." Theodate said, "Come, Robinson," and followed Edwin Friend into the water.[76]

Robert Timmis and Ralph Moodie helped two sailors lower a boat on the starboard side. As they labored, George Kessler, who was calmly smoking a cigar, joined them and helped women into the boat in "a spirit of convention." Kessler believed the *Lusitania* would not sink. Both Timmis and Moodie gave their life jackets to women before going down with the ship.

James Baker, another first-class passenger, assisted with the boats on the port side after having been in his cabin when the torpedo first struck. He rushed outside but returned for his life belt, finding his stateroom suddenly dark and "thick with smoke." Baker went topside where he assisted in lowering boats; he then jumped into the water.[77] Alfred Vanderbilt also did whatever he could to help. Emerging from the grand entrance, he told his valet, "Find all the kiddies you can." He carried as many children into the lifeboats in his arms as he could, and his friend Thomas Slidell watched him offer his life jacket to another passenger, Alice Middleton.[78]

Lady Mackworth descended the stairway to her cabin through a tilt so pronounced she had to walk partly on the wall. On the way to her cabin she bumped into a stewardess; they apologized and each went her way. She took her life jacket from the cabin wall and her father's from his cabin and made her way back on deck.

During the confusion Lady Mackworth had been separated from her father, David Thomas. She went to the port side of the Boat Deck, where she met Dr. Fisher and his sister-in-law, Dorothy Conner. "Do you mind," she asked Fisher, "if I stay beside you until father returns?" Dr. Fisher by this time wondered when an officer would instruct them; he had come to the opinion that discipline among the crew was sub-standard. Finally an officer arrived and said to the three of them, "Don't worry, the ship will right itself." Just then a group of passengers appeared from below, stampeding toward a lifeboat and knocking down an officer. To Lady Mackworth the group was like "a swarm of bees who do not know where the queen has gone."[79]

Meanwhile, David Thomas arrived on deck where he also witnessed the scramble for lifeboats. His secretary offered him an inflatable life belt, but he felt it wasn't secure and decided to retrieve the life jacket from his stateroom. He reached his cabin only to discover his life jacket gone, but found three others in the wardrobe. He quickly made his way topside and surveyed the scene. The ship was listing sharply to star-board, and confusion near the lifeboats was rife. He found "an entire absence of discipline" among the crew of the sinking ship.

Jane MacFarquhar and her daughter Grace left the second-class dining saloon to make their way topside. Maneuvering their way through a mob of panic-stricken passengers was tough, and by the time they reached the Boat Deck Jane told her daughter, "There's no chance here. We must get to the other side." Grace lost her footing and slid to the edge of the deck. A steward assured Jane, "I'll look after her." The steward helped Jane up and led them "from chair to chair through a first-class saloon until they reached the companionway leading to one of the lifeboats." The officer directed Jane to board a lifeboat, and her daughter was passed to her.[80]

Charles Bowring realized the end was near. He placed his glasses into a pocket of his coat, climbed over the rail and jumped into the water. He then began swimming away from the *Lusitania*. When Bowring looked back, he saw a crowded lifeboat being dragged under by the sinking ship.[81]

Signs of panic became more conspicuous. One man jumped into a lifeboat and refused to get out until a seaman jumped in with an ax and shouted, "Hop it!" Meekly, the man complied. There were other passengers still without life jackets. Among them was a weeping Charlotte Pye with her infant Marjorie in her arms. A man noticed her distress and said to her, "Don't cry, lady. It's all right."

"No it's not all right," she cried, "I haven't got a life jacket."

"I'll get you one," the man said sympathetically, but was unable to find one. "Here," he said to her, "take mine." He strapped the life jacket on her, then tied her baby to the jacket and led her to a lifeboat on the starboard side. Pye was expected to walk across two oars laid together, which extended from the rail of the ship to the lifeboat, but a crewman told her she would have to unstrap her baby first. She did so, and when she reached the boat she was handed her baby.[82]

Norah Bretherton made her way along the starboard side with infant Betty in her arms and her son Paul in tow. She pushed and shoved her way toward two lifeboats in hopes of boarding one of them—without success. Luckily an officer helped her to board a third boat, and as she surveyed the boat's passengers, she was surprised to see more men than women. Julia and Flor Sullivan made their way to the starboard side, where they saw passengers throwing wooden gratings, tables and deckchairs into the water to use as rafts. The couple decided the time was right: they held hands, leapt into the water, and Julie called out to Flor, "Hold on to me." Flor held onto Julie's life jacket, and she swam as fast as possible away from the doomed liner.[83]

Lucy Taylor refused to leave her husband, Harold. As she embraced her husband on the slanting deck, she said emphatically, "I won't go." Harold broke from her embrace, and forcibly dropped her into a lifeboat—she tried to climb back on deck but found it impossible, as the boat was lowered too quickly. Lucy saw her husband standing by the rail without a life jacket, knowing he could not swim.

Despite the chaos, there were those who kept a calm head. Among them was Patrick Jones, a photographer and reporter with the International News Service. He was doing what his profession called for—taking photographs of the sinking ship. "You better get off this boat!" Charles Jeffrey said to him. "These'll be the greatest pictures ever!" replied Jones.

As he returned to the forward part of the deck, Charles Lauriat noticed a lifeboat that the sinking ship would soon upset. About 35 people sat in the boat, mostly women and children. Lauriat judged that the lifeboat had been lowered to the water and floated early on, but fouled lines in the bow and stern kept it tethered to the ship's davits. As the ship listed and sank, the davits moved closer and closer to the boat; one was now about a foot above the bow.

He noticed a steward struggling to cut the forward rope with a knife. Lauriat yelled to try an axe but neither he nor the steward could find one. Lauriat "climbed into the stern and threw clear my end, but before I had time to cast off the block it was done for me by a seaman..." Lauriat, trying to move forward to help the steward, stood up into the aft davit and fell into the bottom of the boat. When he got to his feet he stepped on an oar that rolled. He regained his footing and saw that "the end of the davit had gripped the bow of the boat and had just begun to press it under." Realizing it was too late to cut the boat free, Lauriat urged and then begged the passengers to jump. Two men and two women jumped. Lauriat followed, showed the two women and a third they found nearby how to hold onto one another's shoulders, and "pushed them ahead" as he swam away from the ship.[84]

While Oliver Bernard handed out life jackets to women, he came across Alfred Vanderbilt holding what appeared to be a jewel case. He thought Vanderbilt seemed to be "amused by the excitement." Bernard found, for the most part, that the women passengers "kept cool." He did hear a number of them shouting, "Where's my husband?" "Where is my child?" but he was amazed that the great majority of women did not panic.[85]

Bernard realized, however, that the end would come soon. He climbed to the Marconi Deck and removed his coat, tie and vest. He folded each piece of clothing in his usual ritual, and laid them at the base of the funnel "as on an altar." He pondered his life, realizing that his whole existence "amounted to just nothing." While untying his boots Bernard looked around and saw the Chief Electrician talking to somebody. He walked over and saw Leith, the wireless operator, tapping out an SOS. An engineer appeared and said, "The watertight doors are all right, quite all right, don't worry."

Bernard, Leith and the Chief Electrician grinned at each other. Then the electrician asked, "Any amount of other ships about?"

"That doesn't interest me much," replied Bernard, "I can't swim a yard and that's not enough."

The wireless operator stood up and pushed his swivel chair out of the wireless cabin, offering it to Bernard as something to hang on to. Bernard said, "No good at working water-wheels either." The three laughed as the chair rolled down the sloping deck and crashed against the railing. Leith took out a small camera and took a snapshot of the view forward. Bernard left the wireless cabin.[86]

By this time Dr. Fisher had realized that he and his sister-in-law should have life belts, so he went below to find some. While he was away, Lady Mackworth joked to Dorothy, "Well you've had your thrill all right." "I never want another," she replied. The doctor soon returned with life belts, informing them that water below was knee deep. The three decided their best chance was to jump overboard. At first Lady Mackworth was afraid to leap over the side, believing it was a 60-foot drop. Then suddenly she saw "the water green" just up to her knees. In the next instant, she was in the ocean.[87]

Wireless Operator Leith stayed on at his post. The list forced him to hang on to his transmitter. He persistently sent out the SOS, tapping, "SEND HELP QUICKLY—AM LISTING BADLY." On the bridge, Quartermaster Johnston hollered out that the ship was now listing 25° to starboard. "Then save yourself," the Captain called back. Strapping on a life belt, the quartermaster stepped into the water, which by then was level with the bow.

Father Basil Maturin was standing on the sloping deck without a life jacket, offering absolution to several of the people still aboard. The priest handed a child into one of the lifeboats saying, "Find its mother."

Seaman Thomas Mahoney went aft, and lowered himself into the water by a rope. He was halfway down when he thought he saw the propellers still revolving. Fearfully, he climbed back on deck. He then climbed over the railing, dove overboard, and swam to a raft. Stewardesses Marian Bird and Fannie Morecroft threw the life jackets they found into a pile on the Boat Deck. They then climbed aboard one of the last lifeboats to leave. The Marconi wires came down on the boat but the oarsmen pushed off and managed to get the boat clear.

Junior Third Officer Bestic directed his efforts to helping the passengers who remained. He found Alfred Vanderbilt and Charles Frohman tying life jackets to baskets containing infants. Bestic warned them that they had only seconds to save themselves, but the two continued their work undeterred.[88]

Michael Byrne heard an officer say, "We can beach her." To which Byrne replied, "How can you when the engines are dead?" At that moment the water washed over his shoes, prompting Bryne to dive off the liner and swim from the ship. William Adams and his father sat in a crowded lifeboat that had fallen from a davit, though still attached to the davit ropes. Adams' father tried his best to release the falls but was unable to do so. He called out to his son, "Jump!" The two leapt over the side of the boat and swam from the wreckage. George Wynne was waiting for his father to return with a life jacket when a man pushed him toward the rail and told him not to wait any longer. Wynne, fearful of the water but more afraid of staying where he was, leapt overboard.

The slanting deck caused many people to slide down its surface. Among them was Fred Gauntlett, who managed to grab a davit and from there jump into an empty boat. The davits then heeled over, carrying the boat down with it. Nine-year-old Edith Williams and her younger sister arrived at the poop deck only to encounter a slanting deck rapidly disappearing beneath their feet. As the water engulfed them, Edith gripped her sister by the hand. They were parted when Edith's life belt slipped off, and forced her to release her hold on her sister.[89]

Suddenly, a bulkhead collapsed and the number-three boiler exploded. Everyone still on board, if they remained conscious, realized that time had run out. The liner rolled over on its side. Seconds later, at 2:28 p.m. on May 7, 1915, the *Lusitania* sank.

CHAPTER 9

THE STRUGGLE
IN THE WATER

There was relatively little suction as the *Lusitania* sank—an unusual effect given the size of the ocean liner. Charles Lauriat perceptively noted that, but then he heard explosions from the funnels as the cold water made contact with the steam, which "added to the horror of the disaster."[1] "The reverse force after the vortex, on the other hand—a sort of regurgitation by the ocean of human bodies and debris—astonished the survivors by its violence. . . . A swimmer looking back described the spot as "a mound of water," foaming above the general level of the sea for an appreciable space of time."[2]

James Brooks had gotten tangled in the ship's wireless antenna but managed to wiggle free, cutting his hand in the process. Brooks turned his gaze and watched as the sea closed over the *Lusitania*. "There was a thunderous roar, as of the collapse of a great building on fire: then she disappeared, dragging with her hundreds of fellow creatures into the vortex. Many never rose to the surface, but the sea rapidly grew black with the figures of struggling men and women and children."[3]

The ship's wireless antenna dragged Charles Lauriat under, but he "kicked" his way free and swam to the surface. The experience reminded him of "one of my various trips down to see 'Susy the Mermaid' at camp when the older boys would repeatedly shove the young ones from six to 16 feet underwater for 'sins' they had committed."[4]

When he looked around he did not see the three women he had ferried safely away from the ship. Amid the deluge of wreckage from the sinking liner he had lost sight of them.[5]

Steward Robert Barnes felt a "violent underwater explosion" as he was dragged under. He surfaced only to be seized by two terror-stricken men. Barnes managed to dive beneath the chaos and break free of the two, and then resurfaced.[6] Seaman Leslie Morton and his brother were in Lifeboat 3, still fastened to the ship as it was dragged under. Morton swam clear of the boat, and he ran into a floating collapsible. With the assistance of another seaman they assembled the boat, and set out to rescue some of those still struggling in the water. In all they saved 34 lives.[7]

Immediately after the *Lusitania* sank the air was charged with cries of agony. One survivor recalled that "we could hear the dying shrieks of men and women in the water." W.G.E. Meyers said, "Their shrieks were appalling." Likewise, Dr. Daniel Moore heard screams of "'My God!' 'Save me!' and 'Help!'" It made him heartsick. G.B. Lane recalled that "Their cries and shrieks could be heard above the hiss of escaping steam and the crash of bursting boilers. Then the water closed over them and the big liner disappeared, leaving scarcely a ripple behind her."[8] From a lifeboat George Kessler observed a spot foaming. He then cried, "My God—the *Lusitania*'s gone!"

As the liner sank, Robert Wiemann felt an explosion and went under, thinking a boiler had exploded. When he resurfaced he was surprised to see "a circle of people and wreckage about half a mile across."[9] Matt Freeman had cut his head while diving from the sinking ship. He came across a floating barrel, and along with five other men clung to it until it was clear the barrel could not support all six of them. Giving up, Freeman left the other five men and grabbed on to the keel of a capsized boat.

Walter Moore and his wife Nettie were also hanging onto a capsized lifeboat. Walter struggled to hold their infant son up above the water line, until it became obvious that their son was dead. After a while Walter felt the effects of the cold water and began to lose his grip on the lifeboat. He said to his wife, "I can't hold on any more, Nettie," and at that moment released his grip and went under, still cradling his dead son.

After jumping off the ship when the gray hull became visible, the next thing Theodate Pope knew

> …was that I could not reach the surface, because I was being washed and whirled up against wood. I was swallowing and breathing the salt water, but felt no special discomfort nor anguish of mind—was strangely apathetic. I opened my eyes and through the green water I could see what I was being dashed up against. (It looked like the bottom and keel of one of the ship's boats.) It was the under part of a deck. I could see the matched boarding and the angle iron over the railing. I had been swept between decks. I closed my eyes and thought, "This is of course the end of life for me"…[10]

The architect reflected hat she was grateful that she'd recently made a will; she thought of loved ones and peacefully committed herself to "God's care." She became unconscious after a blow to her head and revived "surrounded and jostled by hundreds of frantic, screaming, shouting humans in this grey and watery inferno. The ship must just have gone down." A man without a life belt seized her by the shoulders. Pope saw sheer terror in his eyes. Without any impetus to struggle, she pleaded, "Oh, please don't" and the two went under, Pope sinking again into unconsciousness.

She surfaced a second time to find herself floating under a blue sky, now surrounded by fewer people spaced farther apart.[11] She did see two men and a woman, one of them an elderly gentleman swimming. Pope called out to him, asking if he'd seen any rescue ships. The elderly man answered in the negative. She then caught sight of an oar floating close by that she was able to take hold of, putting an ankle over the oar and holding it with the opposite hand. "This helped to save me," she later wrote. She again lost consciousness. Her next recollection was waking in front of a "small, open-grate fire," her first thought was "that the opening of the grate measured about 18 by 24 inches." She was aboard one of the rescue ships.[12] As the suction of the sinking vessel pulled Alice Middleton down, she got her head caught in an open porthole. She managed to break free, and upon surfacing was shocked to see scores of dead bodies floating nearby.

Margaret Cox found her way to a lifeboat with her son, but as the *Lusitania* heeled over, the funnels threatened to crush the lifeboat and everyone in it. She screamed, "Oh God, if I've got to die, let me die in the water." When the boat miraculously escaped the funnels' direction, she was thankful that she and her son were out of immediate danger.[13] In the overcrowded boat, the sight of hundreds of people in the water whom she knew could not be helped drove her "a little mad."[14]

Deep in the black water after going down with the ship, Lady Mackworth feared being caught on part of the ship and prevented from swimming to the surface. "That was the worst moment of terror, the only moment of acute terror," she experienced. She accidentally swallowed seawater and then, remembering that a person should never swallow seawater, deliberately kept her mouth closed. When she got to the surface, she grabbed a piece of wood a few feet long and found that she "formed part of a large, round, floating island composed of people and debris of all sorts, lying so close together that at first there was not very much water noticeable in between. People, boats, hencoops, chairs, rafts, boards and goodness knows what besides, all floating cheek by jowl."[15] Surrounded by people chanting, "Boat!" Mackworth joined the chorus until she realized it was futile. Just then a white-faced man with a yellow mustache took hold of the other end of her piece of wood, causing her to wonder if the board was big enough for both of them. When she noticed the man moving toward her end of the board, she told him to stay at his end, explaining that his movement would destabilize the wood. A short time later the man disappeared; Mackworth was never sure if he swam away or drowned.[16]

Margaret noticed that a few boats had picked up people nearby. Summoning her courage, she tried swimming toward one of the boats, but abandoned the idea after taking a few strokes and realizing the extent of her exhaustion. While floating in the water Lady Mackworth contemplated her fate, wondering if perhaps this were a nightmare from which she'd wake. She felt dazed and cold, but not afraid. Instead, she understood how lucky she was to be alive.[17] She slowly drifted away from the island of people. Acute loneliness overwhelmed her.

There were many bodies floating over the *Lusitania*'s grave, with some people clinging to the deceased to stay afloat. Michael Byrne was appalled by the multitude of infant corpses floating by, and was forced to push them aside as he swam.

Mabel Henshaw held her baby as she tumbled into the water. The suction dragged her deeper under the surface, causing her to lose hold of her baby. When she surfaced she knew that her daughter was dead. Another mother, Charlotte Pye, fell from a lifeboat while clutching her baby and they both went under; when Pye finally surfaced, the child was no longer in her arms. A collapsible rowed toward her and from it someone shouted, "Take the lady on, for God's sake, she's almost gone." She was pulled aboard, but her shock over losing her baby was inconsolable.

Rita Jolivet clung to an upturned lifeboat. Twice she heard someone shout, "Rescue ships coming!" She was crestfallen to discover these reports were false—it became increasingly obvious that rescue was nowhere to be seen.

Captain Turner survived by hanging on to a floating chair. While floating over the grave of his command he observed sea gulls flying overhead. A couple of birds landed on his body, which he energetically beat off.

William Pierpont was swimming near the Captain when he the ship's suction dragged him down and drew him into one of the *Lusitania*'s funnels. Escaping air ejected him from the funnel, at which point Pierpont flew upward and then splashed down in the water again. Without hesitation he began swimming frantically away from the ship. Margaret Gwyer had a similar experience. After falling from her boat she was sucked into one of the ship's funnels and shot out again, landing her in the water.[18]

Isaac Lehmann, injured but alert, spied a little baby nearby while trying to keep afloat. He and another man tried to secure the infant to a deck chair, and despite being able to keep her alive for an hour or so, the baby eventually succumbed to the elements.

May Barrett suffered from the salt water in her eyes and mouth while she waited in the water. More urgently, she thought of her dear friend Kate, whom she imagined she would never see again. Barrett soon lost consciousness, but was awakened by the crew of a lifeboat that came to her side. "You hold on a little longer," someone in the boat shouted. The crew lifted Barrett aboard where she promptly fell unconscious again.[19]

After drifting afloat in the water, Belle Naish bumped into lifeboat 22 and hung on. A man aboard reached out and said, "Give me your hand. My back is hurt. But I'll do what I can."

"I can hold on," Naish replied selflessly. "Take somebody else."

"Come on," he insisted, "There's no one else I can reach."

Naish was hauled aboard, chattering with cold. She noticed another passenger who was playing his harmonica—until someone suggested the music interfered with their ability to hear cries for help.[20]

Herbert Ehrhardt swam until he came upon two lifeboats, one of which was capsized, the other right-side up. Atop each of the boats he saw the two brothers with whom he shared a cabin, but within a few minutes the righted boat drifted away. Ehrhardt and the older brother helped people aboard the capsized boat. One of the women they pulled onto the boat died only a few seconds later. They then helped to pull an exhausted man gasping for breath aboard. He happened to be the husband of the dead woman, and when he saw his wife, he burst into tears.[21] A corpse then floated by and Ehrhardt lifted it from the water to see if he recognized him—it turned out to be his cabin mates' father.

The rear mast of the *Lusitania* smashed the collapsible boat William Adams had just gained, and he went under. When he kicked to the surface he found a spar to support him, but he was tossed so forcefully about in the swell that he decided to try swimming to an overturned lifeboat in spite of his injuries. He reached the boat and hung on to it until rescue came.

Fifteen-year-old William Holt was nearly crushed by one of the ship's funnels. He clung briefly to an oar but decided to swim away, during which he was seized by a desperate man trying to stay afloat. Holt managed to break free of the man and kept swimming.

Mary Maycock was drifting alone in the water when she came across a man holding onto a piece of wood. After asking the man if he could spare his piece of wood, he shoved it toward her—and for the next four hours Maycock crouched on that narrow piece of wood.

After jumping from the ship, Archibald Donald found himself struggling in the water. He turned and saw the propellers of the *Lusitania,* and saw people in a lifeboat near the stern place oars on one of the propellers to push off. Donald heard an explosion as the *Lusitania* began her plunge beneath the surface. He feared the mast would hit him, a fear eclipsed by a wave that suddenly lifted him up, then drew him under. Donald swam as fast as he could against the ship's suction, and when he surfaced, two pieces of wood shot up beside him. He barely missed being decapitated, but counted himself lucky as he buoyed himself on the wood that had nearly killed him, and waited to be rescued.[22] Looking around, Donald spied several collapsibles in the distance. He swam to one and was hauled aboard, where he met his roommate George Bilbrough.

George and Donald managed to raise the canvas sides of one of the boats, and began hauling aboard whoever they could, including Olive North. In all they rescued 34 people. Donald wanted to pluck more out of the water but the collapsible was too badly damaged and could too easily have been swamped. To complicate matters, most of those aboard did not know how to row or steer. One man aboard made a "nuisance" of himself by endlessly complaining about the loss of his money and his bonds. Donald grew so weary of the man's whining that he hit him on the head with an oar.[23]

Robert Timmis went down with the ship, thinking it must be what plunging down Niagara Falls feels like. He went about sixty feet under, where the scene was "black as the inside of a cow." After several seconds he made his way to the surface, counting each stroke as he swam. Timmis surveyed the scene, and saw that he was over a hundred yards from the majority of debris. There was "a sort of hum" over the scene. Timmis then reached out for a boy floating by whom he hoped to save, but the boy was motionless; he felt for a heartbeat but detected none.

Quartermaster Hugh Johnston was swimming over the *Lusitania*'s grave. He was finally able to reach an overturned boat where he was joined by six other men, and to keep warm they shadowboxed.[24]

Flor Sullivan had lost his grip on his wife Julia as she swam, but somehow he managed to reach a box floating in the water that was being held onto by nine others. "He saw a woman in the water nearby hold up her bag and shout, 'This is my purse. It contains nothing but money and I will give it to anyone who saves me.'"[25] One of the men holding onto the box replied, "I will." She threw her purse in his direction, but as he lunged for it he upset the box and everyone who had been using it to stay afloat went under. Only Flor Sullivan resurfaced.

Charles Hill found himself among others in a lifeboat with no plugs;

the boat flooded and capsized, dumping everyone into the water re-peatedly. As the ship's barber swam away to find another boat, it vague-ly occurred to Hill that he hadn't yet paid him for his services. Hill had unusual difficulty swimming, but turning around he saw the reason why—"a woman with a child in her arms was hanging onto my right leg and an old man was clutching me around the left ankle . . ." Hill struggled to a boat where he heard someone aboard say, "Don't pull them in, they are nearly dead anyway and we must lighten the boat." Fortunately for Hill, a stoker in the lifeboat defied that advice and pulled Hill and his three fellow travelers in.[26]

Junior Third Officer Albert Bestic was lying on an upturned boat, and was suddenly alarmed by people grabbing at its sides. Fearing being swamped, he slid off the boat and began swimming until he encoun-tered another boat. The Junior Third Officer tested it with his weight and, satisfied that it could hold him, climbed over the gunwale. For sev-eral minutes Bestic laid on the boat, until he realized it was sinking. He spotted four watertight tanks floating a few yards away, so he paddled toward them and secured them under the thwarts of the boat. It was then that he discovered a bucket, which he used frantically to bail out the water. Bestic, finally able to locate the leak, plugged it with his knife and a handkerchief. The young officer then saw a swimmer pass by. He shouted, and the swimmer came to him.

"Thanks, old chap," the swimmer said. "I suppose it's no use ask-ing you for a cigarette."

"Sorry," answered Bestic, "Mine have gone rather soggy."

Bestic asked the swimmer if he could row. He replied that he could, but before settling down to row he wanted to help bail out the water, thinking this action would warm him up. After bailing more water out, the two began rowing in search of survivors. They came across a woman whom they helped into the boat.

"Where's my baby?" she asked

"I'm sorry," Bestic told her. "We haven't seen any babies."

Hearing this, the woman jumped back into the water. The other man grabbed for her, and realizing that a lie was the only thing that could save her, said, "Your baby is safe. I saw it taken into another boat." The two rowed until they picked up a dozen more survivors, but they could take on no more, for the boat was taking on water.[27]

Professor Holbourn floated amidst wreckage that reminded him of "a pork pie" when he witnessed the after mast of the *Lusitania* come close to destroying a waterborne lifeboat. Propelling a struggling swimmer who was floating beside him, Holbourn struck out for a lifeboat, only to discover upon reaching it that the man had died. The boat Holbourn swam to was overcrowded and the occupants refused to pull him on board. The sailor in charge decided to have his crew row to a nearly empty boat he spied about a mile away.[28] Holbourn grabbed a line and the rowers pulled him through the cold water. The boat they came to contained two men, almost naked. Some fifteen passengers were transferred to this boat and Holbourn was pulled out of the water, but he made up his mind to stay with the first boat. To keep warm Holbourn rowed, and as the boat moved over the *Lusitania*'s death site, Holbourn saw several people in the water crying out for help. The petty officer in charge of the lifeboat refused to help, though Holbourn believed the boat could safely take on at least ten more people.

Lorna Pavey and John Wilson slid down a line from the *Lusitania* that flayed their hands and feet as they descended, and fell into a boat that was missing its plug and taking on water fast. Frantically they used their shoes to bail out the water. Young Avis Dolphin struggled back up to the surface of the water after the lifeboat she was on capsized, and was suddenly alone. Eventually a man in a collapsible boat pulled her out of the water.[29] Surgeon Major Warren Pearl had been dragged down several times by the suction of the ship but managed to surface each time. He clung to a variety of wreckage for three hours before he was picked up by a collapsible. His wife Amy was clutching a piece of wood when she heard someone shout, "Somebody save that woman," and was hauled aboard an upturned lifeboat.[30]

Charles Lauriat viewed the scene of the *Lusitania*'s destruction. At this point, no shrieks or screaming could be heard. "The mass of wreckage was tremendous. Aside from the people brought out with it, there were deck chairs, oars, boxes, and I can t remember what. I simply know that one moment one was jammed between large objects and the next moment one was under the water. There were many people around one who needed assistance, but all one could do was to push an oar or box or a piece of wreckage to each to grab."[31] Lauriat looked around for a boat and spied an unopened collapsible floating a few yards away.

After he reached it, a sailor and another man joined him. Together, the three began opening the collapsible, only to discover that the boat had no oars. Lauriat was "disgusted" with any authority that would approve a boat not fitted with oars; they went back into the water to get some. They manned the boat and went back to the wreckage. "We took those whom we could help, but there were many, many past human assistance. We loaded our little boat to the full limit of its capacity and started for the fishing smack."[32]

One of those they pulled from the water was Margaret Gwyer, black from head to toe after being sucked into the ship's funnel and then expelled, miraculously unhurt. Lauriat thought they had about filled the boat "when I heard a woman's voice say in just as natural a tone of voice as you would ask for another slice of bread and butter, 'Won't you take me next? You know I can't swim.' When I looked over into the mass of wreckage from which this voice emanated all I could see was a woman's head, with a piece of wreckage under her chin and with her hair streaming out over other pieces of wreckage. She was so jammed in she couldn't even get her arms out, and with it all she had a half smile on her face and was placidly chewing gum. The last I saw of her when I helped her off the boat at Queenstown was that she was still chewing that piece of gum, and I shouldn't be surprised if she had it yet. Of course, we couldn't leave her, and as there was no possible way that I dared try to get her without going into the water for her, I told her that if she'd keep cool, I'd come after her. To my surprise she said it was not at all necessary, just hand her an oar and she'd hang on. That is the last thing in the world I should ever have dared to do, for naturally I thought, in view of the fact that she could not swim, that as soon as I cleared away the wreckage with an oar she'd get rattled and sink. After what she had said I got my huskies to back through the wreckage till my oar would reach to her. Then I placed it as close to her face as I could and she wriggled around and got her two hands on the oar, held fast, and we pulled her through."[33]

Dr. Daniel Moore was in a crowded lifeboat when the ocean liner sank. Water overflowed into the lifeboat, and its occupants desperately bailed it out using their hats. For his part, Moore pitched into the sea a water keg he discovered laying on the bottom of the boat and, believing the situation was hopeless, jumped out of the lifeboat. He swam to the keg and headed toward a steward he saw clinging to a deck chair. The two held onto the keg for more than an hour, kicking to reach a raft. They were eventually fished out of the water.[34]

Unfortunately there were a few safely aboard lifeboats who refused to help others fighting for their lives in the water. Mrs. Henry Adams swam alongside a raft only to be told by the men on board that they wanted to leave her in the water. At the urging of a woman passenger, the men reluctantly hauled her in. Some aboard the lifeboats used force to prevent swimmers from gaining access. Lucy Taylor witnessed occupants of her boat "rapping their knuckles" until people trying to climb aboard let go. Michael Byrne swam to a collapsible where he was told by the people inside, "This boat is full." Undeterred, a few minutes later he returned for a second attempt and this time was recognized by a steward, "Oh, Mr. Byrne, I am glad to see you." "If you are, please pull me in," replied Byrne. The steward hauled the grateful Byrne aboard.[35]

Charles Bowring managed to reach a lifeboat, and one of the ship's officers joined him. The boat was about half-full of water, which they bailed out by hand. They began picking up people struggling in the water, and though many of the bodies turned out to be dead, in all they saved about twenty lives.

Fireman John O'Connell was hanging onto a wooden plank when two men approached and fought him for possession of it. Knowing he wouldn't survive for long fighting over a plank in the water, he made his way to a lifeboat a short distance away. He was pulled aboard, but the boat was so densely packed that people feared moving—any small shift in weight could easily overturn the boat.

After drifting in the water, George Wynne eyed an available lifeboat nearby. He swam over to it and climbed aboard, but the boat was leaking beyond the passenger's capacity to bail it out. The boat soon capsized but Wynne was not discouraged; he clung to the overturned craft for dear life.

William Holton discovered that the Atlantic, even in May, was surprisingly cold. He swam by several dead bodies, and after a while came across a large wooden dog kennel that he pulled himself onto, and three other men joined him. The kennel capsized, and the other three hung on until they lost their grip and floated away. Holton managed to hold on to the kennel until he lost consciousness.

From her lifeboat, Elizabeth Duckworth observed a man in the water having trouble staying afloat. She turned to the petty officer in charge of her boat and asked, "Can we help him?"

"No," the man flatly answered.

"Yes, we can," Duckworth insisted. The petty officer gave in and they rowed to the man, who was dragged aboard by the crew.[36] The boat then set out for Queenstown, assisted by Duckworth at the oars.

Beneath the sea, the *U-20*'s Kapitänleutnant Walther Schwieger viewed the *Lusitania* from his periscope. He noted in his log, "In the distance astern are drifting a number of lifeboats. Of the *Lusitania* nothing is to be seen. The wreck must lie off Old Head of Kinsale Lighthouse 14 sea miles distant."[37]

Satisfied, Schwieger left the area. He had to consider that one or more of the ships in the area could be destroyers, which presented a threat to his command. He assumed the liner had transmitted an SOS, and that its passengers and crew must have known that rescue ships would soon arrive.

In fact, the Admiralty did receive the *Lusitania*'s distress message. Admiral Horace Hood, aboard his flagship *Juno* considered his options. He knew that his ship was a slow-moving old cruiser vulnerable to submarine attack. A single submarine had sunk three similar cruisers, the *Hogue*, the *Aboukir* and the *Cressey*, in the North Sea the previous October. He assumed other vessels would be on their way to help the Cunarder, and he decided to return to Queenstown.

The *Juno* wasn't the only ship ordered to turn back. The *Swanmore* of the Johnston Line received a wireless order from the Admiralty to make port while she was on the Liverpool to Baltimore run, just south of the *Lusitania*. Captain Cowan ordered all off-duty stokers to report to work, and the normally 12-knot ship did 16 knots. She was only 30 miles from the sinking liner, and yet she was not to take part in the rescue.[38]

Other vessels did assist. Although the big ships of the Irish Coast Patrol did not come, two torpedo boats did. Several sailboats also arrived on the scene, as did a local Queenstown lifeboat towed by the tug *Flying Fox*. Fishing boats also put to sea when they were advised of the *Lusitania*'s fate. Though this flotilla arrived after the ship sank, they saved many lives. The *Flying Fox* picked up 80 people, and the trawler *Indian Prince* fished 70 or so from the cold water. The motorboat *Elizabeth* rescued 60 people from one lifeboat and 16 from another. One fishing boat, the *Bluebell,* rescued several individuals, including Captain Turner. Numerous tugs also picked up survivors; one of them, the *Stormcork*, plucked 150 people from the water.

On an upturned lifeboat, Herbert Ehrhardt shivered from the cold, but when he saw streaks of smoke on the horizon he knew rescue was at hand. The *Indian Prince* came up to Ehrhardt's boat and asked if they were all right. "Yes!" replied Ehrhardt. The crew of the trawler promised to come back for them later.

The commanding officer of torpedo boat *055* told his crew to forget about the dead and concentrate on picking up those who were still alive. However, distinguishing between the dead and those who were unconscious proved difficult—and some people died after being rescued. Of the 23 rescued by *055,* two died on the way to Queenstown. The rescue was helped considerably by the arrival of the Greek tramp steamer *Katrina* which picked up the occupants of several lifeboats. Aboard the Greek steamer, the ship's Italian doctor immediately cared for some of the sick and injured.

Oliver Bernard was in a waterlogged boat when he and the other occupants saw a fishing smack. They rowed to the boat and were taken aboard; subsequently the tug *Flying Fish* came alongside and transferred the people from the smack. Aboard the tug, Bernard paced back and forth to keep warm, and then noticed that D.A. Thomas was also aboard.

"An exciting day!" Bernard said, trying to make conversation.

"Outrageous, simply outrageous!" replied Thomas.

"They certainly made a job of it," said Bernard.

"No, no, the boats, the deplorable inefficiency, I mean. Did you see what was happening?"

"Yes," said Bernard, "I saw all I wanted to!" He then told Thomas of what he saw during the final eighteen minutes of the *Lusitania*'s life Thomas paced the deck of the tug exclaiming, "Inefficiency, inefficiency, from beginning to end."[39]

Elizabeth Duckworth was relieved to see the trawler *Peel 12* come to her lifeboat. She along with the others in her boat climbed aboard the

Glasgow trawler, and soon another lifeboat came to the *Peel 12*'s side. There were only three people aboard, and one of its occupants told them that their boat had capsized and the rest of the occupants were fighting for life in the water. The man asked for help, but an officer replied, "I can't spare anyone." "You can spare me!" Duckworth boldly piped up, and with that the 52-year-old weaver jumped into the lifeboat and helped row.[40] The team rescued some 40 survivors and rejoined the trawler.[41]

Fifteen-year-old Kathleen Kaye also assisted in any way she could. She helped lift several people out of the water and into her boat, and when one of the sailors aboard fainted from his frantic efforts to escape swamping, she took his oar and rowed hard until the boat was out of danger.[42]

James Leary, with a badly injured leg, clung to a collapsible lifeboat while waiting for rescue, with twenty or so others huddled alongside him. Since the canvas cover could not be removed to raise the sides of the boat, waves repeatedly washed them from the platform. As they waited for rescue, "one by one, weakened by chill and exhaustion and buffeted by the waves, they dropped back into the water, to be seen no more, until only six of us were left."[43] Fortunately for Leary and the other survivors, they were fished out of the water before they succumbed to exposure.

Charles Lauriat and his companions, still in the collapsible, continued to help those who were struggling in the water. When they'd done all they could, he and the others began rowing to a fishing boat and noticed smoke on the horizon, a sign that other vessels were on their way. When they reached the fishing smack, he saw two lifeboats alongside, busy discharging their occupants. He noticed that the fifty or so people from the first two lifeboats were suspiciously dry, apparently having departed before the *Lusitania* sank. Puzzled as to why these two lifeboats contained so few people, Lauriat concluded they must have rowed away before the *Lusitania* sank. Each boat could have carried 75 or 80 passengers, and the tow lines an added number—had the boats stayed in the area to rescue survivors.[44] Lauriat and the others in the collapsible were hauled aboard. By contrast, he and his companions were saturated from their ordeal in the water. The crew of the fishing boat, the *Flying Fish*, tended to them as best they could.

Aboard one of the rescue vessels, the *Julia*, Belle Naish gulped down tea to keep warm while trying to comfort a seven-year-old boy who had lost his mother. The crew meanwhile looked for socks or slippers for the survivors. Mrs. Naish watched as men pulled the insert body of Theodate Pope on board using boat hooks, and laid her with the dead. "Mrs. Naish touched me," Theodate later wrote to her mother, "and says I felt like a sack of cement, I was so stiff with salt water. She was convinced I could be saved and induced two men to work over me, which they did for two hours, after cutting my clothes off with a carving knife hastily brought from the dining saloon." Pope eventually regained consciousness and was taken ashore.[45]

Quite often it was hard to make a distinction between the living and the dead. Ben Holton was accidentally laid among dead bodies, and woke from his oblivion to hear a sailor gasp, "Good gracious, are you alive? We put you amongst the dead ones." The sailor cut off Holton's lifejacket and gave him a cup of coffee.[46]

George Wynne, adrift and barely conscious, was hauled aboard the *Indian Empire* where he was revived by a cup of tea. Upon her rescue, a caring person gave Avis Dolphin a glass of warm milk, wrapped her in a rug and sat her near a stove. Leslie Morton and the others in his collapsible rowed to the *Indian Empire*. After transferring his people to this vessel, Morton noticed about twenty people on top of a capsized lifeboat. He rowed to the upturned boat, and transported them all to the *Indian Empire*.[47]

Meanwhile, in Queenstown the American Consul Wesley Frost was revising his annual commercial report when the vice consul burst into the office "saying that there was a wildfire rumor about town that the *Lusitania* had been attacked. Stepping quickly to the windows, we could see a very unusual stir in the harbor; and as we looked the harbor's 'mosquito fleet' of tugs, tenders and trawlers, some two dozen in all, began to steam past the town toward the harbor-mouth."[48]

Frost telephoned the secretary to Vice-Admiral Sir Charles Coke, who confirmed the report. The *Lusitania* had been sunk. Word also reached J.J. Murphy, the Cunard agent in Queenstown. He in turn sent a wireless to company headquarters informing them of the tragedy. Murphy notified hotels, boarding houses and private homes to be prepared to assist with the survivors' needs. "The British naval and military authorities provided hospital accommodation, stretcher-bearers, and no little private hospitality. The Constabulary and the Queenstown civil authorities made morgue and hospital arrangements." The volunteer motor ambulance corps of Cork, a fleet of 40 or 50 automobiles, ferried the wounded and frail survivors to their destinations as soon as they had been carried to port.[49]

The area where the *Lusitania* went down was littered with bodies. In time a large number of them washed ashore—some 289 in all, of which 65 remained unidentified.[50] Local authorities organized three morgues to accommodate all the bodies either retrieved from the sea or washed up upon shore: one at the town hall, another at the Cunard wharf, and a third in a disused ship chandlery at Harbor Row. On Monday afternoon, 140 bodies that could not be identified were interred in four collective graves, attended by "a large representation of military, naval, and civil officials, and with throngs of sympathetic Irish people."[51]

The human toll of the attack was appalling in its scale and character. Of the 1,959 passengers and crew aboard the liner, 1,198 died. Of these, 128 were neutral Americans, and in addition, three German-speaking stowaways, detained below, went down with the ship. Of the 129 children on board, only 35 survived. Only four of the 39 babies on the *Lusitania* lived through the ordeal.

By U.S. Consul Wesley Frost's account, "The American death-roster included, among others, Elbert Hubbard, Charles Frohman, Charles Klein, and Justus Miles Forman, as men of letters or arts; Alfred G. Vanderbilt, Harry J. Keser, A. C. Bilicke, William S. Hodges, Albert L. Hopkins, and...Dr. J. S. Pearson, as business men; and Lindon W. Bates, Herbert S. Stone, Mrs. R.D. Shymer, and Captain James Blaine Miller, as persons distinguished in various ways. Most of these persons are too well known to warrant any comment; but possibly some of them were not so familiar to the general American public as they might well have been."[52]

CHAPTER 10

THE WORLD REACTS

Great Britain

The torpedoing of the *Lusitania* galvanized British anger over Germany's conduct in the war. With events such as the shelling of Hartlepool, Whitby and Scarborough, in which German warships inflicted heavy civilian casualties; "the dropping of Zeppelin bombs on undefended towns; the use of asphyxiating gases; the reports of ill treatment of British prisoners... public opinion in England was gradually aroused and it was turned to wrath by the sinking of the *Lusitania* in May 1915."[1] Wracked by the loss of many crewmembers, mobs in Liverpool attacked "all German shops, looted them and set fire to them while the police were unable to act effectively because of the simultaneous disorders in different parts of the city."[2] Some descriptions of the "*Lusitania* riots" have police passively looking on while the violence unfolded.

In parts of London, Manchester, Merseyside and Tyneside, crowds—sometimes several thousand men and women—roamed the streets seeking tradesmen with German-sounding names.[3] Shops were torn apart, looted and sometimes set ablaze, and merchants and their families abused. In the East End, Londoners left few "German"-owned shops intact.[4] Rioters sometimes failed to distinguish between German descent and alien status.[5] Mobs roamed West Ham for several days, causing an estimated half-million dollars in damage. More than 200 shops in Liverpool suffered damage or looting, accounting for some $2 million in property loss.[6] In London, half the offenders brought before magistrates were women.[7]

Riots broke out in British Dominions as well. Authorities invoked martial law following an outbreak of violence against German residents in Victoria, British Columbia. Anti-German demonstrations and the destruction of houses and shops took place in Johannesburg, Cape Town, Port Elizabeth, Pretoria, Marizburg, Kimberly, Bloemfontein and other cities in South Africa.[8] Unlike the *Lusitania* riots in England, no looting took place in Cape Town or Johannesburg.[9]

Social and political institutions also enacted reprisals. The London Royal Exchange decided to exclude persons of German birth.[10] The king ordered that Kaiser Wilhelm II, Emperor Franz Josef I of Austria and other German and Austrian nobility be "degraded" from the most noble of British honors, the Royal Order of the Garter. On May 11, businessmen marched on the House of Commons and petitioned the Attorney General to curb the dangerous freedom of Germans living in the country. On May 13, "the Prime Minister announced that the government had decided upon a measure of general internment.[11] The law required all German, Austro-Hungarian and Turkish people from the ages of 17 to 45 be segregated and interned.[12]

The British press, perhaps with government support, blasted the Germans. The London *Times* described the sinking of the *Lusitania* as mass murder designed to incite panic. "The diabolic character of Germany's action in destroying the *Lusitania* must rivet attention," but the public should recognize the underlying motive: "the moral and sensational effect produced by the destruction of the big ship and the wholesale massacre of those on board..."[13] The editors held that the horrific crime had "stirred the people of this country more deeply than even the poison cloud or any of the other wanton and murderous acts committed by the Germans." The attack on the liner was "ruthless and implacable."[14] Many reports added the torpedoing of the *Lusitania* to the list of other atrocities of war committed by the Germans.

British newspapers also expressed sympathy for American losses and included stories from the United States that aligned with British reactions to the tragedy. Articles reflected widespread British belief that the sinking of the *Lusitania* would propel the United States into war, and professed faith that she would "follow the right course."

According to historian Armin Rappaport:

> Editors ... with an almost magnanimous confidence, asserted that it was not Britain's place to advise America. What the United States would do was a foregone conclusion for them. The British public had considerable justification for the confidence that America would now come in on their side, for when summaries of American press opinion of the sinking appeared in England, they revealed a nation inflamed.[15]

British leaders vented their anger, many hoping that the United States would cast aside her neutrality. "At sight this outrageous crime," Admiral Cyprian Bridge said,

> Outdoing the act of the cruelest pirates ever known, seems to have been deliberately perpetrated, with the intentions of defying and exasperating the American people. Considering the warning given Germany by the United States Government, it is hardly conceivable that the United States will abstain from punishing the crime and preventing its repetition by forcible means.[16]

Lord Sydenham, a former governor of Bombay, thought that Americans would "now realize the depth of German barbarism, and respond to the call of humanity."[17] Sir Gilbert Parker—a Canadian novelist and Member of Parliament largely responsible for British propaganda in the United States—expressed what many of his countrymen thought about the *Lusitania*: "It is an international business, and not England alone will take note of it. The United States will have something to say in regard to destruction of life and property, which in one sense, is as much hers as Great Britain's."[18] Lord Weardale, president of the Anglo-American Peace Centennial Committee, found that "Language is inadequate to condemn the atrocious criminals who have deliberately adopted piracy and murder of innocent civilians as the methods of warfare."[19]

This sentiment coming from British subjects is understandable; Britain was at war, and Germany's slaughter of innocent civilians on board the *Lusitania* intensified a hatred of Germany that had already been fueled by the violence of war. Yet there were also those who questioned the competency of the Royal Navy, bringing under scrutiny the Admiralty as a whole and the First Lord of the Admiralty—Winston Churchill—in particular.

Churchill appeared before Parliament on May 10, 1915, three days after the sinking. He expected to be questioned about the Royal Navy's failure to protect the *Lusitania*, and intended to present the Admiralty in the best possible light. He faced several obstacles. He could not give specific details about the instructions given to merchant captains, because that could inadvertently help the enemy. He was also reluctant to criticize Captain Turner since it might prejudice the formal investigation. Furthermore, condemning Turner might help give justification to the German attack.

Parliament questioned Churchill on many points. How fast was the *Lusitania* going when she was torpedoed? Was she standing in to make for Old Head of Kinsale? Was there a naval patrol in the area? Did he know about the German warning in the newspapers? Did the Admiralty know about submarine activity off the south coast of Ireland? Was the First Lord aware that an escort was provided to steamers carrying horses for the war effort? Were all points of departure and arrival now patrolled?[20]

Churchill could not answer all the questions; to do so would risk making classified information public. Since a formal hearing would be conducted by Lord Mersey, "It would be premature to discuss the matter." As a matter of security, he declined to give information regarding the warships patrolling the coast of Ireland. When asked why the *Lusitania* was unprotected, he explained that "the resources at our disposal do not enable us to supply destroyer escort for merchant or passenger ships, more than 200 of which, on the average, arrive or depart safely every day."[21] If the Admiralty provided protection for a singled-out liner, it would be open to charges of favoring one merchant over another.

When asked about the German warnings, Churchill admitted that the Admiralty "had a general knowledge that these threats had been made . . ."[22] The Admiralty had issued two wireless warnings to the *Lusitania* and "directions as to her course." He said he did not wish to elaborate on this point because he did not want to "throw the blame" on her captain.[23]

When pressed as to why no escort was provided, Churchill explained: "We do sometimes attempt, no doubt, to provide escorts for vessels carrying troops, munitions of war, and cargoes vitally needed by the Government. But our principle is that the merchant traffic must look after itself, subject to the general arrangements that are made. There is no reason to show—none whatever—that that principle is not accepted, and shocking exceptions like this ought not to divert the attention of the House ... from the main fact that almost the entire seaborne trade of these Islands is being carried on without appreciable loss."[24] One Member of Parliament asked Churchill if he knew that the *Hydaspes*, which was carrying government horses, received an escort by two destroyers as it neared the coast of Ireland. Churchill answered that he could not "controvert that statement."[25]

Churchill did his best, but some in Parliament believed the Admiralty could have done more. One member observed that "a number of destroyers of the 'L' class and a large number of patrol vessels" 100 miles away were capable of reaching Old Head of Kinsale "in about five hours."[26]

The majority of British opinion, however, placed the blame for the loss of the *Lusitania* squarely on the Germans.

Germany

Soon after the event, the German foreign office dispatched this note of condolence to U.S. Secretary of State William Jennings Bryan, which the *New York Times* published on May 11. Because German censors so carefully monitored newspapers,[27] this note summarizes the core of many articles and editorials written by the German press.

> The German Government desires to express its deepest sympathy at the loss of lives on board the *Lusitania*. The responsibility rests, however, with the British Government, which, through its plan of starving the civilian population of Germany, has forced Germany to resort to retaliatory measures.
>
> In spite of the German offer to stop the submarine war in case the starvation plan was given up, British merchant vessels

are being generally armed with guns, and have repeatedly tried to ram submarines, so that a previous search was impossible.

They cannot, therefore, be treated as ordinary merchant vessels. A recent declaration made to the British Parliament by the Parliamentary Secretary in answer to a question by Lord Charles Beresford said that at the present practically all British merchant vessels were armed and provided with hand grenades.

Besides, it has been openly admitted by the English press that the *Lusitania* on previous voyages repeatedly carried large quantities of war material. On the present voyage the *Lusitania* carried 5,400 cases of ammunition while the rest of her cargo also consisted chiefly of contraband.

If England, after repeated official and unofficial warnings, considered herself able to declare that that boat ran no risk, and thus lightheartedly assume responsibility for the human life on board a steamship which, owing to its armament and cargo, was liable to destruction, the German Government, in spite of its heartfelt sympathy for the loss of American lives, cannot but regret that Americans felt more inclined to trust to English promises than to pay attention to the warnings from the German side.[28]

German newspapers, for the most part, defended the sinking of the *Lusitania* without hesitation. "The fact that she was a fully armed cruiser," the influential *Lokal Anzeiger* of Berlin editorialized, "completely justifies her destruction under the laws of war."[29]

"What have we done?" the *Frankfurter Zeitung* asked. We have destroyed a "mighty asset which lay on the enemy's side," a "ship equipped like a cruiser." Property valued at many millions has been "annihilated, and an immeasurable store of moral power and self-confidence of a people whose whole life is centered in the prosperity of its shipping and commerce sank to the bottom with the proud vessel." "This maritime people," the editorial continued, has been taken in its very sanctuary. As for the *Lusitania*, she carried munitions of war, which would enable Britain and France to continue the war against Germany. "England, the nation of sailors, the world power, *is overtaken …*"

As for the casualties, "we should have been infinitely better pleased if the ship, which for many months past has been of aid to the enemy," could have been sunk without endangering passengers. If any person finds sinking a passenger liner inhumane, they should consider "England's war of starvation against Germany." Why, the editors asked, should we not retaliate against the British with any means at our disposal? Yet the British "mocked at us" when a clear warning was given. The crime, the *Frankfurter* concluded, was "allowing passengers to travel on a war vessel."[30]

The *Kölnische Volkszeitung*, a voice of the Catholic Center Party in Germany, considered the incident a German victory "to be viewed with joyful pride." The sinking of the *Lusitania* "must be placed beside the greatest achievement of this naval war," a success of "moral significance."[31] "The English wish to abandon the German people to death by starvation. We are more humane. We simply sank an English ship with passengers, who, at their own risk and responsibility, entered the zone of operations."[32]

Supporting the German position, Dr. Edmund von Mach, former Harvard professor and author of *What Germany Wants*, stated in an open letter to Washington officials that "Germany sent the torpedo that struck the blow, but the deaths of the American passengers were due to the criminal inefficiency of the English Company and to the subsequent explosions of the dangerous cargo." Von Mach also blamed the officials at the State Department for not warning the passengers officially, and asked why the American government failed to utter a single word of warning. The *Lusitania* and other British ships were hoisting American flags with the intention of deceiving the Germans. The liner carried dangerous cargo and was not provided an escort for protection.[33]

Dr. Dernburg, head of the German Information Service in New York and accepted as the Kaiser's voice in America, issued a statement about the *Lusitania*. "Any ship carrying goods to Great Britain is to be sunk," he said. The "usage of war" dictates that "vessels could be stopped, seized and searched. Vessels that carried contraband could be destroyed if they could not be taken into port. It has been customary to give innocent people warning and a chance to get away. A submarine is only one hundred and fifty feet long; it has no accommodations for others than its crew of probably twenty-four men. Consequently it is unable to take off passengers. . . . Everybody takes a risk if they want to. Anybody can commit suicide if they want to."[34]

In contrast to this response is the collective picture described by a roving Associated Press correspondent, George Abel Schreiner, who moved among the capitals and front lines of Europe during the war:

> The greatest shock the German public received was the news that the *Lusitania* had been sunk. For a day or two a minority held that the action was eminently correct. But even that minority dwindled rapidly.
>
> For many weeks the German public was in doubt as to what it all meant. The thinking element was groping about in the dark. What was the purpose of picking out a ship with so many passengers aboard? Then the news came that the passengers had been warned not to travel on the steamer. That removed all doubt that the vessel had not been singled out for attack.
>
> The government remained silent. It had nothing to say. The press standing in fear of the censor and his power to suspend publication was mute. Little by little, it became known that there had been an accident. The commander of the submarine sent out to torpedo the ship had been instructed to fire at the forward hold so that the passengers could get off before the vessel sank. Somehow that plan had miscarried. Either a boiler of the ship or an ammunition cargo had given unlooked for assistance to the torpedo. The ship had gone down . . .[35]

United States

News of the *Lusitania* disaster reached the United States within hours. When the unimaginable tragedy became clear, "A cry of mingled horror and rage rose from every part of it."[36]

The Cunard offices in New York released what information they had as the facts unfolded in wire after wire from their Liverpool office. An unconfirmed report of the *Lusitania's* fate first arrived at their office late in the morning of May 7. Word spread through the city and by three o'clock, family and friends of *Lusitania* passengers had "besieged" the office. Late that afternoon Cunard made a formal statement that the

Lusitania had been torpedoed without warning and sunk, and promised to announce any news of passengers as it came. Company officials later made public an unconfirmed report that all passengers had been saved, and many of those waiting ended their vigil. By ten that night, more accurate reports estimating the number of surviving passengers and crew to be 500 to 600 came in, with scraps of information about individual passengers.[37]

President Wilson and Secretary of State Bryan learned of the *Lusitania*'s sinking in the afternoon, when it was believed that all passengers had safely abandoned ship. By the end of the day, they knew that some 1,000 lives had been lost. Neither made a statement to the press. Before setting a course for the government, the administration's task would be to ascertain the facts.[38]

Washington, according to a *New York Times* report from the capital, quietly prepared for crisis. Following Germany's declaration in February 1915 of a war zone surrounding Great Britain, the United States had warned Germany that she would be held to "strict accountability" if she attacked American ships or harmed Americans traveling on any ship.[39] The sinking of the *Lusitania* would test Washington's commitment to neutrality.

The following day, headlines across the country such as this one from the *New York Times* brought the European war to life for Americans.

LUSITANIA SUNK BY A SUBMARINE, PROBABLY 1,260 DEAD; TWICE TORPEDOED OFF IRISH COAST; SINKS IN 15 MINUTES; CAPT. TURNER SAVED; FROHMAN AND VANDERBILT MISSING; WASHINGTON BELIEVES THAT A GRAVE CRISIS IS AT HAND[40]

News of the *Lusitania*'s sinking, a State Department official observed, "sent a wave of horror throughout the country, particularly in the east. The public denunciation of German barbarism was bitter."[41] The *Nation* magazine editorialized: "Germany ought not be left in a moment's doubt how the civilized world regards her latest display of 'frightfulness.' It is a deed for which a Hun would blush, a Turk be ashamed, and a Barbary pirate apologize. To speak of technicalities and the rules of war, in the face of such wholesale murder on the high seas, is a waste of time. The law of nations and the law of God have been alike trampled upon."[42] The New York *Herald* held that "The civilized world stands appalled at the torpedoing of the *Lusitania*, with the terrible loss of life—non-combatants, many of them citizens of neutral countries." The German warnings published before the liner's last voyage defined the character of the act. "If ever wholesale murder was premeditated," the paper concluded, "this slaughter on the high seas was."[43]

The New York *World* declared, "The American people do not want war with Germany if war can be honorably avoided, but that question must be decided in Berlin, not Washington." The editorial then spoke of Americans' rights. "We know our rights under international law, and we are not without means of enforcing those rights. Furthermore those rights will be enforced—peaceably if possible, but by force if necessary."[44] According to the *New York Times*, the State Department should demand that Germany cease making "war, like savages drunk with blood, that they shall cease to seek the attainment of their ends by the assassination of non-combatants and neutrals. In the history of wars there is no single deed comparable in its inhumanity and its horror ..."[45]

Newspapers outside New York added their voices to the chorus. The *Evening Journal* of Richmond branded the attack as "wholesale, cowardly, deliberate assassination. No massacre ever done by savage people, by Indians and wild Africans, was so base, cruel and ruthless. The savages at least attack in the open and encountered some risk."[46]

The *Richmond Virginian* declared that "If Germany has one single, other friend in the world today the world is in ignorance of it. And the condition is Germany's fault." The editors recognized that sinking the *Lusitania* was not as much "a stab in the side of this country" as torpedoing the *Gulflight*. Nevertheless, there existed "no greater crime against the record of any nation than the dastardly, infamous murder of the passengers and crew of the *Lusitania*—unless it be the ravishing of Belgium." The editors branded Germany "a moral and international leper." They conceded that Germany was at war and burdened with her own particular conflicts, but still she had no more right to attack neutrals than "a mob of outlaws has over the persons and lives of helpless women." "Slapped in the face," the world is "stunned by this atrocity." Nevertheless, the editors did not recommend force. "It is our task," they summed up, "to use every honorable means to lessen rather than increase the horrors that have encompassed the world . . ."[47]

The *Richmond Times Dispatch* proclaimed that Germany "must have gone mad." The editors insisted that the Germans had to have known that Americans were on board the liner. The sinking of the Cunarder was "a *reckless* disregard" of world opinion, especially American opinion. Germany's desire to win the war by any means revealed that "*blood lust has toppled reason from its throne.*"[48]

Newspapers in the Midwest expressed the same belief. The Akron *Beacon Journal* went on record as saying, "It matters not how much one may sympathize with Germany—it is impossible to contemplate the *Lusitania* tragedy without a shudder of horror." "The act was unprecedented. Had it happened in any other war the civilized world would arise against it."[49]

Many newspapers advocated forbearance, among them *The Independent.* "National indignation is inevitable," the editors believed, "its expression is a national duty." But the American people had a "higher duty. We must practice the sternest self-control. In demanding justice we must weigh our every act and word and thought in the scales with even hand."[50] The Cleveland *Plain Dealer* expressed a similar view: "Seldom has the American people stood in greater need of calmness and deliberation." The torpedoing was "a deliberate act," but the *Lusitania*, the editorial pointed out, was British, not American. Those who booked passage on her "voluntarily" took the risk.[51] An informal poll of a thousand newspaper editors who were asked for their opinions yielded only six calling for war.[52]

Americans criticized their leaders' interpretation of "neutrality." An anonymous letter to the *Washington Post,* signed "Neutral," said that it was "unwarranted" to consider the *Lusitania* an unarmed and unresisting ship since British merchantmen were under orders from the Admiralty to ram submarines. "How does the collector of the port of New York," Neutral asked, "the official representative of our government, see it his duty to clear vessels whose captains openly announce their determination to destroy German submarines? Let our Government be right, and then go ahead," the writer suggested. "It is better to start right and then there is more chance of finishing in good shape."[53]

Neutral opinions such as this must have disturbed former President Theodore Roosevelt, who publicly stated, "When the German decree establishing the war zone was issued, and of course plainly threatened exactly the type of tragedy which has occurred, our Government notified Germany that in the event of any such wrongdoing at the expense of our citizens we would hold the German Government to 'a strict accountability.' The use of this phrase, 'strict accountability,' of course, must mean, and can only mean, that action will be taken by us without an hour's unnecessary delay."[54]

Taking the opposite stance, former President William H. Taft warned against precipitous action in a speech in Philadelphia. "I agree that the inhumanity of the circumstances in the case now presses us on, but in the heat of even just indignation is this the best time to act, when action involves such momentous consequences and means untold loss of life and treasure? There are things worse than war, but delay, due to calm deliberation, cannot change the situation or minimize the effect of what we finally conclude to do."[55]

Diverse positions were held by American politicians, most favoring continued neutrality. Governor Simeon Baldwin of Connecticut recalled the warning to Germany about attacking American ships. "The phrase 'strict accountability' used in the dispatch did not," as he recollected it, "refer to a foreign vessel sailing under her true colors. The responsibility now under the present circumstances of our declaring our policy is somewhat different in character."[56] Senator Charles Thomas agreed that the situation was not as clear as the Germans' attack on the *Gulflight*. "The attitude of the Government upon the sinking of the *Lusitania* should, in my judgment, be in accord with its note to Germany. The *Lusitania* tragedy differs only in degree from that of the *Fabala*."[57] Governor Brewer of Mississippi believed that since passengers were warned not to take passage on the liner, we had no quarrel with Germany. "Americans were given fair warning to stay off," he said, "The passengers knew what to expect and took the risk."[58]

There were similar reactions on Capitol Hill. Vice President Thomas Marshall thought it was reckless for any American to have booked passage on the *Lusitania*. They were on "British soil" when they boarded the Cunarder and "must expect to stand the consequences."[59] Americans should "deplore the attack," suggested Representative Caleb Powers, but he also thought that Americans who booked passage on a British liner put themselves at risk.[60] Senator William Walsh took the position that Americans "must yield to the warning given to keep out of the water surrounding Great Britain." Otherwise the United States was obliged to make war, though neither interest nor honor requires it, he concluded.[61] Representative W.L. Jones concurred. "Our citizens have rights," he admitted, "but they should not insist on exercising them in a way likely to involve us in war." "Innocent people at home," Jones insisted, "should not be embroiled in war on their account."[62]

Senator Henry Cabot Lodge disagreed. "An American citizen lawfully in a foreign country or on a foreign ship," he believed, "is entitled to the protection of his Government." The fact that there is a war does not give a belligerent the "right to kill him."[63] The attack was labeled as "common piracy and murder" by Senator John Shields of Tennessee, who looked to the President to protect the rights of Americans.[64] Senator Hoke Smith referred to the sinking of the liner as "heathen," while insisting that Americans should not forget about the deaths of German civilians caused by the British blockade. American rights included the right of freedom of the seas, which the British, by their use of the blockade, denied the United States.[65] Senator Works of California felt that Germany should be held responsible for the American lives lost, and suggested the possibility of an embargo of munitions of war to all belligerents.[66]

Some in Congress agreed with Wilson's measured approach to the problem. Senator Morris Sheppard of Texas described the sinking of the *Lusitania* as an "unspeakable horror" of modern war, advocated disarmament after the war, and counseled patience in the meantime.[67] Senator E.D. Smith from South Carolina suggested that Americans should wait until all the facts were in before taking action, and expressed his utmost confidence in the President.[68] Since Wilson had "kept us free from entanglements so far," Congressman R.E. Difenderfer also had trust in the president's judgment.[69]

Americans also defended Germany's action. They reminded the world that the British blockade, also illegal, was killing German civilians, many of them women and children. Professor John Walse, head of

Harvard's German department, asked, "Which is the harder death—by starvation or drowning?" That said, Walse also believed the commander of the German U-boat "made a grave mistake" by not allowing the *Lusitania*'s passengers a chance to abandon the ship safely.[70] Professor Heinrich C. Bierwirth took a legal view: "International law has been tossed about like a dirty rag through this war. About every rule has been broken, and I don't see how one can especially blame the Germans" in the sinking of the *Lusitania*.[71] Roland B. Grom, writing for the *Richmond Times-Dispatch*, defended Germany's actions because the *Lusitania* displayed an enemy flag and carried war goods. The illegal British blockade of Germany compelled Germany to conduct the submarine blockade. The fact that the British armed their merchant marine ships and instructed them to ram submarines caused German U-boats to attack without warning.

The *Washington Post* pointed out that Captain John Black of the *Transylvania* boasted that he would ram submarines if necessary, and a ship owner named Joseph Holt offered $2,000 each to "the next four merchantmen or trawlers which sink German submarines." The *Post* reminded its readers that the *Baltic's* captain volunteered his willingness to ram U-boats. Therefore, the *Lusitania* and other British merchant ships "can neither be classed as peaceful merchant vessels nor properly deemed such, in the view of many naval officers."[72] Some German apologists hinted that policies which allowed merchant ships to resist German submarines were designed to embroil the United States in war.[73]

A publication called the *Fatherland* agreed. "Legally and morally," this paper declared, "there is no basis for any protest on the part of the United States." The *Lusitania* was a British vessel instructed to ram submarines. "Hence every British ship must be considered in the light of a warship."[74] Writers at the *Gaelic American* accused the British of arming their passenger liners, including the *Lusitania*. According to this newspaper she carried rifles and concealed guns.

Other voices advocated a more balanced view of Germany. J.P. Leaf wrote in the *Nashville Banner*, "Now that the English-owned or English-subsidized papers are ransacking the dictionaries in search of expletives to give vent to their feelings of horror and indignation over the sinking of the *Lusitania*, let us in a spirit of fairness look at the other side also." Germany, Leaf argued, was being exposed to slow starvation by the British blockade. More lives were threatened by this action than by torpedoing the Cunarder. Leaf asked:

[I]s it less cruel, less criminal, less barbarous to kill forty millions of women and children by slow starvation than to sink the ship of the enemy, loaded with war material to the gunwales, on which unfortunately hundreds of passengers had taken passage, despite the warnings of the German Government?" This government would be only too glad to give up this kind of warfare and has repeatedly offered to do so, if England would allow the entrance of foodstuffs into Germany for its civilian population. England has, however, contemptuously spurned this humane proposal. It prefers to conquer Germany by starving its women and children and then insure its transports of war material and reservists against German attacks by taking on board passengers from neutral countries. And if hundreds of them should perish, what do the lords of England care for that. Not enough to send a warship to meet and protect it as it enters the danger zone.

He or she went on to criticize Wilson's government for being "bulldozed" by Great Britain while it denied Americans the right to sell "innocent goods" to whomever they wished, and the right to ship whatever they wished to neutral countries. "Let me repeat that such occurrences as the sinking of the *Lusitania* are deplorable," Leaf said in closing, "But let us put the responsibility where it belongs."[75]

American clergymen were called upon to respond to the tragedy. Among them was the Reverend John Haynes Holmes, who said, "This is an hour for lamentation, but not for anger—an hour for grief, but not for madness." He believed the United States should not go to war. "There is no more reason why we should go to war with Germany today than there was yesterday. On the contrary, there is infinitely more reason why, in the face of this monstrous horror, we should reaffirm our love of peace and our faith in reason and good will." According to Holmes, militarism caused this horror. "War settles nothing," he concluded, "It adds to horror, aggravates madness with madness, sanctifies the insane idea that the slaughter of a thousand men on shipboard can be met by the slaughter of unnumbered other thousands of men upon the fields of battle. . . . [Now is] the time to show that America abhors the crime of war and sincerely believes in peace."[76]

The Reverend Dr. S. Edward Young of the Bedford Presbyterian Church in Brooklyn believed the time had come "for outspoken protest against Germany's conduct of the war by the multitude of preachers, publicists, and laymen who, complying with President Wilson's request for neutrality, have kept silence for over nine months, while Ambassador von Bernstorff, Dr. Dernburg, and a host of other German advocates violated the President's express wish by carrying on a campaign against neutrality. . . . America cannot be silent or inactive after this. We are in an awful and dangerous crisis. One spark could set the land aflame. The wisest friends of Germany here will take care to uphold the hands of President Wilson and cease calling for the impeachment of the Secretary of State for not forbidding Americans to sail on the *Lusitania*. Universal prayer is surely being offered for our calm, brave, God-fearing President, whose task is heavier than any man's since Lincoln."[77]

Where did the majority of Americans stand on the sinking of the *Lusitania*? There is no clear answer. Certainly many Americans defended the Germans, but most of them resented Germany for what she did. The act—perhaps accidentally—had the potential of prodding the United States into a war.

Many besides William Jennings Bryan questioned whether Americans should be travelling on belligerent passenger liners. William W. Fiske wrote to the *Philadelphia Ledger* that "the sensible suggestion" was that Americans should travel on American or other neutral ships. After all, Germany up until now had shown a disposition to make reparations when she was in the wrong.[78]

Not surprisingly, there were those who placed at least some of the blame with the British. The *Washington Post*, while doubting Captain Turner deliberately set out to have his ship torpedoed, declared that if he had "decided to facilitate in every way a successful torpedo attack, he could not have taken a more effective means to carry out his purpose." The *Post* asked why the *Lusitania* took the usual route on scheduled time, slowed her speed, and blew her foghorn. The newspaper also wondered why there was no escort.[79]

The Cunard Line did not escape blame for its part in the tragedy. The *Richmond Evening Journal* pointed out that not all of the *Lusitania*'s boilers were in use on her last voyage, in order to save coal. What the editors overlooked was that there was a shortage of crew to work those boilers because of the war. The *Richmond Evening Journal* also asked why there was no convoy for the liner.

On May 18, the *Post* railed at the American government for illegally allowing a passenger vessel to "carry arms and ammunition or other explosives." The collector of the port in New York should have known it was "his duty to withhold clearance papers" for the *Lusitania*. The 1882 "act to regulate the carriage of passengers by sea" states that "it shall not be lawful to take, carry or have on board any such steamship or other vessel any nitroglycerin or any other explosive article or compound, nor vitriol or like acids, nor gunpowder, except for the ship's use," nor anything else "likely to endanger the health or lives of the passengers or the safety of the vessel." The *Washington Post* asked, "Why is not this law enforced?"[80]

Two days later the *Post* reported that the Department of Commerce and Labor's solicitor had, in 1911, offered the opinion that small arms ammunition could be carried on passenger ships. To this the newspaper responded that, "Obviously, if a passenger steamer is loaded with ammunition in such quantity as to endanger the lives of passengers, the law has been violated, notwithstanding departmental opinions... The safest rule to follow would be refusal to clear any passenger vessel that has any ammunition on board, regardless of quanity."[81]

Others agreed. Francis J.L. Dorl wrote to *Vital Issues* quoting the law of 1882. The writer pointed out that it was unlawful to carry explosives on passenger trains and "it certainly is even more dangerous on a passenger ship." "A collision with another ship, the striking of a submerged rock, the possibility of internal combustion, the likelihood of fire on board the ship—the mere shock—might cause an explosion and sink the ship."[82]

Some people wondered if it was wise for the United States Government to protest the use of submarines. Albert Pelter wrote to the *Washington Post*, making the point that international law was largely made up of precedent. If one day the United States were forced into war, and found that our opponent shipped arms and ammunition on ships advertised as luxury liners, what recourse would our submarine commanders have to protect themselves and our country? He believed no passenger liners should be allowed to carry contraband of war.

One writer to the *Washington Post*, George P. Eustis, wondered if the United States should be selling war materials to belligerents. "The President proclaimed our neutrality and called on all citizens of this country to observe the same to the best of their abilities, and yet millions of dollars' worth of ammunition have been shipped to the Allies." This ammunition was responsible for thousands of deaths. Eustis admitted that under international law America had the right to sell arms, but Congress has the right to outlaw such shipments. He called it a "national disgrace" to sell arms to either side.[83]

Thomas C. Hall, president of the Union Theological Seminary in New York, considered the loss of the *Lusitania* "a tragedy for which the United States and the Cunard Company are about equally responsible." To allow a passenger liner carrying women and children also to contain a cargo of powerful explosives was "a shocking exhibition of lawlessness and greed." The passengers were warned prior to sailing, and since the United States was shipping arms, she was "the only neutral nation thus sinning."[84]

CHAPTER 11
THE FORMAL HEARINGS

Britain was at war and losing about two dozen ships each month. Though the government could not possibly investigate every sinking, the loss of 1,201 lives and a vessel of the *Lusitania's* size unquestionably required a formal inquiry into the circumstances and the cause. Thus it was determined that a formal hearing would proceed according to the Merchant Shipping Acts of 1894 and 1906.

A Harsh Verdict

Before this could take place, a surprise came from another quarter. The coroner at Kinsale, John J. Horgan, formed a coroner's inquest into the matter. He convened a jury of twelve men, mostly shopkeepers and fishermen, to hear the evidence. The inquest opened on May 8, 1915, one day after the sinking. It lasted two days. The Admiralty caught wind of the matter and sent orders for its adjournment, but the message arrived after the last witness quit the stand. The Royal Navy tried to squash the inquest results, fearing that information regarding secret instructions to ship's masters and code-breaking clues might be made public, risking its transfer into enemy hands.

Captain Turner appeared as a witness, visibly shaken by his ordeal. Neither the Admiralty, Cunard officials nor their lawyers were available to prepare him for the inquest. Sailors in this predicament were well aware of the dangers of being questioned by "land sharks." A thought-less word might hurt the company, or even worse, help the enemy. Turner did the best he could.

Among the questions put to the captain was whether or not the *Lusitania* was armed. Turner gave an unequivocal "No."[1] The coroner then asked whether or not the Cunarder had been warned of the at-tack. "Had you personally any warning?" he asked Turner.

"No, only through the [news]papers."

"You were aware that threats had been made that this ship would be torpedoed?" inquired Horgan. It must be remembered that the no-tice published by the Germans in the newspapers prior to the *Lusitania*'s last sailing did not specify any ship.

"Fully aware of it," was the captain's reply.[2] If that were so, Turner must have known that his ship could be attacked, and that he could be held responsible for taking inadequate—or not any—precautions.

Horgan raised a few questions about wireless messages. Turner stated that he remained in wireless contact "all the way across, to re-ceive but not to send messages." He also admitted that he'd received wireless warnings about submarine activity. The witness stated that he had no knowledge of the *Earl of Lathom,* which had been sunk off Old Head of Kinsale not far from where his ship was torpedoed. The cap-tain insisted that it was best, for the sake of national security, that the coroner query the Admiralty about specifics.

At one point Horgan asked the witness if he had received "any spe-cial instructions as to the voyage." Captain Turner replied that he had, but could not divulge what they were.

"Did you carry them out?" came the question.

"Yes," insisted Turner, "to the best of my ability."

"Tell us in your own words what happened after passing Fastnet," the coroner requested. Turner explained:

The weather was clear. We were going at a speed of eighteen knots. I was on the port side and heard Second Officer Hefford call out, "Here's a torpedo!"

I ran to the other side and saw clearly the wake of a tor-pedo. Smoke and steam came up between the last two funnels. There was a slight shock. Immediately after the first explosion there was another report, but that may possibly have been internal.

I at once gave the order to lower the boats down to the rails, and I directed that women and children should get into them.

I also gave orders to stop the ship, but we could not stop as the engines were out of commission. It was not safe to lower boats until the speed was off the vessel.

When she was struck she listed to the starboard. I stood on the bridge when she sank and the *Lusitania* went down under me. She floated about eighteen minutes after the torpedo struck her. I was picked up from among the wreckage and afterwards brought aboard a trawler.

No warship was convoying us. I saw no warship and none was reported to me as having been seen. At the time I was picked up I noticed bodies floating on the surface but saw no living persons.[3]

Horgan asked about the speed of Turner's command. "Eighteen knots was not the normal speed of the *Lusitania,* was it?"

This was an embarrassing question for the witness, but he answered, "At ordinary times she could make 25 knots, but in war times her speed was reduced to 21 knots." Turner then elaborated. "My reason for going 18 knots was that I wanted to arrive at Liverpool bar without stopping, and within two or three hours of high waters."[4]

The witness was asked several questions about the orders he issued. "Was a lookout kept for submarines, having regard to previous warnings?" Turner answered that the lookouts were doubled. The examiner also inquired whether the ship had zigzagged, and asked for details about launching the lifeboats.

"Were your orders promptly carried out?" was the next question.

"Yes," insisted Turner.

"Was there any panic [on board]?"

"No, there was no panic at all. It was almost calm," the captain claimed. Of course, other observers noted clear signs of panic during the eighteen minutes following the torpedoing.[5]

The foreman of the jury had a question for the witness. "In face of the warnings at New York that the *Lusitania* would be torpedoed, did you make application to the Admiralty for an escort?"

"No," answered Turner, "I left that to them. It is their business, not mine. I simply had to carry out my orders to go—and I would do it again." Turner said this last word emphatically.

The coroner responded, "I am very glad to hear you say so, Captain."

A juror asked, "Do you think it would have been advisable for patrol boats to have accompanied you?"

This raised an awkward point, for if the answer were "yes," then some blame had to be laid with the Admiralty. Horgan stepped in.

"I suppose it might not have prevented [the attack] in the slightest degree?"

"No," agreed Turner, "they might have torpedoed them [the escorts] as well."[6]

After hearing all the evidence, the coroner addressed the jury. "I propose to ask the jury," Horgan said to them, "to return the only verdict possible for a self-respecting jury, that the men in charge of the German submarine were guilty of willful murder."[7] The verdict the jury reached fulfilled the coroner's expectations:

> The jury find that this appalling crime was contrary to international law and the conventions of all civilizations, and we therefore charge the officers of the submarine, and the German emperor and the Government of Germany, under whose orders they acted, with the crime of willful and wholesale murder.[8]

The Whole Blame

After the coroner's inquest came a formal investigation by the British Board of Trade in the Wreck Commissioner's Court in London. The Merchant Shipping Acts of 1894 and 1906 provided legal grounds for the action. Britain was at war, emotions were high, and an adverse finding against Turner or the Admiralty would weaken Allied propaganda. While there was an inclination to "whitewash" on the British side,[9] there was also a strong appetite to condemn the Germans.

The man chairing the inquiry was jurist and Wreck Commissioner Lord Mersey. Mersey, above all an establishment man, had garnered fame earlier when he headed the investigation into the *Titanic* disaster. Four assessors assisted Mersey, two officers in the Royal Navy and two in the Merchant Service. The solicitor general, Sir Frederick Smith (later Earl of Birkenhead), represented the government and would cross-examine witnesses. By all accounts a brilliant lawyer, he subsequently prosecuted Irish nationalist Sir Roger Casement for treason in connection with the Easter Rebellion.[10] The attorney general, Sir Edward Henry Carson, also represented the British government. Carson was a superb cross-examiner, well known for successfully defending the Marquis of Queensberry in a criminal libel suit brought by Oscar Wilde in 1895.[11]

Parties involved in the sinking hired their own lawyers. Butler Aspinall represented Turner and the Cunard Line. There were also four lawyers for litigating passengers, one for certain members of the crew, one for the National Union of Sailors, one for the Marine Engineers Association, and one for the Canadian government.

The court opened its hearing on June 15, 1915, thirty-nine days after the *Lusitania* sank. The six sittings of the formal hearing ended on July 1 of that year. Some of the sessions were conducted behind closed doors, during which sensitive Admiralty instructions were discussed, along with wireless messages that could provide clues for code-breaking if the Germans were to learn of them.

Some early witnesses testified to the condition of the vessel. Albert Laslett, the Board of Trade Engineer and Ship Surveyor at Liverpool, and Captain O.A. Barrand, the Board of Trade Emigration Officer at Liverpool, had examined the *Lusitania* earlier that year and found her to be satisfactory.[12]

By far the most important witness was Captain Turner. Several questions were put before him, including whether the ship was armed.

"Was she [the *Lusitania*] armed or unarmed?" asked the attorney general.

"Unarmed," was Turner's answer.

"Had she any weapons of offense or defense against an enemy at all?"

"None whatever."

"Or any masked guns?"

"None whatever."[13]

Several days later the board of inquiry called Captain Turner back to testify about ferrying troops.

"Were there any Canadian troops on board?" inquired Mersey.

"None whatever."

"Were there any troops on board?"

"None whatever."[14]

Turner gave the most crucial testimony during the secret hearings on June 15th. Attorney General Carson established that Tuner had received instructions from the Admiralty prior to sailing, and grilled him about following those instructions:

"What I want to ask you first is why, with the information before you, did you come so close to Old Kinsale Head?"

"To get a fix. We were not quite sure what land it was, we were so far off."

"Is that all you have to say? You say you were warned especially to avoid the headlands and to stay in mid-channel, those were the two instructions which were given?"

"Yes, but I wanted to find out where I was."

"Do you mean to say you had no idea where you were?"

"Yes," admitted Turner, "I had an approximate idea, but I wanted to be sure."

At this point Lord Mersey interjected.

"Why?"

"Well, my Lord, I do not navigate a ship on guess-work."

"But why did you go groping about to try and find where land was?"

"So I could get a proper course."

"I do not understand this. Do you mean to say it was not possible for you to follow the Admiralty directions which were given you?"

"Yes, it was possible," the witness conceded.

"Then why did you not do it?"

"I considered I followed them as well as I could."[15]

There then began an argument between Captain Turner and his interrogators about what constitutes a mid-channel course. Turner insisted that he gave land a wide berth, while others at the hearing believed that ten miles is not enough in a channel 140 miles wide. Then there was another important matter—the question of why Turner did not zigzag.

"You would have plenty of time," the attorney general pointed out, "I understand zigzagging takes more time but why did not you zigzag?"

"Because I thought it was not necessary until I saw a submarine."

"But the whole point of that is that it is the submarine that is looking at you?" asked the Commissioner.

"Yes."

"And if you are zigzagging you confuse him and put him into difficulties."

At this point the attorney general read the instructions: " 'War experience has shown that fast steamers can considerably reduce the chance of a successful submarine attack by zigzagging'—nothing about when you see the submarine. You see, when you are torpedoed it is too late."

"Of course it is."

"Do not you see now that you really disobeyed a very important instruction?"

Turner had no answer to that question.[16]

Mersey issued the official report on July 17, 1915. It dealt with the quality of the lifeboats and life-saving equipment. The report found that the boats, life jackets and life buoys examined a month prior to the ship's sailing were in satisfactory condition.[17] The report also considered the quality of the crew; Mersey concluded that the officers and crew were competent. Although he conceded that Cunard had lost some of its best men to the Royal Navy when the war broke out, Mersey judged the crew proficient in handling lifeboats. They were "well able to handle the boats" and carried out "the orders given to them in a capable manner."[18] Actually, the boat drill was perfunctory at best, and some of the crew attempted to lower the boats contrary to the captain's orders, which were to wait until the liner stopped.

Lord Mersey also dealt with the questions about cargo and armament. He insisted that the liner carried only rifle ammunition and "no other explosive." Mersey mentioned that a French passenger heard a second explosion "similar to the rattling of a maxim gun for a short period" and responded: "I do not believe this gentleman."[19] As for the German claim that the *Lusitania* was armed, Mersey bluntly said: "These statements are untrue, they are nothing but baseless inventions and they serve only to condemn the persons who make use of them."[20]

The report claimed that two torpedoes had been fired at the liner—the first striking and the second missing the ship. However, we now know that Schwieger launched only one torpedo. Mersey dealt kindly with Captain Turner. Although he failed to follow his instructions from the Admiralty, he "exercised his judgment for the best. It was the judgment of a skilled and experienced man . . . [H]e ought not, in my opinion, to be blamed.[21]

Severely critical of Germany, Mersey's report denounced the enemy's murderous intent. "The defenseless creatures on board," Mersey angrily stated, "made up of harmless men and women, and of helpless children, were done to death by the crew of the German submarine acting under the directions of the officials of the German Government . . . It was a murderous attack because made with a deliberate and wholly unjustifiable intention of killing the people on board." Mersey concluded that "The whole blame for the cruel destruction of life in this catastrophe must rest solely with those who plotted and with those who committed the crime."[22]

This embittered report perhaps deliberately overlooked the negligence of the Cunard Line and Captain Turner in order to focus the responsibility on German actions. Mersey's judgment might also have pleased and emboldened Captain Turner. A few months later he gave an interview to the *New York Times*. According to the reporter, Turner appeared to be a "trifle" thinner and his hair grayer than when the *Lusitania* sailed from New York on that tragic voyage. In the interview Turner defended his crew, saying they were "as good as most sailors that go to sea nowadays," and shared his opinion that regardless of the ship's speed, "the submarines would have got her."[23]

"A Pirate and Common Enemy of Mankind"

Many survivors and relatives of those lost on the ill-fated liner felt that the wreck commissioner was too lenient toward the Cunard Line and Captain Turner. Francis Jenkins bitterly stated, "It was outrageous that the *Lusitania* pushed ahead right into the path of danger." Another survivor agreed. "How the *Lusitania*'s officers can account for letting her creep through waters known to be dangerous is beyond me," commented R.T. Taylor, a Canadian manufacturer.[24]

The passengers' anger at the alleged negligence of Cunard and her officers expressèd itself in lawsuits; some 67 actions were initiated in the United States alone. The suits claimed $5,883,479 in total, most for loss of life. United States law allowed many of these claims to be consolidated into one, thereby limiting the liability of the Cunard Line.[25]

The case was heard before Judge Julius M. Mayer in the United States District Court, Southern District of New York. Mayer, a graduate of Columbia University Law School, had practiced law for many years and had held several government posts, including that of attorney general of New York State. In 1912 President Taft appointed him to the bench, where he heard the case against the White Star Line over the *Titanic* disaster. Since he held the "not guilty of negligence" line in that case, the plaintiffs and Cunard waived the right to a jury and entrusted the case to him.[26] The fact that the hearing didn't begin until April 17, 1918, after the United States had already joined the war on the Allied side, helped Cunard considerably.

Mayer considered "all of the testimony taken before Lord Mersey which was deemed material by either side" and new testimony from both sides of the Atlantic. Because of the war, the court appointed three commissions to interview witnesses: two in the United States and one in London. Testimony that was heard in court from additional passengers, crew and experts completed the record.[27]

Mayer weighed evidence about the crew's competence and the life-saving equipment. One witness, Junior Third Officer Albert Bestic, stated that it was his first voyage on the *Lusitania*. Cunard's lawyer Butler Aspinall asked him about the boat drills.

"When you were in New York and before you left, is it within your knowledge whether you had a boat drill?

"It is," he answered.

"Were any of the boats put in the water at New York?"

"That I cannot say."

"By that answer do you mean you do not remember or you do not know or what do you mean?"

"I do not know; I do not remember it."

"After you left New York had you got a boat?"

"Yes.

"What was your boat?"

"No. 10."

Bestic went on to say that he was taking soundings while the liner was in fog, and then mentioned that he'd taken part in the four-point bearing. Later he went off duty, heard the explosion and immediately reported to the bridge for orders.

"What orders did you receive?"

"To stand by our boat stations."

"Did you do so?"

"Yes."

"Where did you go to for that purpose?"

"I went to No. 10 boat."

"That is the boat on the port side?"

"Yes, on the port side."

"When you got to the boat deck were there passengers there?"

"Yes, they were crowded there."

"Did you have any difficulty with any foreign passengers?" Aspinall inquired.

"Yes, some foreign passengers jumped into the boat and they had to be taken out."

"Into your boat No. 10?"

"Yes, male passengers."

"And you had to clear them out?"

"Yes."

"I hope you succeeded?"

"I did."

The attorney for the plaintiffs cross-examined Bestic on the issue of boat drills. He began, "The state of your recollection about boat drill is that you do not know whether there was or was not a boat drill in New York?"

"I know there was a boat drill in New York," Bestic replied.

"Why did you say to Mr. Butler Aspinall that you did not know or could not remember?"

"I said I could not remember whether the boats were lowered in the water or not."

"Or whether any boat was lowered into the water?"

"I cannot remember."

"You yourself I think had nothing to do with the boat drill; is that so?"

"I had to attend my station at boat drill."

"You gave evidence before Lord Mersey's Enquiry?"

"Yes."

"Did you say there: 'I had nothing to do with the boat drill'?"

"No, I did not say that."

"I will read the whole question to you. This is the question asked you by Mr. Rose Innes: 'Will you describe what you mean by the usual boat practice?' And this is your recorded answer: 'My watch in the morning is from 8 to 12 and boat practice and fire drill is at 11 o'clock, and as far as my connection with the boat drill is concerned I have nothing to do with the boat drill, but I telephoned down about the fire drill. So far as boat drill is concerned I have nothing to do with it; I was on watch on bridge at the time'."

This put Bestic on the spot. He answered the best he could.

"That refers to the emergency boat drill held about 10 o'clock in the morning."

"I think that that was your recollection then; do you think it necessary to change it now?"

"No," Bestic insisted.

"Then you were asked this question by Lord Mersey: 'But can you tell that gentleman what the boat drill consists of?' and your answer was 'I could not'."

"Yes."

"You did not know what the boat drill was?"

"I know what the boat drill in New York was."[28]

"I am speaking about the boat drill you were referring to when you were giving evidence before Lord Mersey, the daily boat practice."

"No."

Bestic was questioned about the condition of the lifeboats.

"As regards the life boats which the *Lusitania* carried, I think you never examined those boats?"

"I examined the contents of them, not the boats themselves."

"What did you examine?"

"I examined the number of oars and the provisions; what the Board of Trade require."

The attorney examined Bestic closely about the fog and visibility conditions.

"During your watch on the 7th from 8 o'clock to noon, at one time there was a haze or fog I think?"

"Yes."

"Can you tell me when it cleared off?"

"As far as I recollect it was about 11:30."

"When the haze lifted at 11:30 the weather I understand was very clear?"

"It was not quite clear at 11:30; it lifted but it did not become quite clear."

"When did it become quite clear that morning?"

"I should say shortly after noon."

"If the Captain says it became clear about 11:40 do you agree with him or not?"

"As far as I remember it was shortly after noon."

"I think you said that the fog had lifted at 11:30; do you mean that or not?"

"The weather cleared before then, it was better; it improved."

"I am putting this to you on your recollection of what took place. Can you say whether or not before your watch ended at noon it was clear; that the sky was clear, the fog having lifted and that the sea was as nearly as could be perfectly calm?"

"As far as I recollect at noon there was a slight haze on the horizon."

"Could you see the land during your watch?"

"No."

"Do you mean not at any time?"

"Not on my morning watch from 8 to 12."

"Did you know on this journey when you made the land fall off the Irish coast?"

"No."[29]

Bestic was then questioned on what he did after lunch.

"When did you go on the bridge again after lunch?"

"About 25 minutes to two."

"You were then within sight of land?"

"Yes."

"Was it perfectly clear then?"

"I do not remember that it was perfectly clear."

The attorney was growing impatient with the witness.

"You seem to remember some things remarkably well and others not so well. To the best of your recollection tell the learned Commissioner as to the weather condition about twenty minutes to two when you went on the bridge after lunch?"

"To the best of my recollection it was quite clear."

"That is the best you can be expected to say in answer to a question like that. You had a good view of land then?"

"Yes."

"And the ship was pursuing her ordinary course?"

"Yes."[30]

Bestic then told of how he rushed to his boat station after the torpedo struck.

"In that condition of affairs [the ship's list], could boats have been lowered on the port side?"

"If she had come up far enough they could have been."

"Was any attempt made to lower any of the boats on the port side?"

"Yes."

"How many boats did those responsible try to lower?"

"They tried to lower them all."

"Were any of them lowered?"

"There was one to my knowledge."

"With passengers in it?"

"Yes."

"Were all the crews of the boats at their boat stations on the port side?"

"Not when I got there."

"They were not there at the time when she temporarily righted herself?"

"They would be there by then."

"You are being asked a question; do you know of your own knowledge whether they were there or not?"

"I could not tell you whether they were all there or not."

"You do not know even with regard to your own boat No. 10 whether the whole crew was there or not?"

"No, I cannot tell you if they were all there."[31]

Several other witnesses took the stand. Among them was Alfred

Booth, chairman of the Cunard Line. He was closely questioned on issues such as instructions the captain received from the Admiralty. First he was asked about the conservation of coal on the *Lusitania*

"After war broke out did a question arise in the office of the Cunard Company as to whether or not you should continue running the two big ships the *Lusitania* and the *Mauretania*?"

"Yes."

"What were the reasons which gave rise to that question being considered?"

"The large amount of west-bound travel which followed the outbreak of war, returning Americans, had come to an end and it was a question whether there would be sufficient traffic to warrant one or both of the steamers being maintained in the service."

"Was this matter very carefully considered by you and your colleagues?"

"Yes."

"What conclusion did you arrive at?"

"The conclusion we arrived at was that there would be sufficient traffic to justify running one of the steamers say once a month but not both, and only at reduced speed, that is to say at reduced coal consumption, and the *Lusitania* was chosen."

"What orders were given with a view to running her at a reduced speed?"

"That she was to run at three-quarter boiler power, which meant a reduction of speed from about 24 knots to about 21."

"How many boilers was she fitted with?"

"She was fitted with 24 double-ended boilers, that is counting a single-ended boiler as half a double-ended boiler, and we proposed to run her with 18 double-ended boilers."

"The others were closed down?"

"The others were closed down."

"Running her at that reduced speed, how would her speed compare with the speed of other passenger vessels crossing the Atlantic?"

"She was considerably faster than any other steamer crossing at the time," insisted Booth.

"First of all, as you say, it would save her consumption of coal?"

"Yes."

"And in addition to that would it also save something else which was of importance to you?"

"Yes wages. The crew would be considerably reduced. Roughly speaking the number of firemen and trimmers would be reduced in proportion to the reduction of the boiler power."

"So that you would be burning less coal and you would be using less labour."

"Yes."

"Quite apart from any consideration that might apply to the Cunard Company, did other and greater considerations weigh with you in arriving at that conclusion?"

"We felt that the question of economy of coal and labour in time of war had to be taken into account as well as the purely financial considerations of the Cunard Company," Booth pointed out.

"I propose to pass away from the topic now. After the German submarines began to make their first raids on our western coasts, did you and your colleagues discuss what could be done in order to combat it?"

"The matter was not discussed at a Board Meeting. It was discussed in the way I ordinarily discuss these matters. I am in constant touch with the Directors and the Managers and ascertain their views, and my own feeling and the feeling of all concerned was that there was no reason for withdrawing the steamer from the service."

"And in order to deal with the peril were any special measures taken to bring it home to the minds of your captains that special precautions should be taken?"

"The matter was discussed with each of the captains as he went on his voyage, either by myself or by the general manager or one of the assistant managers, whoever was available at the moment, with a view of seeing how far he realized the general aspects of the peril, not from the point of view of trying to give him specific instructions, which we considered dangerous, but general considerations which we wanted to be sure were present to his mind."

"Did you think it wise or otherwise to fetter his discretion in dealing with particular circumstances as they arose?"

"We thought it very unwise to fetter his discretion, as when an emergency arose he would have knowledge of facts which we could not have knowledge of."

"Unfortunately we have had a great experience of this submarine peril since, but do you still adhere to that opinion?"

"I am more than ever confirmed in the view that if one mistake has been made by those in authority it has been in making their instructions too specific and not leaving enough discretion of the individual commander."

At this point the commander intervened.

"May I ask what is meant by 'those in authority'?"

"I mean the Admiralty," answered the witness.[32]

The attorney for the Cunard Line resumed his questioning.

"We have been told that the *Lusitania* left New York on her last voyage on May 1st; when did you first hear of what one may call the warning advertisement which appeared in the American papers?"

"Either on Saturday evening or Sunday morning."

"May 1st was a Saturday?"

"Yes; I learnt it through the press."

"In consequence of that did you take any measures or were you able to take any measures?"

"We were not able to take any measures," Booth explained.

"I think later on in the course of the week you did hear, did you not, of the sinking of two large liners in St. Georges Channel?"

"That was on a Thursday I think; would you remind me what date it was." Booth stated that he heard of these two ships before the *Lusitania* was sunk.

"It was on Friday morning May 7th you heard of the sinking of these two liners, they were two Harrison liners."

"That is right, I remember the ships perfectly well but I could not remember whether it was Thursday evening or Friday morning that I heard. I heard that these two vessels had been sunk in the Channel, and knowing that the *Lusitania* was likely to be coming along that afternoon or sometime before very long, I became anxious with regard to her and asked the senior naval officer to send out a wireless message to the ship—we could not do it ourselves—to advise the captain of the sinking of those two ships and the position. I felt confident that the Admiralty would do so in any case, but I wanted to do it myself as well if possible in that way."

"Did he give effect to your wishes; did he send a wireless?"

"I believe he did but I believe it never arrived; it was too late."[33]

Booth was questioned on the time of arrival at the Mersey Bar.

"Were any instructions or warning given to the captains with regard to the time of their arrival at the Mersey Bar?"

"That was one of the general topics that we discussed with all captains, to see whether they realized what appeared to us to be the danger of coming to the Mersey Bar and having to anchor to remain at rest there, owing to there not being enough water to enable them to come up. That appeared to us, and we found the captains agreed with us, to be a dangerous thing if there were any submarines about [and] that the ships would then be an easy target."

"Was the question of whether he should enter the Mersey with or without a pilot discussed?"

"Yes, and for the same reason we authorized the Captain to come up without a pilot, if there was no pilot there, rather than wait."

Some of the plaintiffs asserted that Captain Turner and his crew were incompetent. Booth met this question head on.

"In answer to your petition [the statements of two women named Genevieve Cox Bancroft and Ethel Ann Rowell appear in this allegation in paragraph 6], 'That the Petitioner well knowing prior to the sailing of the steamship *Lusitania* of the danger of an attack upon her by submarines failed to provide the said ship with a prudent and competent master and crew and a crew competent and properly trained to handle the life boats and to rescue the passengers and other persons on board the said vessel in the event of the destruction of the said vessel.' Is that an accurate statement or not?"

"No," said Booth flatly.

"Speaking of Captain Turner (it may be that it does not immediately come within your province but in the course of your duties I have no doubt that you do have reports from time to time from your superintendents) is there any justification in your opinion for suggesting that Captain Turner is an incompetent Master?"

"Quite the reverse," Booth insisted, "I do not rely only on my superintendents; I am able to form my own judgment with regard to leading captains. At any rate I am able to see a good deal of them and I know them personally and I have and had the very highest opinion of Captain Turner's ability." Booth based this on observations of him before the war. In fact Turner's pre-war record was outstanding, but it would appear that he was unable or unwilling to adjust to wartime conditions. Booth could not admit to this.

"He has told us he has been in the service of your company for a very large number of years; is that accurate?"

"Yes."

"And I suppose has worked his way up from a subordinate position to the very high position he now occupies?"

"Yes."

"And I believe from time to time he has been put in charge of most of your great steamers?"

"Yes."[34]

Booth was cross-examined by the attorney for the plaintiffs. He was asked about any discussions with the captain regarding the submarine peril.

"So far as guarding against submarine perils goes, had you discussions with the captains of your company, the masters of your ships?"

"Yes."

"Had you any discussion with Captain Turner?"

"My recollection is that it was the general manager who had the discussion with him."

"Can you say as a fact whether or not you yourself discussed with Captain Turner either on this voyage or the previous voyage the risks from submarines?"

"I am perfectly certain that I had had some conversation with Captain Turner, but I think this specific conversation I am thinking of, the one before he sailed on his voyage was with the general manager and not with me."

"Were you present at it?"

"No, I was away."

"All you mean to convey, I presume, is that it was related to you, it was told you in the office subsequently that such a conversation did take place?"

"Yes."[35]

By far the most important witness, as twice before, was Captain Turner. Fate had not been kind to Turner in the time since the *Lusitania*. On New Year's Day in 1917, while in command of the liner *Iver-*

nia, which had been converted to a troop ship, he was again torpedoed. The ship sank but Turner once again survived.

On the witness stand, the captain was asked when he had first heard that the Germans would sink passenger ships. He replied, "I heard that in New York. I do not know about passenger ships, but I heard they were going to sink the *Lusitania* in New York." He later was asked, "Of course you knew, in consequence of the information you had before you left Liverpool, of the German submarine campaign, and this publication in the American papers, that your ship was seriously threatened?"

"Yes, certainly," was the answer.

The questioning then shifted to the instructions Turner received concerning the submarines.

"The instructions issued by the Admiralty and all their [advice] to you were instructions and [advice] supplied to you for the purpose of helping you to avoid submarine peril?"

"No doubt."

"And you realized, I suppose, that the British Admiralty were in a better position to form an opinion as to the location of submarines, as to the spheres in which they were operating, than you could?"

"Yes," admitted Turner.

"Did you feel that it was your duty to obey the instructions of the Admiralty in so far as they were conveyed to you?"

"Yes, consistent with the welfare of the ship."

"You realized, did you not, that the Admiralty, having better means of knowing where submarines might be encountered than you could have, the course which prudence dictated was to follow out the Admiralty instructions?"

"Yes, that is right," the witness conceded.

"In some particulars I think you claim that you did follow their instructions?"

"Yes."

"And I think, to be equally frank, you admit that in other particulars you neglected their instructions and pursued your own course?"

This was a tough question for Turner. He answered, "I do not admit anything of the kind."

"Did you carry out the advice given to you by the Admiralty in every particular?"

"As far as possible," the captain insisted, "Yes, as far as it was consistent with the welfare of the ship."[36]

Later he was asked if he used his own discretion and disobeyed part of the instructions given to him by the Admiralty. His response was, "That may be some people's idea, but it is not mine. I considered I followed out all instructions to the best of my ability—what I thought were the instructions."[37] Turner was asked what instructions he thought were wise to ignore. He explained that had he steered a mid-channel course, "I would run right foul of a submarine off Coninbeg." He went on to say that, "I am sure I was right. I do not think I was right, I am sure I was right."

"You take up this position," he was asked, "that although the Admiralty had sent you a message about Coninbeg, you were right in disregarding it?"

"Yes. We never got there, though, we never got that far."[38]

It would appear that Captain Turner felt justified in disregarding his instructions or some of the advice given him by the Admiralty. Actually, the advice to avoid land, steer a mid-channel course and zigzag at top speed was sound advice.

After litigation lasting more than a year,[39] Judge Mayer dismissed the case against Cunard. In his decision he stated that "It is fortunate for many reasons, that such a comprehensive judicial investigation has been had; for in addition to a mass of facts which give opportunity for a clear understanding of the case in its various aspects, the evidence presented has disposed, without question and for all time, of any false claims brought forward to justify this inexpressibly cowardly attack upon an unarmed passenger liner."[40]

Mayer dealt with the issue of cargo. He concluded that the Lusitania "did not carry any explosives." He observed that she did carry "18 fuse cases and 125 shrapnel cases consisting merely of empty shells without any powder charge." The liner was also transporting 4,200 cases of "safety cartridges."[41] As for armament, the "proof is absolute that she was not and never had been armed ..."[42]

As for competence, Mayer found the crew "highly intelligent and capable." Boat "drills were both sufficient and efficient." He dismissed the passengers' claims that the boat drill was inadequate, merely because they were not present to see them.[43]

With respect to the warning published in the newspaper prior to sailing, Mayer found that:

> [T]he master was fully justified in sailing on the appointed day from a neutral port with many neutral and non-combatant passengers unless he and his company were willing to yield to the attempt of the German Government to terrify British shipping. No one familiar with the British character, would expect that such a threat would accomplish more than to emphasize the necessity of taking every precaution to protect life and property, which the exercise of judgment would invite.[44]

Yet it may be said that not every precaution was taken, and in fact Turner failed to follow all of his instructions.

Judge Mayer dismissed the accusation that Captain Turner was negligent. He quoted Lord Mersey's analysis of Turner's performance, and agreed with Mersey's judgment that Turner ought not "to be blamed." According to Mayer, if "a foe employs such tactics, it is idle and purely speculative to say that the action of the captain of a merchant ship, in doing or not doing something, or in taking one course and not another, was a contributing cause of disaster, or that had the captain not done what he did or had he done something else, then the ship and her passengers would have evaded their assassins."[45]

Mayer lambasted the German government. "The cause of the sinking of the *Lusitania*," he found, "was the illegal act of the Imperial German Government, acting through its instrument, the submarine commander and violating a cherished and humane rule observed, until this war, by even the bitterest antagonists."[46]

The finding gave no surprise, as it came when the United States was at war with Germany. But that was then—an objective tribunal today might very likely find for the plaintiffs.

These three formal hearings—the coroner's inquest, Lord Mersey's investigation, and the liability trial in New York—for the most part reached the same conclusions. The Cunard Line and Captain Turner were innocent of negligence, while the Germans were guilty of atrocity.

All three hearings, conducted in a wartime climate, did not succeed in ending the controversy surrounding the sinking of the *Lusitania*. On the contrary, the controversy continues to this day.

CHAPTER 12
CHARGES AND COUNTER-CHARGES

Though the investigations were complete, controversy surrounding the *Lusitania* continued to rage. Few sinkings during World War I have evoked as much passion as the *Lusitania*; charges and counter-charges over the incident multiplied and flourished. One charge—that the Germans had planned the attack on the liner—reasoned that Germany's published warning prior to the Cunarder's last voyage and its timing were not accidental. In one of the newspapers the warning went so far as to appear alongside the timetable for the *Lusitania*.

With the gift of hindsight we can see the Germans were not being manipulative; the placement of the warning near the *Lusitania*'s advertisement was very likely coincidental. Count von Bernstorff, the German ambassador to the United States at the time explained, "Our notice to the press had no particular reference to the *Lusitania*, but was simply a general warning."[1] It appears that the German embassy was unaware of any plot by Berlin to sink the liner. Ambassador Bernstorff later wrote, "Whether the action of our naval authorities was planned beforehand or not, we in America had no knowledge of any such plan."[2]

After the war, a search was conducted through the archives of the German Navy. The orders Schwieger received read, "Large English troop transports expected starting from Liverpool, Bristol (south of

Liverpool), Bartmouth. Get to stations on fastest possible route around Scotland. Hold as long as supplies permit. Submarines to attack transport ships, merchant ships and warships."[3] Nothing specific was mentioned about the *Lusitania*. Also, if the Cunarder were the intended target, Schwieger would not have alerted the British of his presence by the pre-*Lusitania* sinkings of the *Earl of Lathom*, the *Candidate*, and the *Centurion*—these actions should have given Turner notice that a submarine was in the vicinity. The Germans had no idea that the *Lusitania*'s captain would take such a casual attitude toward these obvious warnings.

Another charge made against the Germans was that the U-boat fired more than one torpedo at the liner, based on the many reports of passengers that there were two explosions. Lord Mersey and Judge Mayer hinted at the possibility of more than one torpedo, and even Winston Churchill, known for his accuracy as an historian, wrote in his *The World Crisis*, "Two torpedoes were fired, the first striking her [the *Lusitania*] amidship with a tremendous explosion, and the second a few minutes later striking her aft."[4]

Some witnesses claimed to have seen a second torpedo coming toward the ship on the portside. This could only indicate that another submarine was present, but we now know that only one U-boat was on the scene. Seaman Leslie Morton, the first to see the torpedo, testified that there were two streaks of bubbles—yet to an inexperienced sailor such as Morton it is possible to mistake the trail of one torpedo for two. German records, including Schwieger's logbook, show without a doubt that only one torpedo was fired.

The Germans received the brunt of the criticism over the sinking of the *Lusitania*. It is therefore not surprising, given the atmosphere of war, that German and pro-German groups would level counter-charges against the British and their accusations. Many of these charges were revived by a British journalist, Colin Simpson, in his book *The Lusitania*. His argument also appeared in an article he wrote for the October 13, 1972 issue of *Life*. Simpson echoed the original charges against the British—that the Cunarder was armed with guns and carrying Canadian troops and war contraband. He even goes so far as to claim that the British Admiralty, under the First Sea Lord, Winston Churchill, deliberately allowed the liner to be torpedoed to draw the U.S. into the war on the Allied side. Under close scrutiny, these charges prove groundless.

The crucial charge that the defenders of Germany, and later Simpson, made was that the *Lusitania* was armed with naval guns during her last voyage. If that were true, then the Germans would have had a legal right to sink her under international law. However, if the Cunarder were only defensively armed, she would be protected by international law. The State Department on September 20, 1914, set the rules for defensively armed status. The caliber of the guns must not exceed six inches, be few in number and not be placed in the forward part of the ship. The quantity of the ammunition must be small, and the vessel must be manned by the usual officers and crew.[5]

Simpson argues that the liner was armed beyond these guidelines, but his proof is weak. Simpson cites that there were plans for 12 six-inch guns to be installed on the *Lusitania* at the Admiralty's wishes.[6] There is no denying that the ship was designated an auxiliary cruiser and that blueprints for guns existed. But plans are just pieces of paper, and there are no other pieces of physical evidence beyond paper to support his argument.

Simpson relies on five affidavits which claim that the *Lusitania* was armed. Two of these affidavits were hearsay, and two others concern a January 1915 sailing. The affidavit he relies on heavily is that of Gustav Stahl, a German reservist. Stahl stated that he had visited the Cunarder the night before she sailed on her last voyage, and saw four mounted guns, two on the bow and two aft. It is worthwhile to note that Stahl later pled guilty to perjury and was sentenced to 18 months in jail.[7] At the sentencing, the judge remarked that "His crime is far more serious against the United States than it would seem."[8]

Another important piece of evidence Simpson uses to support his claim that the *Lusitania* was armed with guns were the findings of diver John Light. Light dived on the derelict in the 1960s and claimed to have seen the barrel of a gun, though what he probably saw was a simple pipe. At that depth, the unaided eye is not reliable.

Numerous British merchant ships did not have guns during that stage of the war because there were just not enough guns to provide for every ship. During the period January 1, 1916 to January 25, 1917, the year after the *Lusitania*'s final voyage, 612 ships were attacked or stopped by German U-boats. Of these vessels, 302, or roughly half, did not have guns, proving that even that late in the war guns were scarce.[9]

This being the case, priority had to be given to the most vulnerable ships. It was understood that the *Lusitania,* with her great speed, did not need guns, but more significantly, to arm the liner would have given the Germans an airtight excuse to sink her. Evidently the Admiralty did not realize that the U-boat commander would torpedo her whether she was armed or not.

There is abundant evidence that the *Lusitania* was gunless on her last voyage. The crew flatly denied having any such weapons, and Captain Turner, as we have seen, testified under oath that he had no naval cannons aboard. On May 1, 1962, John Lewis said in an interview, "I was third officer at the time and in a position to know. The *Lusitania* didn't have any guns at all to defend itself against a German attack—not even a machine gun on deck."[10] This assertion coming from the crew is to be expected, yet the passengers, even those from neutral countries, also witnessed no guns.

Then there are the findings of Dudley Malone and his "neutrality squad," who examined the liner before departure and found no traces of guns. When accusations were made that the ship was armed, Malone went on record as saying, "This report is not correct. The *Lusitania* was inspected before sailing, as is customary. No guns were found, mounted or unmounted, and the vessel sailed without any armament."[11]

There is also photographic evidence that the *Lusitania* was unarmed on her last voyage. Many still photos of the liner, taken by reporters and others, reveal no guns on board. The editor of the Philadelphia *Evening Ledger* reported that a motion picture photographer had taken 1,000 feet of film of the *Lusitania*'s departure. And again, there were no signs of guns.[12] Finally, a Signal Corps film of the Cunarder's leaving New York also shows that she was gunless.[13]

Perhaps the greatest evidence that the *Lusitania* had no naval armament was the information provided by Dr. Robert Ballard, whose team examined the wreck thoroughly. As one key team member stated, "I did not see any guns," and Ballard himself stated, "We did not find guns or any evidence of guns on her."[14] The inescapable conclusion, therefore, was that the *Lusitania* was not armed on her final voyage.

Another charge Simpson made was that the liner was transporting

Canadian troops on her last voyage. According to him, on April 30, 1915, the Admiralty had 70 passengers transferred from the *Queen Margaret* to the Cunarder.[15] In reality, the *Queen Margaret* had no accommodations for passengers, and sailed from New York on the 29th of April. Apparently Simpson confused this ship with the *Cameronia* of the Anchor Line. The *Cameronia* was taken over by the Admiralty and some 40 passengers were transferred to the *Lusitania*. Many of these people were women and children and had reported American locales, such as New York, as their residence.

Simpson builds his case on the witness of one Robert Matthews. According to him, Matthews belonged to the 6th Winnipeg Rifles, when records show he belonged to the 60th Rifles, 21st Infantry Brigade.[16] Matthews joined on January 15, 1913. He had unsuccessfully tried to secure a commission in the Canadian Expeditionary Force and was on the *Lusitania* to enlist in the British Army. The 60th did not depart until November 6 of that year on the *Scandinavian*.[17] With this being the only evidence Simpson has to offer, we cannot take the argument for Canadian troops seriously. There were some 360 Canadians on the liner during her last voyage, and a good number of them were women and children. Dudley Malone, the collector of the port, insisted that the Cunarder "did not have Canadian troops or troops of any nationality on board."[18] There is simply no reason to believe that the liner was used to ferry an organized body of troops.

What of the charge that the *Lusitania* was carrying contraband on her final voyage? The answer is an unequivocal yes—for one thing the liner was carrying foodstuffs. Sometime earlier in the war the British themselves declared that food would be treated as contraband, resulting in several German-bound ships being seized on the grounds that they were loaded with food. By the British government's own definition, then, the Cunarder was transporting contraband.

It is also true that the liner was transporting munitions of war. On her final voyage the *Lusitania* carried 42,000 cases of rifle ammunition and 100 cases of empty shrapnel shells in her cargo holds. However, this did not violate the federal laws of the United States.[19] Nor did it violate international law. Private citizens or private organizations of a neutral nation had the right to sell arms and ammunition to belligerents. The representative of Germany at the 1907 Hague Convention made this point when he said, "The neutral boats which engage in such trade, committed a violation of the duties of neutrality. However, according to a principle generally recognized, the State of which the boat flies the flag is not responsible for this violation. The neutral States are not called upon to forbid their subjects a commerce which, from the point of view of the belligerents, ought to be considered as unlawful."[20]

Nevertheless, the Germans deeply resented American firms supplying the Allies. "The German press," according to James Gerard, the American ambassador to Germany, "continually published articles to the effect that the war would be finished if it were not for the shipment of supplies from America."[21] Gerard also recalled an incident when the German colonial minister said to him, "You are the American Ambassador and I want to tell you that the conduct of America in furnishing arms and ammunition to the enemies of Germany is stamped deep on the German heart, that we will never forget it and will some day have our revenge."[22] Gerard tactfully replied that the Hague Convention allowed these shipments, also reminding him that Germany had supplied Britain's enemies during the Boer War.[23]

Although it was legal for the *Lusitania* to carry rifle ammunition, there are some people, such as Simpson, who claim the liner was carrying a great deal of explosives besides. Unfortunately, Dudley Malone and his "neutrality squad" were unable to examine every box and crate on ships leaving New York. As he later explained, this was "practically a physical impossibility."[24] Simpson's evidence that the ship carried such explosives is based on the second explosion that followed the torpedo. This, according to him, was caused by the detonation of munitions. However, Simpson overlooks the fact that the torpedo struck more than a hundred feet from the cargo space. There were two and possibly three bulkheads to absorb the shock, and the doors to these bulkheads were closed in accordance with Captain Turner's orders. Dr. Ballard in his 1993 examination of the wreck found the cargo hold undamaged.

One charge concerning the questionable cargo of the *Lusitania* was made by Dr. John Braun, a chemist, shortly after the news of the disaster. He claimed that the liner was carrying 250,000 pounds of tetrachloride, a chemical used in making gas bombs. He based his assumption on the fact that some of the survivors were suffocated by gas fumes.[25] Yet in all likelihood, what suffocated them was probably steam—there is just not enough evidence to support Braun's claim.

The most absurd theory to be advanced about the disaster claimed that the *Lusitania* was deliberately sunk in hopes of embroiling the U.S. in the war on the Allied side. It originated shortly after the event and was voiced anew by Simpson in the 1970s. Many Germans believed in that scenario. Ambassador Gerard was told by the Kaiser that the British government "made the *Lusitania* go slowly in English waters so that the Germans could torpedo it and so bring on trouble."[26] This view was also voiced by the German-American press, such as the *Friedensbote*, the *New Yorker Staats-Zeitung* and *The Fatherland*.

Some Americans also expressed this view. Among them was Congressman Richmond Pearson Hobson, who became a hero during the Spanish-American War by sinking the *Merrimac* in Santiago harbor in an attempt to bottle up the Spanish fleet. He went on record as saying, "A widowed cousin of mine applied at the New York office of the Cunard Line for passage on the *Lusitania*. The booking agent, an old friend, took her apart and told her that the vessel was acting under Admiralty orders and that she simply must not take passage on it. He pledged her to secrecy until after the trip."

Hobson brought up pertinent questions:

1. Why did not the Cunard Company give to all parties applying for passage the same humane advice its agent, for old friendship sake, gave to my cousin, instead of loading the vessel down with a full passenger list, including many distinguished Americans, whose loss would necessarily strike the American imagination?

2. Knowing that German submarines were operating south of the Irish coast, why did not the British Admiralty, which controlled the *Lusitania*'s movements, order her to use the uninfested route around the north of Ireland?

3. Why was the ship, having a speed of twenty-five-and-a-half knots—a very substantial aid to security—ordered by the British Admiralty to slow down to seventeen knots in the danger zone?

4. How could a torpedo sink such a ship in twenty minutes? An elementary knowledge of naval architecture would con-

vince anyone that such a thing is impossible unless there was a contributing cause inside the vessel, such as open water-tight doors or an inside explosion.

5. Why was there no protecting convoy in the danger zone?
6. Why was there no consort for the great ship's passengers' lives, ready for rescue work?
7. Why was there no preparation along the shore? Why was rescue work so slow in reaching the scene?
8. Why was it possible, in a smooth sea, within sight of land, in the middle of the day, to lose so many lives?
9. Why was censorship thrown open to all the harrowing details throughout the slow and inexplicable work of the recovery of the bodies, while secrecy was ordered for the Admiralty instructions, under which the ship proceeded to its doom?[27]

Hobson raised some interesting and pertinent questions, but some of his assumptions can be easily disputed. The *Lusitania* was going at 18 knots, not 17 knots, and the Admiralty did not order her to slow down. The Cunard Line had to leave some of the liner's boilers cold because of the shortage of hands, and Turner chose to slow down from 21 knots to 18 knots without orders from the Admiralty—on the contrary, the Royal Navy stressed the need for him to go at top speed. The Admiralty urged Turner to steer a mid-channel course and to zigzag, both of which the captain failed to do. The watertight doors were not left open, but were, in fact, closed by the captain's orders. The second explosion, he maintained, was due to coal dust.

Churchill, who was then First Lord of the Admiralty, has been at the center of many conspiracy theories. This larger-than-life individual was in later years accused by Nazi propagandists of planting a bomb on the *Athenia*, a British passenger liner torpedoed in World War II, for the sole purpose of heaping blame on the Germans. This view does not take into consideration that the *Athenia* was torpedoed on the first day of the conflict—meaning that the British simply would not have had enough time to carry out such a task. Some have accused him of having the airplane carrying Wladyslaw Sikorski, the Premier of the Polish government in exile, sabotaged. The accusation follows that Churchill wanted this Pole eliminated merely because he was at odds with him.

Some have also accused Churchill of concealing intelligence from President Roosevelt that revealed the Japanese planned to attack Pearl Harbor.

Churchill, the chief architect (or villain) of the alleged conspiracy to have the *Lusitania* sunk in order to compel the United States into war, did in fact write, three months before the Cunarder met her demise, "In hopes of especially embroiling the United States with Germany, for our part, we want traffic, the more the better, and if some of it gets into trouble, better still."[28]

One basis of the theory is the May 7, 1915, conversation between Colonel Edward House, an advisor to President Wilson, and the King of England just a few hours before the Cunarder met her doom. The King asked, "Colonel, what will America do if the Germans sink the *Lusitania*?"[29]

Another point raised was why there was no escort provided for the liner. It seems suspicious to some that the Admiralty would allow a ship with a large number of passengers to enter waters unprotected, where there was established submarine activity, unless there were a plan deliberately to sink her. What the proponents of this theory overlook is that the Admiralty had sent wireless warnings to Turner informing him of the presence of a U-boat in the area. One of the messages closed with the words, "Make sure *Lusitania* gets this." Had the Admiralty intended to have the ship sunk they would not have gone out of their way to warn her.

Nor would the British be foolish enough to divulge their plan by asking such a direct question to Colonel House. More than likely the King wished to know what America's position would be if a large liner were to be sunk. The British may have wanted to prepare their diplomatic strategy and propaganda machine for such an occasion; the mention of the *Lusitania* was merely a coincidence.

The absence of an escort was not due to a conspiracy but rather to the shortage of warships. Although the British had the largest navy in the world at this time, they were unable to provide protection to every civilian vessel. Warships were needed to enforce the blockade of Germany and for other operations. Many vessels would have to be on their own.

Ironically, the fact that the *Lusitania* was a passenger liner may have been partly the reason why she was not given an escort. The Admiralty may mistakenly have believed the Germans were morally incapable of attacking a ship carrying women and children. If nothing else, the force of world opinion might deter them from sinking a vessel such as the *Lusitania* without first giving the conventional warning. Thus, to provide warships for protection would not only be unnecessary, but would give the Germans justification under international law to sink her. The British evidently did not take into consideration the possibility of a rash judgment made by a U-boat commander who simply saw the liner as an auxiliary cruiser and possible troopship.

Another reason why the Admiralty may not have offered the Cunarder protection was the fact of her speed. As mentioned previously, the *Lusitania* was capable of nearly three times the speed of a submerged submarine. Her speed for ramming or fleeing was her best defense against U-boats, and it was for this reason the British Navy did not deem an escort necessary. Up until that time no ship faster than 15 knots had been sunk by a German submarine. Had Captain Turner followed his instructions and zigzagged, it is safe to assume that he would have reached Liverpool unharmed.

As evidence for his theory, Simpson presents a sentence in the book *Freedom of the Seas* by Joseph Kenworthy, a Royal Navy officer. Simpson claims that Kenworthy wrote, "The *Lusitania* was sent at considerably reduced speed into an area where a U-boat was known to be waiting and with her escorts withdrawn." According to Simpson, Kenworthy had originally written "was *deliberately* sent," but the Admiralty put pressure on the publisher to delete the word "deliberately."[30] Yet Kenworthy's book was examined and found to have no such revision made.

As late as 1987, Simpson insisted that the Admiralty had set up the *Lusitania*. He stated that the instructions to zigzag were issued after Turner sailed, and then after the disaster the orders were predated.[31] This runs counter to Turner's admission under oath that he received instructions to zigzag from the Royal Navy prior to sailing.[32]

The private reactions of high-ranking officers in the Royal Navy must also be considered. Captain Richard Webb, director of the Admiralty's trade division, wrote a report that expressed the opinion that German agents had infiltrated Cunard's New York office and discovered the *Lusitania*'s route to Liverpool. He concluded that Captain Turner was guilty of "almost inconceivable negligence."[33] Admiral John Fisher, the First Sea Lord, bitterly stated that Turner was either totally incompetent, or had been "got at by the Germans." "As the Cunard Company would not have employed an incompetent man, the certainty is absolute that Captain Turner is not a fool but a knave!" wrote Fisher. He hoped that the captain would be arrested "immediately after the inquiry whatever the verdict or finding may be. No seaman in his senses would have acted as he did." Fisher concluded that the *Lusitania*'s master was a "scoundrel."[34]

The biggest flaw with this theory is the fact that Britain in May of 1915 was not of the opinion that it needed the United States in the war—many Allied leaders at this time believed the war could be won even without American intervention. To carry out a scheme such as this would have risked driving the United States into the Central Powers camp if her leaders were to discover the plot. But in actuality, to bring the United States into the war at this time, by any means, would have hurt the Allies more than helped them. The American army was small and unprepared to fight a major war in Europe. To raise and equip a sizeable army would have drained many of the supplies the British were purchasing for their own army.

A better conspiracy case can be made for the torpedoing of the *Sussex,* a cross-channel passenger ferry, on March 24, 1916. By this time the war had turned gruesome and was mired in deadlock on the Western front. One of the passengers aboard the *Sussex,* Samuel Flagg Bemis, who would later become a famous historian, offered the theory that the ferry was "lumbering along, without escort, through a sea littered with wreckage of torpedoed [and mined] vessels." True, the *Sussex* was "lumbering along," but she was a ferryboat and inherently slow. There were no escorts because, as mentioned previously, there was not enough for every civilian vessel. The Allies may have felt none were needed, for up to this time the Germans were holding to their promise not to attack passenger ships.

If there were no deliberate plot on the part of the British to sink the *Lusitania*, there was undoubtedly a great deal of negligence. As the *Washington Post* reported, "But we do say that if Captain Turner had desired to give the German submarine notice of his identity and whereabouts, and had desired to facilitate in every way a successful torpedo attack, he could not have taken a more effective means to carry out his purpose."[35]

The Cunard Line did not escape blame. Though the company provided enough boats for the ship's company, they failed to install the necessary number of davits. Nor did the company adequately train the crew in the loading and lowering of lifeboats. The boat drill, as we have seen, was laughable.

Although there is no reason to believe there was a deliberate plot on the part of the Admiralty, some blame is justified. One shipmaster recalled a conversation with a representative from the Admiralty in which he asked what was meant by a zigzag course.

"To tell you the truth, I don't exactly know," the Admiralty representative replied.

When the shipmaster informed him that his ship's top speed was 17½ knots, the Royal Navy officer stated flatly, "You need not worry about submarines. You are immune going at that speed."[36]

Turner, it must be remembered, was doing 18 knots when he was torpedoed, and it was Turner who viewed the submarine peril with some indifference. Even Thomas Bailey and Paul Ryan in their book, *The Lusitania Disaster*, while absolving the British government of deliberately allowing the liner to be sunk, concluded, "With the benefit of hindsight we can see that the Admiralty should have spelled out with diagrams as it later did, and probably also with demonstrations, precisely how zigzag tactics worked with optimum effectiveness."[37]

But how far should we blame the Admiralty? In his book, *The Lusitania: Unravelling the Mysteries*, Patrick O'Sullivan claims that Turner requested permission from the Admiralty to go around the north of Ireland, but was refused. Later, according to O'Sullivan, the captain was instructed to divert to Queenstown. O'Sullivan cites Turner's pre-war record, his jumping into the cold water of the Mersey to save a boy, and his rescue work for the *West Point*. "These are hardly the actions of a captain who was later accused of negligence, disobedience and reckless handling of the *Lusitania* in a war zone," O'Sullivan concluded. He finds that Turner testified as he did in order to cover for the Admiralty.[38] Some of O'Sullivan's evidence is weak, relying on the recollections of a Miss Mabel Every, Turner's housekeeper and companion.

She stated that the captain told her he intended to go the northern route around Ireland. He also cites a quartermaster named Johnson, who stated that the liner was heading to Queenstown. But even O'Sullivan himself admits that these recollections are hearsay.

It is difficult to defend Turner. There is no way of avoiding the fact that he was guilty of "negligence, disobedience and reckless handling" of his command. As has been previously mentioned, he failed to zigzag, steer a mid-channel course and steam at top speed. His decision to conduct a four-point bearing was sound if he had been travelling in peacetime, but there was an ongoing war, and moreover, reports of submarine activity. Turner, who had a brilliant pre-war record, was simply unable to adjust to the new situation.

O'Sullivan would have us believe that Turner fell on his sword and took the rap for the Admiralty like a good British sailor. In reality, he was not above openly criticizing the Admiralty. Shortly after the disaster he publicly stated, "The Admiralty never troubled to send out to meet the *Lusitania*. They only look after the ships that are bringing the big guns over, like the *Orduna* and the *Transylvania*—last voyage on the eastbound trip I never saw a warship until we reached Liverpool."[39]

We then come to the morality of Schwieger's decision to fire the torpedo. Hundreds of civilians perished in this act, many of them women and children. On behalf of Schwieger, it could be said he was doing what was expected of a submarine commander on behalf of a country engaged in a total war with Britain. His actions were no less legal than the British long-range blockade.

There is little doubt in this writer's mind that if Germany had the larger navy and Britain faced the same geographical disadvantages as Germany, the Germans would have been the ones conducting a blockade. Since guns were now more powerful than in the past, the Germans would have carried out a long-range blockade, and the British most likely would have responded by using their submarines. In this connection it must be remembered that during World War II, Allied submarines, mostly American, sank without warning a large number of Japanese merchant ships. The argument used to justify this course of action was that the Japanese ships had the capacity for ramming surfaced submarines—an argument with which we are by now familiar.

Some have argued that the long-range blockade by the British meant German civilian deaths by slow starvation. Alternatively, giving the passengers of a large ship time to surrender before torpedoing would doubtless jeopardize the crew of the submarine. Others have argued that people have time to surrender before sailing on liners, and neutrals can take passage on the ships of non-combatants, such as the *New York*. The German actions were no less moral than the British, but at the same time, no more ethical.

The question remains to this day: was the sinking of the *Lusitania* an immoral atrocity or a legitimate act of war?

There is also the question of whether it was pragmatically justified. On the tactical level the Germans sank over 30,000 tons of enemy shipping, but on the strategic level they suffered egregious damage to their propaganda and international image, thereby allowing Allied propaganda to fill the vacuum. They directed America's fury away from the British blockade and redirected it toward Germany, which lost any support through world opinion it might have had. In the end, pragmatically speaking, the sinking was tactically sound but strategically foolish. The disadvantages outweighed the advantages tremendously.

This had been an ongoing problem with Germany's war effort. One historian, Correlli Barnett in his book, *The Swordbearers*, pointed out the vast gulf between Germany's advanced technological/industrial base, and its political primitiveness. Germany's decision to invade Belgium was an example of this gulf, revealing their failure to take into account possible British, as well as world, reaction. Later, as we shall see, the Germans would conduct unrestricted submarine warfare, not realizing the effect it would have on the United States' willingness to enter the war, thus ensuring Germany's doom.

Perhaps it would have been better for the Germans had they refrained from sinking passenger liners, and instead concentrated their efforts on cargo ships. As a point of fact, the German high command issued orders following the *Lusitania* disaster to no longer attack large passenger ships. Had such orders been issued earlier and been followed, the Germans would have saved themselves much international scorn.

Another development in the *Lusitania* case is the alleged mutiny aboard the *U-20*. In their book *Seven Days to Disaster*, Des Hickey and Gus Smith tell the story of a crewmember of the German submarine, a seaman name Ulbricht. Ulbricht, along with other members of the crew, was taking turns observing through the periscope the sinking of the *Lusitania*. At one point Ulbricht, whom Hickey and Smith describe as "temperamental," drew a revolver and pointed it at Captain Schwieger, but was overpowered by an officer.[40] This writer doubts the story, for the incident was not recorded in Schwieger's log.

Another story about the lost liner, one that is neither pro-Allies nor pro-German, is that the vessel was carrying bullion on her last voyage. It is not unusual for rumors to circulate that a sunken ship has gold aboard—similar stories surround the *Titanic* and other ships that foundered. The *Lusitania*'s manifest does not list bullion, and in fact the British were exporting gold at this time.

There will always be controversy surrounding the last voyage of the *Lusitania*. Many stories and theories about the tragic liner have been confirmed and others debunked—and still others remain open to interpretation. Unfortunately it is difficult to sift out the truth from fancy when it comes to this Cunarder.

CHAPTER 13
STRICT ACCOUNTABILITY

Senator William J. Stone of Missouri, chairman of the Senate Foreign Relations Committee, made a public statement on May 8, offering advice to President Wilson and the rest of the country. "Good sense," he said, "dictates that we keep our heads until we get our bearings. It is a bad time to get rattled and act impulsively. 'Don't rock the boat.'"[1]

Ambassador James Gerard, the American representative to Berlin, believed that war with Germany was imminent. "Of course, the news of the torpedoing of the *Lusitania* on May seventh and the great loss of American lives brought about a very critical situation."[2] He prepared to leave his post.

Colonel Edward House heard of the sinking of the *Lusitania* at four o'clock on the day she was torpedoed, while at the American Embassy in London. He and his wife were having dinner when the story broke. Though there were no immediate details concerning the extent of the tragedy, House responded quickly. He sent a message to President Wilson describing the urgency of the situation. "I cannot see any way out," the Colonel wrote, "unless Germany promises to cease her policy of making war upon non-combatants. If you do not call her to account over the loss of American lives caused by the sinking of the *Lusitania*, her next act will probably be the sinking of an American liner, giving as an excuse that she carried munitions of war and that we had been warned not to send ships into the danger zone."[3]

Secretary of State William Jennings Bryan wanted nothing less than a peaceful resolution. In an interview with the press, Bryan stated that the president still hoped for peace. "I pray, as earnestly as he," the Secretary of State told the interviewer, "that Germany may do nothing to aggravate further the situation."[4] Because a patriot's duty is to support his country "in time of war," Bryan said, "he has a right in time of peace to try to prevent war. I shall live up to a patriot's duty if war comes—until that time I shall do what I can to save my country from its horrors."[5]

However, Bryan was becoming aware that he and his superior were no longer in complete agreement. In a letter to Wilson after the sinking of the *Fabala* and the first American death of World War I, he warned that he had "not been able to reach the same conclusion" as the president. To send a stiff note to Germany over her violations of international law without a similar protest to London about their blockade of Germany would leave the United States government "embarrassed." Bryan pointed out that Germany was willing to negotiate on the issue of freedom of the seas, but Britain refused. Furthermore, by allowing shipments of munitions to the Allies and letting British merchant vessels hoist the American flag, Germany is given "not justification but an excuse for charging that we now favor the Allies."[6]

President Wilson's initial statements after the sinking of the *Lusitania* indicated that he, too, wanted to avoid war. During a May 10 speech in Philadelphia to newly naturalized citizens, the president went on record as saying,

> The example of America must be the example not merely of peace because it will not fight, but of peace because peace is the healing and elevating influence of the world, and strife is not. There is such a thing as a man being too proud to fight. There is such a thing as a nation being so right that it does not need to convince others by force that it is right.[7]

The phrase "too proud to fight" suggested that Wilson did not wish to go to war over the *Lusitania* incident, as probably the great majority of his fellow Americans did not, but editorials immediately raised an outcry against a position "inclined to meet insult and outrage with nothing more terrible than superior airs and fine phrases."[8] The speech undercut his diplomatic leverage, leaving the Germans to conclude that the administration had ruled out the use of force.

Wilson, however, would push to "convince others" of what was right in a patient, unyielding campaign of diplomatic letters. His first "*Lusitania* note" dated May 13 began this work to defend American rights, persuade Germany to disavow submarine warfare, and secure reparation for American parties injured by German actions against merchant vessels. Wilson opened negotiations thus:

> In view of recent acts of the German authorities in violation of American rights on the high seas which culminated in the torpedoing and sinking of the British steamer *Lusitania* on May 7, 1915, by which over 100 American citizens lost their lives, it is clearly wise and desirable that the Government of the United States and the Imperial German Government should come to a clear and full understanding as to the grave situation which has resulted.[9]

He then joined previous German attacks with the loss of the *Lusitania*, reminding the Germans that the American Leon Thrasher lost his life when a German submarine attacked the *Falaba,* that the American vessel *Cushing* had been attacked by a German airplane, and that "American citizens met their death" in the German assault on the *Gulflight*. These incidents, he summarized, "constitute a series of events which the Government of the United States has observed with growing concern, distress and amazement."[10]

Wilson also provided room for the German government to change direction. He praised the "humane and enlightened attitude hitherto" of the Germans and described their laudable respect for freedom of the seas. Because recent acts of the Imperial German Navy were contrary to international law and to the "spirit of modern warfare," the United States assumed the German government did not sanction them. Wilson invited the German government to "correct the unfortunate impressions which have been created."[11]

At the core of his message, Wilson acknowledged that the blockade of Germany by Britain and her Allies had "obliged" Germany to adopt measures contrary to international law, such as declaring certain areas to be a war zone which neutral ships should avoid. But, he reminded Germany, the United States had already informed the Imperial German government that it would not submit to "an abbreviation of the rights of American shipmasters or of American citizens bound on lawful errands as passengers on merchant ships" of any nationality.[12] The United States would hold Germany to "strict accountability for any infringement of those rights."[13] Further, Washington assumes that Germany will continue to respect the lives of non-combatants by taking the legal and "usual precaution of visit and search" to determine whether a merchant vessel is of "belligerent nationality" or carries "the contraband of war under a neutral flag."[14]

The use of submarines to disrupt enemy commerce, Wilson pointed out, disregards "those rules of fairness, reason, justice, and humanity, which all modern opinion regards as imperative." Because it is "practically impossible" for a submarine to visit and inspect a merchant ship or take it as a prize, they must sink the merchant, leaving the crew and passengers—if they received adequate warning—adrift. "Manifestly," Wilson concluded, "submarines can not be used against merchantmen, as the last few weeks have shown, without an inevitable violation of many sacred principles of justice and humanity."[15] The German embassy's published "warning that an unlawful and inhumane act will be committed" cannot excuse the act or diminish the responsibility for its execution.[16]

Wilson then suggested that since Germany was known to follow international law, the fault might lie with the individual U-boat commanders acting on a "misapprehension" of their orders. Since the commanders should have realized the critical importance of following humane and lawful practices, the German government should willingly disavow their actions, make reparation to the injured parties, and "prevent the recurrence of anything so obviously subversive of the principles of warfare."[17]

In closing, Wilson declared that the United States government would stand by the rights of its citizens. "The Imperial Government will not expect the Government of the United States to omit any word or any act necessary to the performance of its sacred duty of maintaining the rights of the United States and its citizens and of safeguarding their free exercise and enjoyment."[18]

On May 17, a conversation between the Austro-Hungarian ambassador, Dr. Constantin Dumba, and Secretary of State Bryan resulted in a misunderstanding that compromised Wilson's message. After a friendly exchange in which both men assured one another that their countries "had no desire for war,"[19] Dumba asked Bryan why Washington had not been equally harsh in response to the illegal British blockade. Bryan "answered at once, 'Because the American people cannot regard the holding up of merchandise by Great Britain in the same light that they regard the taking of life by the sinking of the *Lusitania*'."[20] (It must be remembered that many German women and children were slowly dying of malnutrition by the "holding up of merchandise.") A few days later the American ambassador in Berlin informed Washington that "Dumba sent a telegram saying in substance that the *Lusitania* note was 'not meant in earnest and was only sent as a sop to public opinion.'"[21]

Privately, Bryan did have misgivings about the note Wilson dispatched to Berlin. He felt that everything the United States had done strictly fulfilled the international laws of neutrality, but that an equally firm protest was needed against British violations of international law in their blockade of Germany. Bryan would later characterize the administration's "lack of neutrality" not as one of "commission" but rather "omission."[22]

The official German reply to Wilson's first note was over two weeks in coming. It arrived on May 29, declaring the German government's intention to "contribute" to an effort to "clear up any misunderstandings which may have entered into the relations of the two Governments." The attacks on the *Cushing* and *Gulflight* were "traceable to the misuse of flags by the British Government" or "carelessness or suspicious actions on the part of the captains of the vessels."[23] Should German submarines or aircraft harm any neutral vessel, and an investigation by the German government show it was through no fault of their own, Germany will offer indemnification. In the matter of the *Falaba*, the U-boat captain intended to allow the passengers and crew of this steamer to take to the boats, but the master of the British vessel tried to flee and fired distress rockets. Only then, the German note continued, did the U-boat captain tell passengers and crew that they had ten minutes to abandon ship. He fired a torpedo after 23 minutes when suspicious vessels were approaching the scene.

The official reply then addressed the sinking of the *Lusitania*. The Imperial government regretted the loss of lives, especially of those from neutral countries. However, some facts relevant to the sinking may have "escaped the attention of the American Government." The note attempted to correct the American assumption that the *Lusitania* was an unarmed merchant vessel, and explained that she was on the official navy list of the British government as an auxiliary cruiser, and, like many British merchant ships, was armed. "According to reports at hand here, the *Lusitania,* when she left New York undoubtedly had guns on board ..."[24]

The German government reminded Washington that the British Admiralty had issued instructions for merchantmen to display flags of neutral nations to mislead German U-boats and "even when so disguised to attack German submarines by ramming them." "High rewards have been offered by the British Government as a special incentive" to destroy German submarines with the result that Germany could no longer consider British merchant vessels as unarmed or "observe the rules of capture otherwise usual."[25]

The official reply pointed out that the *Lusitania* had carried contraband on her last voyage. She carried ammunition "intended for the destruction of the brave German soldiers." The reply also asserted that the liner had on board Canadian troops being ferried across the Atlantic. For these reasons the Imperial government "believes it acts in just self-defense" in protecting the lives of its soldiers by "destroying ammunition destined for the enemy with the means of war at hand."[26]

The United States must understand, the note continued, that Cunard had "quite deliberately tried to use the lives of Americans as protection for the ammunition carried." The company "wantonly caused" the deaths of these people by ignoring American laws and taking passengers on board a vessel carrying explosives. Had there been no ammunition to explode when the *Lusitania* was torpedoed, there would have been time to save the passengers.[27]

The Imperial government closed by asking the United States to examine the facts presented. It "would reserve a final statement of its position" in relation to the American demands set out on May 13 until Washington sent a reply. Berlin appreciated American efforts to help Germany and Great Britain negotiate the terms of their maritime conflict. The German government had provided "ample evidence of its good will by its willingness to consider these proposals," but the government of Great Britain proved to be unwilling negotiators.[28]

The German lack of contrition posed a problem for the administration in Washington. As one cabinet member concluded, "The German reply was unsatisfactory. It was insincere and cynical."[29] The American press was nearly unanimous in its agreement. British newspapers were less circumspect. The *Daily Mail*, for instance, said that "A more sneering or contemptuous reply or a flatter refusal to take the American government seriously could hardly be imagined." Other newspapers published comments that left readers waiting to hear whether Wilson would join the war or "submit" to Germany's outrages.[30]

Wilson would soon be faced with another knotty problem. Secretary of State Bryan decided he could no longer remain in an administration with which he so deeply differed, and on June 8, 1915, he resigned. Bryan explained that he could not support Wilson's note to Germany, for it went against his obligations to his country. He feared a strong stand against Germany would pull the United States into war, and instead favored resolutions that imposed restrictions on Americans traveling on belligerent ships."[31] After concerted efforts to dissuade Bryan, Wilson bowed to Bryan's insistence on resigning "with much more than deep regret, with a feeling of personal sorrow." The president's warm letter to Bryan emphasized: "Even now we are not separated in the object we seek but only in the method by which we seek it."[32]

Bryan's resignation was a serious blow to Wilson and his administration. William Jennings Bryan had a significant following among the American people, having been a three-time presidential candidate for the Democratic Party. His resignation "would not only send a signal of disunity to Germany," it could divide the Democratic Party.[33] Bryan declared he would continue to work for peace as a private citizen. He informed Wilson that he would "promote the end," which the administration does "not feel at liberty to use."[34] His resignation during a time of diplomatic conflict brought with it a storm of abuse, even from his own party.

Wilson chose the State Department's counselor, Robert Lansing, to replace Bryan as secretary of state. His attitudes were consistent with Wilson's, though Lansing did not have Bryan's popular following. However, Wilson believed Lansing would not "sufficiently or vigorously combat his [Wilson's] views"[35] where Bryan had been "virtually an equal partner in "framing and executing foreign policy." Following his resignation, Wilson largely made foreign policy decisions on his own and used Lansing to facilitate those decisions.[36]

The day after Bryan's resignation Wilson sent his second *Lusitania* note, this time meeting German accusations head on but moving his protest to higher moral ground. The *Lusitania* was not armed, as the Germans alleged, nor was she carrying Canadian troops; if she were, the United States government would not have granted her clearance as a merchantman. The American government had performed its "duty and enforced its statutes" vigorously. The note asked the German government to produce any evidence to the contrary.[37] Wilson acknowledged that the *Lusitania* carried contraband, allowable by nongovernmental entities under law, and reminded Germany that in any circumstance the lives of non-combatants "cannot lawfully or rightfully be put in jeopardy by the capture or destruction of an unresisting merchantman." The United States government, Wilson responded, "is contending for nothing less high and sacred than the rights of humanity," and expects the Imperial German government to put humanitarian principles into practice to preserve American lives.[38]

The German response came on July 8, 1915. The Imperial government agreed with Wilson on the issue of freedom of the seas, and the British had violated this principle by their long-range blockade of Germany and the mining of the North Sea. The German government insisted that the rights of humanity should also encompass the starving civilian population of Germany. The British blockade of neutral ports in contravention of international law had required Germany to act in self-defense for her very existence. The sinking of the *Lusitania* showed with "horrible clearness" how human lives are jeopardized using the methods of war employed by Germany's adversaries.[39] The reply also set forth a plan which would eliminate the need for Americans to travel on merchantmen belonging to a belligerent nation.

Undaunted, Wilson sent his third "*Lusitania* note" on July 21, adhering to his demand for the rights of neutral citizens. The United States rejected Germany's arguments, saying that 'The lives of noncombatants may in no case be put in jeopardy unless the vessel resists or seeks to escape after being summoned to submit to an examination.'"[40] The need for retaliation could not justify acts that injured the lives or property of neutrals; "humanity" should dictate that such retaliation should be discontinued. The American government expected a disavowal from the Imperial government of the "wanton act of its naval commander in sinking the *Lusitania*." "Friendship itself" prompted Wilson to say that if such an incident were to happen again involving American citizens, Washington would regard the act "as being deliberately unfriendly."[41]

Less than a month later, another crisis would occur that Wilson would indeed regard as "deliberately unfriendly."

CHAPTER 14

TOWARD WAR

Despite protests from the United States, the German government pressed ahead with its submarine warfare. Three months after the sinking of the *Lusitania* came the *Arabic* crisis. An important ship of the White Star Line, the *Arabic* was a 15,801 gross ton vessel, 600 feet/seven inches in length and 65 feet/five inches across the beam. Her twin screws were driven by quadruple expansion engines, producing 10,000 horsepower. The liner spent most of her first seven years chartered for cruises to Egypt and Palestine, carrying between 600 and 700 passengers.[1] A few years before the war, White Star eliminated her first-class accommodations and she was turned into a two-class passenger ship.

On August 18, 1915, she left Liverpool bound for the United States. There were 423 people aboard, 261 of them passengers. Most of the passengers came from Allied countries such as Britain, France, Russia, Italy and Belgium. Some, however, came from neutral nations. The passenger list for this voyage included 25 Americans.[2]

Among those aboard was Stella Carol, a promising young English soprano en route to her performance debut in New York. The passengers included playwright Zellah Covington and his wife, who were returning from opening the play "Some Baby" in London.[3] Actor Kenneth S. Douglas and a vaudeville acrobatic team known as the Flying Martins also took passage on the *Arabic*. The ship carried 2,813 bags of mail, and since she was outbound from Britain, she carried no contraband of war.

Captain William Finch, who had previously served on the Pacific mail service, had commanded the *Arabic* for more than six years, and though he was offered promotions he turned them all down—he loved the *Arabic* and refused to part from her.

Unlike the *Lusitania*'s Captain Turner, Finch took the U-boat menace seriously. When the war broke out, he placed sandbags around the wheelhouse to protect the steering gear from shellfire, and formed a rifle club for the crew to practice shooting at a stick towed behind a lifeboat.[4] He kept the lifeboats loaded with provisions and swung out, ready for lowering. Lifebelts were placed on deck, and the passengers were instructed how to fasten them. A lifeboat drill—not a token drill like the *Lusitania*'s, but a complete lifeboat drill—took place on the first night at sea. Finch followed the instructions he received from the Admiralty to the letter, avoiding headlands and zigzagging at his top speed of sixteen knots. He routinely chose the nighttime hours to pass the coast of Ireland, with all lights out. The captain had reasons to worry: rumors had circulated that the Germans intended to sink the *Arabic* as well as a sister ship, the *Arcadia*.

The *Arabic* would be a tempting target for the Germans, as on her previous voyage she had carried several tons of war goods. On that voyage her cargo included airplane parts, 4,000 cases of cartridges and several cases of fuses.[5] During that same voyage, detectives had discovered two sticks of dynamite under a settee in the women's retiring room amidships. The slightest concussion could have set them off. The authorities never found the person responsible, but German saboteurs could not be ruled out.[6]

The dynamite, along with rumors that the Germans had targeted the *Arabic*, led Finch to take strict precautions to ensure the safety of his command and the people aboard. While in the war zone, the engine room was staffed with off-duty personnel and two lookouts were posted in the stern and two in the bow in addition to the two already in the crow's nest. They were "scanning every inch of sea within reach" of their binoculars.[7]

Nothing had happened since leaving Liverpool the day before. On this day, August 19, 1915, Finch seemed to have everything under control. The precautions he had taken boosted the confidence of his passengers. One of them, J. Edward Usher, believed there was only one chance in a hundred of being "submarined."[8]

Finch then noticed the British steamer *Dunsley*, and became aware that something was amiss. Two of her boats had set sail for the land. Finch immediately set course for the stricken vessel, still zigzagging at 16 knots, her top speed.

The *Dunsley* was under attack by the *U-24*, commanded by Kapitänleutnant Rudolf Schneider. The German submarine had surfaced and begun firing on the *Dunsley* with her deck gun, but when Schneider saw a steamship approaching he quickly submerged.[9]

Suddenly Finch saw an object 300 feet away, under the water and speeding for the *Arabic* at a right angle from the north. There was no doubt in the captain's mind what it was—a torpedo. Finch at once ordered the engines stopped and the ship put astern, but it was, in his words, "absolutely impossible" to avoid it.[10] The torpedo struck the starboard side of the *Arabic* about 100 feet from the stern.

In the next instant the captain heard a "terrible explosion." It was "so loud I never heard anything like it." Apparently one or more of the ship's boilers had exploded. Water and debris were blown into the air; the explosion reduced one starboard lifeboat to splinters. Immediately, the *Arabic* developed a pronounced list to starboard.[11]

The liner's bugler also saw it coming. "By the time the torpedo reached us," he later explained, "we had moved a couple of hundred feet, but so well was the speed calculated by the submarine's commander that the torpedo struck us about 100 feet from the stern and near the engine room." Hearing a "tremendous explosion," he sounded his bugle as loud as possible.

One passenger later recalled talking with friends as they observed the *Dunsley*, and a few seconds later he heard a "roar such as I never heard and hope to never hear again."[12]

Alfred Still, a professor of electrical design, also saw the torpedo. At first he thought it would miss the ship, but a few moments later he "knew we were done for." Still heard a "dull explosion" and saw water shooting up in the air.[13] From the Promenade Deck, Mr. Usher heard a woman shout, "There's a submarine!" Usher was about to get out of his chair when he felt a "terrible jar" and heard an "awful roar."[14]

Joseph G. DeLorimer and a friend observed a white line in the water. DeLorimer's friend shouted, "We are gone!" Quickly DeLorimer rushed to his cabin to fetch a life jacket. Playwright Zellah Covington and his wife put on their lifejackets; they had seen the *Dunsley* and knew immediately that their lives were in danger. While still in the cabin they heard the explosion.

The falling debris wrecked the ship's wireless, but the wireless operator still managed to get off two SOS messages before the equipment failed.[15]

Captain Finch reacted immediately. He ordered the engines full speed astern to stop the vessel's forward progress. He then ordered the crew to abandon ship. The ten lifeboats and numerous life rafts had a total capacity of 2,092—more than adequate for the number of people on board.[16] However, the ship's condition created difficulties. One lifeboat had been destroyed, and the ship was sinking at such an alarming rate that the list, first to starboard and then to port, hindered the lowering of the boats.[17]

The crew did the best they could. Two lifeboats capsized while being lowered, but the crew launched six boats without incident. There was little panic. According to the captain, both passengers and crew behaved "splendidly."[18]

James Calmon seized his wife "the minute I felt the impact." He took her to one of the lifeboats and together they boarded.[19] Another passenger, Louis Bruguiere, immediately became concerned for the safety of his mother. He rushed to her cabin, where he found her breakfasting in bed. He quickly fastened life jackets around her and her maid, and took them topside. When he arrived, Bruguiere discovered that all the lifeboats had been lowered, but also saw his two beloved bulldogs still on deck. Bruguiere tossed them into a lifeboat below, then grabbed his mother and dove overboard.

From a lifeboat, Mr. Usher saw the liner dip by the stern and caught a glimpse of Finch on the bridge. "His face was calm and pale," Usher noticed, "as if he was facing death with the grim resolve not to desert his post."[20] The White Star liner began to sink deeper in the water and as it did, the remaining lifeboats tore from their fastenings and floated away. She rose up at the bow and went down by the stern, and then plunged with a "sizzling roar."[21] Only nine minutes after the torpedo struck, the *Arabic* disappeared beneath the surface of the water.

Louis Bruguiere had been swimming on his back supporting his mother for about 20 minutes, when suddenly he bumped his head on a piece of wreckage and went under. In that moment, he lost hold of his mother. He quickly resurfaced, only to discover that his mother was lost.[22]

"I thought I was all in," Finch later said, "but after a time I found myself in the water floating among rafts and patent boats, which were banging the life out of me, until a patent boat to which I could cling came along and I was able to hold on to it. I was too tired and weak to haul myself on board. Then two firemen came along, and I succeeded in shoving them into it. ... After that a woman and her baby were met and taken on board, and I got a piece of raft under me, and a swell then washed me on board the boat."[23]

Lifeboats picked up survivors from the water, and drifted in the heavy swell over the ship's grave. After more than an hour, the first sign of hope came when the patrol boats *Primrose* and *Mongolian* arrived. They picked up 379 survivors, including Captain Finch. Two of the 44 people lost in the attack were American.

Finch and his crew had performed admirably. Finch had steamed at top speed, avoided headlands and travelled in a zigzag pattern. The engineers and firemen "remained below and never came above, but kept at their duties and did their work like heroes."[24] They were all lost. The task of abandoning the ship had been well organized and rehearsed in advance, and its execution was coolheaded and efficient. About 90 percent of those aboard the White Star liner survived, compared with 38 percent from the *Lusitania*. On the surface this seems especially impressive since the crew of the *Arabic* had only nine minutes to evacuate the ship while the Cunarder had twice as much time, but the Arabic carried only 423 people to the *Lusitania's* 1,959.

The incident is important for other reasons. At the beginning of the war, it was believed that ships faster than 15 knots could not successfully be attacked by submarines. The *Arabic* was travelling at 16 knots when the torpedo struck. This episode showed that zigzagging at top speed did not guarantee a ship's safety from torpedoes, and debunked the notion that a ship's speed makes it invulnerable to submarine attack.

The fact that the liner sank so quickly also may be relevant to the *Lusitania*. Bound for America, the *Arabic* carried no munitions, so the rapid sinking can only be attributed to a boiler or coal dust explosion. Linked to the unexploded munitions recently found in the wreck of the *Lusitania*, the *Arabic's* quick descent makes it easier to attribute the 18-minute sinking of the Cunarder to the same cause or causes.

There was another outcry in the United States. The *New York Times* summed up American opinion thus: "Americans look to the President to uphold the nation's dignity and self-respect and to keep its binding engagements for the protection of the rights of Americans by whatever measures the undertaking may demand. 'Peacefully, if we may, forcibly, if we must' is a principle of action not unworthy of the most pacific of nations, and one which where its rights are involved, no nation can disregard without menace to its future peace and security."[25]

Theodore Roosevelt thought that, "The time for words on the part of this nation has long passed, and it is inconceivable to American citizens, who claim to be inheritors of the tradition of Washington and Lincoln, that our government representatives shall not see that the time for deeds has come." The *Plain Dealer* of Cleveland expressed the view that "The destruction of a passenger liner, outward bound, is mere wantonness. There is no palliation possible."[26]

Secretary of State Lansing summed up the anxiety of many Americans. With the sinking of the *Arabic* happening as it did "when the whole country was growing impatient at the apparent intentional delay of the German Government in answering our note of July Twenty-First, this new outrage created another critical situation."[27] Ambassador Page concluded, "Berlin has the Napoleonic disease."[28]

The German government explained that the commander of the *U-24*, Kapitänleutnant Schneider, believed that the *Arabic* was attempting to ram him. He mistakenly fired the torpedo in self-defense.[29] The Berlin press was virtually silent on the matter.[30]

Wilson's ultimatum following the sinking of the *Lusitania* left little room to negotiate. He desired to remain neutral, but realized that he could not be seen to be weak. After a period of solitude in which to consider the situation, "Wilson hit upon the expedient of a deliberate news leak. On August 23, newspapers published reports that 'speculation in Government circles' predicted that the president might break relations with Germany. The 'highest authority' stated that he would take such action if the facts of the case showed that the Germans had 'disregarded his solemn warning in the last note on the *Lusitania* tragedy. He also had Lansing tell Bernstorff how gravely the president regarded the situation."[31]

This strategy achieved results. On September 1, 1915, the German Ambassador to the United States, Count Johann von Bernstorff, wrote to Secretary of State Lansing,

> With reference to our conversation of this morning, I beg to inform you that my instructions concerning our answer to your last *Lusitania* note contain the following passage:
> 'Liners will not be sunk by our submarines without warning and without safety of the lives of noncombatants, provided the liners do not try to escape or offer resistance.'[32]

This was the "*Arabic* pledge." The country hailed the pledge, and the formal disavowal of the sinking of the *Arabic* that followed, as a diplomatic victory for Wilson. But would the Germans keep their promise?

In Europe the war dragged on. The Germans struck at Verdun in February 1916, and both the French and Germans poured hundreds of thousands of troops into the battle. Casualties mounted, roughly averaging between 25,000 and 65,000 casualties per month for each side. In the end, the French held the line and their commander, General Philippe Petain, became a national hero. With the setback at Verdun, the Germans decided to shift their emphasis to the Eastern front. There they faced the impoverished Russian Empire. Underequipped and poorly led, Russian soldiers fought bravely but ineffectively, as their home front suffered hunger and strife. It was only a matter of time before the Russians would be overwhelmed and knocked out of the war.

In March, 1916, another incident resulted in friction between the United States and Germany. On March 24, a German submarine torpedoed the French ferry *Sussex*. The severely damaged *Sussex* did not sink, but the attack killed or injured 80 people, and four Americans were among the injured. The attack violated the months-old *Arabic* pledge and angered Wilson. He told Congress that "We owe it to a due regard of our own rights as a nation, to our sense of duty as a representative of rights of neutrals to take this stand [against submarine warfare] now with the utmost solemnity and firmness."[33] The note that Wilson wrote and Lansing conveyed on April 18 to the German secretary of foreign affairs concluded,

> Unless the Imperial Government should now immediately declare and effect an abandonment of its present methods of submarine warfare against passenger and freight-carrying vessels, the Government of the United States can have no choice but to sever diplomatic relations with the German Empire altogether.

The German government responded two weeks later with a promise to limit submarine activity to established rules of warfare, with a condition that the United States would help persuade the British to moderate the blockade. A separate note apologized for the attack on the *Sussex,* and explained that the submarine commander had mistaken her for a minelayer. With this *"Sussex* pledge," the situation cooled down considerably.

Then came the greatest naval battle of World War I, the Battle of Jutland. On May 31, 1916, two opposing armadas, the British Grand Fleet and the German High Seas Fleet, set sail. Until then, the German surface fleet had stayed in port, fearful of the Royal Navy's superior numbers. Now under the command of Vice Admiral Reinhard Scheer, the German High Seas Fleet would attempt a bold effort to destroy a large portion of the British fleet. If they succeeded, the British blockade would be broken and a path forced open for German victory.

Admiral Scheer intended to lure out the British battlecruiser squadrons and trap them among a submarine picket line and the main German fleet. The British intercepted messages leading them to expect a major fleet action, and Admiral Sir John Jellicoe sailed with the Grand Fleet to rendezvous with the battlecruiser squadrons. The early timing of the British fleet eliminated any submarine action, and the German Navy faced a much larger force than planned. In all, some 250 ships took part in the action.

The battle began on the afternoon of May 31, 1916 and raged

through the night. In the end, the German Navy fled back to its base, despite heavier British losses. The British lost 111,980 tons of warships and suffered 6,945 dead; German losses totaled 62,233 tons in material and 2,921 dead. Although a material victory for the Imperial German Navy, their fleet was diminished in size and some remaining ships badly damaged. However, the Royal Navy—in spite of heavy losses—maintained its superiority. The Germans never again would challenge the Royal Navy using surface ships; instead they would use submarines.

After the Battle of Jutland, Scheer told his superiors in Berlin that the only way to bring Britain to her knees was through unrestricted submarine warfare. Though that method could risk bringing the United States into the war, many in German naval circles believed they could force Great Britain out of the way before America could raise and equip an adequate army. An intense anger suffused Germany over the British blockade. Hunger and malnutrition had become widespread. Why not give the British a taste of their own medicine? Late in January 1917, the German government announced it would conduct unrestricted submarine warfare. Any ship, enemy or neutral, heading to Britain would be sunk without warning. The die had been cast.

Wilson was furious with this latest announcement. Earlier that month he had addressed Congress and called for a "peace without victory," asking the belligerents to state their terms for peace. It was now clear the Germans would not hesitate to sink American ships deliberately. Wilson reacted by severing ties with Germany. The American Ambassador was recalled from Berlin and the German Ambassador to the United States was sent home. Determined to protect American shipping, Wilson decided to arm merchant ships. He went before Congress and asked for its support so that American ships could at least protect themselves "against the unwarranted infringements they are suffering at the hands of Germany."[34]

Then came another blow: the Zimmerman telegram. The German Foreign Minister, Arthur Zimmerman, secretly cabled his government's representative in Mexico; however, the message was intercepted and decoded by British intelligence. It read:

On the first of February we intend to begin submarine warfare unrestricted. In spite of this it is our intention to keep neutral the United States of America.

If this attempt is not successful we propose an alliance on the following basis with Mexico. That we shall make war together and together make peace. We shall give general financial support and it is understood that Mexico is to reconquer the lost territory of New Mexico, Texas, and Arkansas. The details are left for your settlement.

You are instructed to inform the President of Mexico of the above in the greatest confidence, as soon as it is certain there will be an outbreak of war with the United States, and we suggest that the president of Mexico on his own initiative should communicate with Japan suggesting adherence at once to this plan, at the same time offer to mediate between Germany and Japan.

Please call to the attention of the President of Mexico that the employment of ruthless submarine warfare now promises to compel England to make peace in a few months.[35]

Americans were outraged. The Chicago *Daily Tribune* declared, "Germany recognizes us as an enemy."[36] The Cleveland *Plain Dealer* said there was "neither virtue nor dignity" in refusing to fight Germany.[37] Even German-American papers hastened to express their loyalty to America.

German submarines began sinking ships heading to Britain. On March 18, 1917, German U-boats attacked three American ships. Soon Wilson was forced to an agonizing conclusion: America must enter the war.

On April 2, 1917, President Wilson appeared before a joint session of Congress to seek a declaration of war. Germany's "new policy has swept our restrictions aside," Wilson pointed out. Unrestricted submarine warfare "is a war against all nations. American ships have been sunk." With the Zimmerman telegram, it is clear that Germany "means to stir up enemies against us at our very doors." In "unhesitating obedience to what I deem my constitutional duty," Wilson advised "that Congress declare the recent course of the Imperial German Government to be in fact nothing less than war against the Government and people of the United States; that it formally accept the status of belligerent which has thus been thrust upon it, and that it take immediate steps not only to put the country in a more thorough state of defense but also to exert all its power and employ all its resources to bring the Government of the German Empire to terms and end the war."[38]

Four days later, Congress voted to declare war on Germany.

It would take a year before the United States could field an army large enough to enter the war in any significant way. In the meantime, the British developed the convoy system in which ships would travel in groups protected by naval vessels. Allied shipping losses were reduced to an acceptable level, and Germany's effort to cut off Allied supplies failed. In the spring of 1918, the Germans made one final effort to drive the Allies out of the war. Codenamed Michael, the offensive began on the first day of spring. At first the venture went well for Germany, but the Allies held the line. It was Germany's last gesture.

With the arrival of two million American troops, the situation began to improve for the Allies. A counter-offensive was launched in the summer of 1918, and one-by-one Germany's allies dropped out of the war—Bulgaria, the Ottoman Empire and the Austrian-Hungarian Empire. On November 11, 1918, the Germans agreed to an armistice.

The sinking of the *Lusitania* played a part in the United States' entry into World War I. This departure from the rules of war that resulted in the slaughter of hundreds of noncombatants, including neutral American men, women and children, made the consequences of the "European" war real to many Americans. Wilson negotiated tenaciously for American rights, and began to define America's humanitarian responsibilities and the limits of her tolerance in the *Lusitania* notes. He took a stronger and more confident stand against unlimited submarine warfare following the *Arabic* and *Sussex* incidents.

Submarine warfare proved to be Germany's downfall. As Winston Churchill noted, "Nothing could have deprived Germany of victory in the first year of war except the invasion of Belgium; nothing could have denied it to her in its last year except for the unlimited submarine campaign. Not to the number of enemies, nor to their resources or wisdom; not to the mistakes of her Admirals and Generals in open battle; not to the weakness of her allies; not assuredly to any fault in the valour or loyalty of her population or her armies; but only to these two grand crimes and blunders of history, were her undoing and our salvation due."[39]

The final irony was the date of the peace settlement. The Allies handed the defeated Germans harsh terms, which included reparations, severe limitation on their military resources and loss of territory. The day these terms were given to Germany was May 7, 1919, the fourth anniversary of the sinking of the *Lusitania*. The German delegation may have wondered how things might have been different had Schwieger never sunk the *Lusitania*.

CHAPTER 15
AFTERWARD

After several other commands, Cunard gave William Thomas Turner the steamer *Ivernia*, which was then a British transport ship. In January 1917, the German submarine *UB-47* torpedoed the *Ivernia* off the coast of Greece. Once again, Turner oversaw the evacuation of passengers and crew, and only survived personally after first going down with the ship and then swimming clear as she went down.[1] When he returned to Great Britain, he remained on land with shore duty for the duration of the war. The United Kingdom recognized Turner with the British Order of the Empire in 1918, and Cunard promoted Turner to commodore of the line. He left the company in November 1919 at Cunard's mandatory retirement age of 63.[2] Turner lived in seclusion until he died of cancer in 1933.[3]

Walther Schwieger lived for two more years after sinking the *Lusitania*. On September 4, 1915, Schwieger, without warning, torpedoed the passenger liner *Hesperian*, which resulted in the loss of 32 lives. This was contrary to his orders but the U-boat commander pleaded—this time successfully—that he'd mistaken the vessel for an auxiliary cruiser. Though he was called to headquarters to give an account of this sinking, his superiors accepted his explanation; he was only warned to "follow your instructions exactly" in the future.[4]

The *U-20* itself became a casualty of war in November 1916. Called to rescue the *U-30* off the coast of Denmark, the *U-20* ran aground in a heavy fog. Neither the crew nor the ships sent to protect and assist the *U-20* could refloat the vessel. Schwieger chose to scuttle the notorious submarine using her own torpedoes.[5]

Schwieger next commanded the larger *U-88*. On September 5, 1917, while on patrol, the *U-88* unwittingly entered a nautical mine-field off Terschelling. The crew of the nearby *U-54* recorded a heavy detonation and ten minutes later a second explosion. It is believed that the *U-88* had struck a mine and was lost, with Schwieger aboard.[6] During his time as a commander, Schwieger had sunk more than 190,000 tons of Allied shipping.[7]

The *Lusitania* remains a few hundred feet beneath the water off Old Head of Kinsale. In 1935, the crew of the salvage ship *Orphir* used an early sonar device to locate the wreck. The Tritonia Corporation and Joseph Peress, who had developed a cast magnesium atmospheric diving suit popularly known as the "Iron Man," planned to send a man to investigate the wreck.[8] Peress' assistant Jim Jarrett completed the dive without incident. He actually stood on the *Lusitania*, but due to the lack of light he mistakenly reported that the liner was lying on her port side.

The lost liner became the subject of gossip. In 1936, rumors in Kinsale and Queenstown (now Cobh) held that an Italian salvage firm, Sorima, had made an attempt on the *Lusitania,* only to be driven away by a British naval vessel. Sorima denied any such claim, insisting they had considered going after the sunken ship but decided it was too dangerous. In the following decade rumors floated that a British vessel had depth-charged the liner. There were also stories of Americans trying to procure the *Lusitania's* alleged gold, though no one living near Old Head of Kinsale ever admitted to seeing Americans diving for the wreck.

In 1950 came another story. According to gossip, a British salvage team had been at work on the wreck, setting off charges placed by a crane. The charges, the story goes, were directed by a diver suspended in a pressure-proof chamber. The British firm denied any attempt on the *Lusitania*, responding, "You just cannot get any further with it. You're just wasting your time."[9]

In 1960, John Light, a former U.S. Navy diver who achieved noto- riety from a 300-foot dive to film a submarine exercise, began his stub- born investigation of the *Lustiania*.[10] He visited the British salvage firm to ask for advice about diving for the wreck. The British firm treated Light in a curt manner, but he did manage to talk to a crewmember of one of the company's ships. According to this man, in 1954 a diver had been sent down to the wreck to set off a charge.[11]

Light encountered problems from the outset—he needed money and men, and to get both he had first to prove that the diving and photog- raphy could be done. So on July 20, 1960, he descended 245 feet while operating a camera. The pressure at that depth caused him to suffer from narcosis, but he still came back with pictures.

A few weeks later Light acquired two men and equipment for a dive to the *Lusitania*. The trio soon began to grapple with the project's chal- lenges. Because of the strong tide, dives could be made only when the current was still, and time spent at the bottom was limited to a meager ten minutes. Anchoring the buoys also proved difficult. Light and his men needed lines from surface floats to mark known points of the derelict. They initially used manila lines with heavy anchors, but the tide carried them away. Lines tied at the bottom soon frayed, and the more durable iron chain was stolen during the night. Finally they used steel cables shackled to the wreck.[12]

According to Gustav Stahl, in an affidavit produced by the German ambassador in 1915, a gun was just outboard of the children's nursery, so Light targeted that location for his first descent. He saw no gun where Stahl had indicated, but noticed that the metal had been cut. Someone had been there before.

The weather permitted Light to return to the same location the fol- lowing day. He noticed a hole some eight feet across, which appeared to him "as if some heavy object had dropped straight down *after* the ship had settled on her side, maybe long after. The superstructure is made of light materials, and it looked as if something had just gone on through." He observed three steel cables leading into the hole. "Maybe," speculated Light, "they were attached to whatever had fallen through. Maybe somebody was trying to hoist that thing away, and it broke loose."[13]

Light had used up his time and was forced to surface, but a few days later a mysterious ship appeared over the wreck. Light was told that this ship belonged to the same salvagers who had earlier denied any involvement with the wreck. "When she left," Light reported, "I didn't have any buoys." Speculation was that the buoys had been stolen by whoever was on this boat, which angered Light. "Why would anyone care what a bunch of free divers were doing?" he bitterly asked, "We couldn't take anything away. We could only look; maybe there was something we weren't suppose to see."[14]

Light and his men set up new buoys and resumed exploring the hulk. They discovered a huge gash in the hull opposite the point where the torpedo entered, indicating that an internal explosion had occurred after the torpedo struck. They found a cargo door lying some distance from the doorway and concluded that the door had detached itself after the ship settled. They also saw cables and chains which did not belong to the liner.

John Light returned the following year, this time equipped with better gear and more men. Among the party was an officer of the United States Navy. The first dives were arranged to set up cables; on the fourth dive they strung a cable near the hole where a gun might have been. On a subsequent dive, the naval officer called Light's attention to a long, tapered object, but because of time constraints, they were forced to surface before thoroughly examining the object. The naval officer saw what he "felt was a gun barrel and questionably a gun emplacement or turret near by: a semispherical piece of metal, riveted."[15]

The Light expeditions were hampered by the effect that depth had on the divers, plus a host of other variables, including weather. It is possible that they did in fact see a gun, but Light thought it could also have been a pipe or a spar.

In the early 1980s, Oceaneering International set out to explore the sunken Cunarder. Included in the crew were two British engineers who planned to test their method of raising heavy weights from the ocean floor. The goal was to recover gold bullion the wreck was purported to contain. After examining the wreck from photographs, they retrieved three bronze propellers, one of which is displayed on the docks at Liverpool; two anchors; and various small objects such as silverware and chronometers.[16] The undertaking did not meet the company's financial expectations.

The British Ministry of Defense warned the team that "it would be imprudent not to point out the obvious but real danger inherent if explosives did happen to be present..." Some thought this could be an admission that the *Lusitania* had carried highly explosive cargo in addition to the rifle ammunition. In response to this, the Ministry issued a statement that it "does not know of any evidence whatsoever that might substantiate rumours of other explosives."[17]

A more detailed examination of the *Lusitania* came years later, in 1993. Dr. Robert Ballard, who in 1985 discovered the wreck of the *Titanic* and the German battleship *Bismarck*, decided to examine the torpedoed Cunarder using his state-of-the-art equipment.

Ballard was the ideal man for the mission. With a Ph.D. in marine geology and geophysics, he had been involved in the development of small, unmanned submersibles and worked at the Woods Hole Oceanographic Institute for many years. In the 1990s, he founded the Institute for Exploration to pursue deep-water archeology. As one colleague summed it up, "Bob has an extraordinary ability to find interesting things on the bottom."[18] Ballard and his wife had visited Old Head of Kinsale in 1992, finding it a "breathtakingly beautiful spot."[19] From the start, he fell in love with the locale, and that affection led to his decision to investigate why the liner sank.

Aspects of the *Lusitania's* sinking puzzled Ballard. The *Titanic*, which wasn't as well constructed as the *Lusitania*, foundered two hours and forty minutes after striking an iceberg. The *Lusitania* sank in eighteen minutes. Furthermore, the *Lusitania* had listed heavily, while the *Titanic* suffered only a slight list.

At first Ballard thought the magazine had exploded. It made perfect sense, assuming the torpedo hit the starboard side of the ship and ignited a cargo of explosives.[20] However, Ballard faced an uncomfortable fact: the torpedo had struck below or just in front of the bridge, well away from the magazine. So what caused the second explosion that made the ship sink so fast?

One important advantage Ballard would have with the *Lusitania*, compared with the *Titanic* and *Bismarck* projects, was that they knew the liner's exact location. It wasn't necessary to comb the ocean for an indeterminate number of days. Local fishermen knew the exact spot where their nets repeatedly got tangled in the derelict.

The Ballards made a preliminary map of the area using sonar, and in 1993 returned with a fine team. His wife Barbara handled the most advance planning for the expedition. In addition to Ballard and his wife, the team included three people to adapt and handle the maneuverable, remote-controlled photographic robots, a maritime artist and two historians. They studied the *Lusitania*'s history, and found themselves empathizing with everyone involved—not only the passengers and crew, but the politicians who condemned or defended the sinking as well. They also gained an understanding of the *U-20*'s crew.

The investigators' ship, the *Northern Horizon*, took up position over the *Lusitania*. The first step was a sonar reconnaissance of the derelict, and from this they made an outline of the wreck. The hull had been broken up between the third and fourth funnels. The break had occurred in about the same area as that of the *Titanic*, near the dining room and first class lounge.[21] This area was not meant to take such stress. The superstructure was badly mangled.

With the sonar reconnaissance completed, Ballard and his team dispatched *Jason*, a 3,000-pound remote-controlled photographic robot. Martin Bowen handled the controls from the *Northern Horizon*. *Jason* provided an excellent view of the *Lusitania* to viewers on the mother ship.[22] Two other robots were dispatched, *Medea* and the smaller *Homer*.

The team watched the view from *Jason* in silence, awed by the sight. This once beautiful ship was a heartbreaking vision—most of her superstructure was gone, and many of her portside doors were thrown wide open. The upper part of the liner was covered with fishing nets; Bowen had to be careful not to bring *Jason* too close to the wreck. As Ballard later explained, "These nylon nets are virtually indestructible, which is good news for fishermen but not for underwater explorers."[23]

Combing over the sunken ship, *Jason* photographed every square inch of the target. High-frequency sonar provided a computerized, color-coded, three-dimensional diagram of the derelict. Ballard could superimpose a 3-D image of the *Lusitania* onto the wreck. This enabled the team, while viewing from above, to see what parts of the ship had been affected by the sinking.[24]

The investigators found that the deck had collapsed. The ship's beam had shrunk from 88 to 40 feet. The cabins, once the epitome of luxurious transatlantic travel, had been reduced to "grotesque caricatures of their elegant former selves."[25] Only the front portion of the bow, bent upward at a 45° angle, at all resembled the original ship. The robot photographed *Lusitania*'s nameplate. The brass letters had been painted over early in the war, and years of being under water had corroded the fasteners that held them in place. The letters had fallen off, leaving only the outlines visible. Ballard and his crew felt as excited as archaeologists deciphering hieroglyphics in some long undiscovered cave.[26]

The images showed many small holes in the ship's hull. They looked as though someone had started to cut each one out, and then pressed the steel plate in. To Ballard they resembled the press-in tops of soft drink cans. The team examined the port side where in the 1960s John Light had seen an eight-foot hole that he attributed to the secondary explosion. In spite of their efforts, they found nothing that matched Light's description.

Because of the ship's position, *Jason* could explore beneath the keel. Again, there was no large hole, but they found instead more of those small, pressed-in punctures. The bow was smashed and bent upward, probably by its collision with the seabed when the *Lusitania* sank. *Homer*, a smaller photographic robot, glided under the hull to photograph the starboard side near the magazine. It was intact.

With *Jason*'s reconnaissance complete, the next step was to see the *Lusitania* firsthand using the submersible, *Delta*. The oceanographer would have excellent visibility, with a large window forward and on either side of the craft. The weather was good and the seas calm. *Delta* descended about 295 feet and traveled across the seabed. Finally the submersible came within view of the great liner. Ballard saw a woman's shoe, size six. He also noticed a boat winch, the ship's stockhold vents and a doorknob. Perhaps the most surprising object was a bathtub with its spindly, birdcage-like shower still attached, found outside the ship. Ballard felt like a bug crawling on a sleeping giant.[27]

Then the submersible came across a depth charge. It was so close that Ballard could see the contact pin only a few inches from *Delta*'s side. "I preferred not to contemplate what would happen if we touched it," the scientist later wrote. The depth charge was used by the Irish Navy for practice, which explained the small holes in the liner's hull.[28]

He and the pilot examined the wreck from every angle. Ballard found the bridge to be one of the most interesting sights. The wooden deck was in better condition than that of the *Titanic*. "Maybe it was the unreliable visibility or the topsy-turvy angle, but everything on the ship looked enormous. The base of the mast reminded me of a giant redwood," though he thought it actually measured about three feet in diameter.[29] They discovered the aft docking bridge, with its own controls for guiding the liner into its berth in port. Originally on the aft Boat Deck, it had been torn off the vessel. The engine room was open to view because the superstructure had slid away. The metal girder running across the room and the metal catwalk were badly battered but still recognizable.

The crew found the magazine where munitions would have been stored "clearly undamaged."[30] Ballard rejected the theory that the second explosion had been caused by illegal contraband. Likewise, he discounted a bursting boiler as the culprit. None of the survivors from the operating boiler rooms testified to an explosion in that section of the ship. What then caused the second explosion?

Ballard concluded the cause was coal dust.[31] By the end of her voyage the *Lusitania* had consumed a great deal of coal—some estimate more than a 1,000 tons (about 2,205,000 pounds) per day.[32] Because coal dust explosions require a mix of coal particles and air, an empty coal bunker presents a greater risk of explosion. The torpedo struck the ship, and the coal dust that became airborne on impact was ignited. This caused a "massive, uncontrollable explosion" throughout the liner's Lower Deck and effectively doomed the ship.[33]

An alternate theory on the cause of the second explosion was advanced by Patrick O'Sullivan in his book *The Lusitania: Unravelling the Mysteries*. He pointed out that the liner was carrying a large amount of aluminum powder, which burns when exposed to moisture.[34] Yet no one has observed evidence of an explosion near the number-two cargo hatch. Furthermore, Ballard found the bow relatively undamaged in the cargo area.

Dr. Robert Ballard's investigation of the *Lusitania* added a great deal of knowledge to the subject that haunts observers to this day. The sinking of the *Lusitania* was more than just the loss of a ship. It ushered in the beginning of unrestrained warfare and rage. May 7, 1915, the day the world was shocked, was the day Western man violently entered the modern era.

ACKNOWLEDGEMENTS

The Story of the *Lusitania* has something in it for everyone. For the liner enthusiast, she was a luxurious record breaker. For disaster buffs, she and the *Titanic* are the two most famous shipwrecks. For the naval historian, the incident was the submarine coming of age. For psychologists, it is a fascinating laboratory. For the moralist, it is an issue that raises complex ethical questions. For the political scientist, it was an event that united and divided a nation. For scholars of international relations, it is an episode of modern diplomacy.

I dealt with the *Lusitania* in my earlier works, *To the Bottom of the Sea* and *Reflections on the Lusitania*. Many people helped me then, and many assisted me with this work.

I would like to thank organizations such as 7 C's, the *Titanic* Historical Society, and the Steamship Historical Society of America for producing reprints of old materials. Also I would like to thank Woods Hole Oceanographic Institute, especially Martin Bowen and the Institute for Exploration, and in particular Dr. Robert Ballard.

Certain government organizations assisted me, such as the National Archives in Britain and the British Embassy in Washington DC. And for putting me in contact with them, I want to thank the Library of Congress, the National Archives in New York, and the Canadian government.

Libraries were also helpful. I would like to thank college libraries such as the ones at Kent State University, Lycoming College, and Arkansas State University. Public libraries deserve a word of thanks as well, including the Stow-Munroe Falls Public Library, the James V. Brown Library, and the Akron-Summit County Public Library, as do their unseen interlibrary loan officers in other libraries.

College professors have helped to enhance my knowledge and insights into the First World War. Among them were Dr. John Piper, Dr. Robert Larson, Dr. Richard Morris of Lycoming College, Dr. W.J. Greenwald, and Dr. Donald Konnold of Arkansas State University.

Some people have read earlier drafts of my work. I would like to thank Dr. Richard Morris, Dr. John Piper, Veronica Huwig, Ernestine Stevenson, and Connie Farr.

All faults and shortcomings of this work are mine and mine alone.

NOTES

Foreword
1 "Submarines: History—Submarines & the American Revolution," from the *Office of Naval Research Science and Technology Focus*, online at http://www.onr.navy.mil/focus/blowballast/sub/history2.htm.

Chapter 1: ". . . Do So at Their Own Risk"
1. Six major New York newspapers published this warning on Saturday, May 1, 1915 according to *The New York Times current history: the European war, Volume 17, The* New York Times Co., 1919. *Eyewitness—American Originals from the National Archives* (available from the National Archives in Washington, DC.) states that the warning ran in 40 U.S. papers on May 1.
2. Louis L. Snyder, *The Military History of the Lusitania* (New York: Franklin Watts Inc., 1965), 2.
3. Des Hickey and Gus Smith, *Seven Days to Disaster* (New York: G.P. Putnam's Sons, 1981), 160.
4. Donald B. Chidsey, *The Day They Sank the Lusitania* (New York: Award Book, 1967), 4.
5. Chidsey, *Day They Sank*, 12.
6. Snyder, *Military History*, 4–5 and Droste, Christian Ludwig, *Documents on the War of the Nations*, vol. 2 (The Dietz Printing Company, 1915), 75.
7. A.A. Hoehling and Mary Hoehling, *The Last Voyage of the Lusitania* (New York: Henry Holt and Co., 1956), 75.
8. *New York Times*, May 1, 1915.
9. Sir Norman Lockyer, *Nature: International Journal of Science*, no. 1977, Vol. 76, September 19, 1907, 523.

10. Chidsey, *Day They Sank*, 19–20.

11. "Wife of Lusitania's Richest Passenger Bears Up Under Strain of No News," *The New York Times*, May 9, 1915.

12. Robert D. Ballard and Spencer Dunmore, *Exploring the Lusitania* (Toronto: Madison Press Books, 1995), 32.

13. "Mrs. Antonio Ruiz A Suicide in London," *New York Times*, June 11, 1909.

14. "Bought Secrecy for Ruiz Suicide," *New York Times*, June 11, 1909.

15. "London to Ostracize Friend of Mrs. Ruiz: King Gave Hint at Horse Show of His Attitude in Sensational Suicide Case," *New York Times*, June 13, 1909.

16. Hickey, *Seven Days*, 24-28.

17. See http://www.roycrofter.com and also Maria Via and Marjorie Searl, *Head Heart and Hand: Elbert Hubbard and the Roycrofters* University of Rochester Press, 1994.

18. "Blow to Arts and Letters," *Literary Digest* (May 22, 1915), 1215.

19. Hoehling, *Last Voyage*, 57–60.

20. *New York Times*, May 1, 1915, 3.

21. F. Champney, *Art and Glory: The Story of Elbert Hubbard* (Kent, Ohio: Kent State University Press, 1983), 194.

22. Frederick D. Ellis, *The Tragedy of the Lusitania* (Philadelphia: National Publishing Company, 1915), 103.

23. Chidsey, *Day They Sank*, 49–52.

24. "Blow to Arts and Letters," *Literary Digest*, 1214.

25. Isaac Frederick Marcosson and Daniel Frohman, *Charles Frohman: Manager and Man* (New York: Harper & Bros., 1916), 382–83.

26. Marcosson, *Charles Frohman*, 421.

27. Marcosson, *Charles Frohman*, 287–289.

28. Chidsey, *Day They Sank*, 56–58.

29. Ibid.

30. Oliver Bernard, *Cock Sparrow* (London: Jonathan Cape, 1936), 145.

31. Hickey, *Seven Days*, 22.

32. Ibid.

33. See the Dublin City Gallery *The Hugh Lane* online at http://www.hughlane.ie.

34. Diana Preston, *Lusitania: An Epic Tragedy* (New York: Walker and Company, 2002), 102.

35. "Grief and Fury in Liverpool," *Times* (London), May 10, 1915; "Cunard Office Here Besieged for News; Fate of 1,918 on Lusitania Long in Doubt," *New York Times*, May 8, 1915.

36. "The Lusitania Case." *New York Times Current History; The European War*, vol. 2, no. 3 (June, 1915), 28.

37. Preston, *Epic Tragedy*, 105.

38. Charlotte Kellogg, *Women of Belgium: Turning Tragedy to Triumph* (New York: Funk & Wagnalls Co., 1917), 4–7.

39. Hoehling, *Last Voyage*, 28.

40. Kolleen M. Guy, *When Champagne Became French: Wine and the Making of a National Identity* (Baltimore: Johns Hopkins University Press, 2003), 33.

41. Frank J. Prial, "Wine Talk; A Bubbly History: Garters, Crowned Heads, Widows," *New York Times*, December 24, 1997.

42. Chidsey, *Day They Sank*, 27–28.

43. Hickey, *Seven Days*, 151.

44. Charles Lauriat, *The Lusitania's Last Voyage* (Boston: Houghton Mifflin Company, 1915), 65–66.

45. *National Geographic Video: The Last Voyage of the Lusitania* (1994).

46. Hickey, *Seven Days*, 35–36.

47. Hoehling, *Last Voyage*, 23–24.

48. Lauriat, *Lusitania's Last Voyage*, 67.

49. Hoehling, *Last Voyage*, 37.

50. *Secrets of the Unknown: The Lusitania* (Oak Forest, Ill.: MPI Home Video, 1989).

51. Hoehling, *Last Voyage*, 38.

52. Hoehling, *Last Voyage*, 64–67.

53. Hickey, *Seven Days*, 44–45.

54. Hickey, *Seven Days*, 53–54.

55. Leslie Morton, *The Long Wake*, (London: Routledge & Kegan Paul, 1968), 98–99.

56. Lauriat, *Lusitania's Last Voyage*, 6.

57. Snyder, *Military History*, 5.

58. Snyder, *Military History*, 6.

59. Douglas R. Burgess, *Seize the Trident: the Race for Superliner Supremacy and How it Altered the Great War* (Camden, Maine: McGraw Hill, 2005), 225.

60. Ellis, *Tragedy of the Lusitania*, 172–174.

61. Hickey, *Seven Days*, 16.

62. *New York Times*, May 1, 1915.

63. Theodate Pope, ". . . And Then the Water Closed Over Me . . . ," *American Heritage* (April 1975): 98.

64. Thomas Bailey, "The Sinking of the Lusitania," *American Historical Review* (October 1935): 68.

65. *Secrets of the Unknown: The Lusitania* (Oak Forest, Ill.: MPI Home Video, 1989).

66. "Found No Guns on the Lusitania," *New York Times*, June 4, 1915.

67. *New York Times*, May 10, 1915.

68. *Shipping Casualties (Loss of the Steamship "Lusitania") Report of a Formal Investigation into the Circumstances Attending the Foundering on the 7th of May, 1915, of the British Steamship "Lusitania," Command 8022.* (London: HMSO, 1915), 6. Hereafter called the *Mersey Report*. A reprint of the *Lusitania*'s cargo manifest can be found in William Tantum and C.L. Droste, *The Lusitania Case* (London: Patrick Stephens, 1972).

Chapter 2: Rivalry on the Atlantic

1. Kay Grant, *Samuel Cunard Pioneer of the Atlantic Steamship* (London: Abelard-Schuman, 1967), 27.
2. Melvin Maddocks, *The Great Liners* (Alexandria, Va.: Time Life Books, 1978), 22.
3. University of Toronto/Université Laval, "Samuel Cunard," Dictionary of Canadian Biography online at http://www.biographi.ca/009004-119.01-e.php?BioId=38502.
4. John Malcolm Brinnin, *The Sway of the Grand Saloon* (New York: Delacorte Press, 1971), 93.
5. Ibid.
6. Grant, *Samuel Cunard*, 88.
7. Maddocks, *Great Liners*, 23.
8. Brinnin, *Grand Saloon*, 107.
9. Brinnin, *Grand Saloon*, 98–99.
10. Brinnin, *Grand Saloon*, 272.
11. Ibid.
12. Brinnin, *Grand Saloon*, 276–277.
13. Robert Wall, *Ocean Liners* (New York: E.P. Dutton, 1977), 48.
14. Ibid.
15. John Maxtone-Graham, *The Only Way to Cross* (New York: Macmillan Company, 1972), 8.
16. Maxtone-Graham, *Only Way*, 8.
17. Walter Lord, *The Night Lives On* (New York: William Morrow and Company, Inc., 1986), 30–32.
18. Lord, *Night Lives On,* 21.
19. Ibid.
20. Wall, *Ocean Liners*, 32.
21. Maxtone-Graham, *Only Way*, 52.
22. *New York Times*, April 30, 1901, 2.
23. Daniel Allen Butler, *The Age of Cunard: A Transatlantic History 1839–2003,* (ProStar Publications, 2004), 139–140.
24. "Alliance with Mr. Morgan Wins Herr Ballin Favor," *New York Times*, July 13, 1902.
25. Brinnin, *Grand Saloon*, 328–329.
26. Ibid.
27. Brinnin, *Grand Saloon*, 328–329.
28. Maxtone-Graham, *Only Way*, 11.

Chapter 3: The Luxury Liner / Auxiliary Cruiser

1. Mark D. Warren, *Cunard Turbine-Driven Quadruple-Screw Atlantic Liner "Lusitania"* (Wellingborough: Patrick Stephens, 1986), 55.
2. "The Atlas Works, Sheffield," *Page's Engineering Weekly*, vol. 7, 774–776.

3. Ibid.

4. Warren, *Cunard Turbine*, 58–59.

5. "The New Turbine Liner *Lusitania*," *Scientific America* (September 14, 1907): 189–190.

6. "New Turbine," *Scientific America*, 188.

7. Warren, *Cunard Turbine*, 36.

8. "Unsolved Problems in the Design and Propulsion of Ship," *Scientific America* (August 24, 1907 Supplement): 122.

9. Warren, *Cunard Turbine*, 55.

10. Warren, *Cunard Turbine*, 55–56.

11. Warren, *Cunard Turbine*, 11.

12. J. Kent Layton, *Lusitania: An Illustrated Biography of a Ship of Splendor* (Lulu.com, 2007), 9; "New Turbine," *Scientific America*, 190.

13. Ballard, *Exploring the Lusitania*, 23.

14. "Steam Trials of the *Lusitania*," *Scientific America* (August 24, 1907): 190.

15. Warren, *Cunard Turbine*, 26.

16. Ibid.

17. American Society of Naval Engineers, "The Cunard Liner *Lusitania*," *Journal of the American Society of Naval Engineers, Inc.*, vol. 19 (1907): 966.

18. Layton, *Lusitania*, 64

19. "Coal Consumption of the *Lusitania*," *Scientific America* (May 9, 1908): 326.

20. Ballard, *Exploring the Lusitania*, 22.

21. "Across the Atlantic in 5 Days and 54 Minutes," *Harper's Weekly* (September 28, 1907): 1417.

22. Warren, *Cunard Turbine*, 51.

23. "New Turbine," *Scientific America*, 189.

24. Layton, *Lusitania*, 12

25. Warren, *Cunard Turbine*, 52.

26. "The 25 Knot Turbine Liner "Lusitania'" *Scientific America* (August 10, 1907): 96.

27. Brinnin, *Grand Saloon*, 343.

28. Brinnin, *Grand Saloon*, 343–344, see also Theodore Dreiser, *A Traveler at Forty* (New York: The Century Company, 1913), 16.

29. Butler, *Age of Cunard*, 467.

30. "25 Knot Turbine," *Scientific America*, 96.

Chapter 4: The Great Naval Race

1. Michael Epkenhans, *Tirpitz: Architect of the German High Seas Fleet* (Washington: Potomac Books, 2008), xi.

2. V.R. Berghahn, *Germany and the Approach of War in 1914* (New York: St. Martin's Press, 1973), 27–28.

3. Epkenhans, *Tirpitz*, 23–30.

4. Epkenhans, *Tirpitz*, 24

5. Berghahn, *Germany*, 29.

6. Berghahn, *Germany*, 34.

7. Richard Hough, *Dreadnought: A History of the Modern Battleship* (Penzance, Cornwall: Periscope Publishing 2003), 33–34.

8. Berghahn, *Germany*, 35.

9. William Mulligan, *Origins of the First World War* (Cambridge: Cambridge University Press, 2010), 51.

10. Volker Rolf Berghahn, *Imperial Germany, 1871–1918: Economy, Society, Culture, and Politics* (New York: Berghahn Books, 2005), 260.

11. Berghahn, *Germany*, 48.

12. Berghahn, *Germany*, 48; see also Mulligan, *Origins of the First World War,* 52.

13. Paul G. Halpern, *Naval History of World War I* (Annapolis: Naval Institute Press, 1995), 7–8.

14. Cornelli Barnett, *The Swordbearers* (New York: William Morrow and Company, 1960), 114.

15. Barnett, *Swordbearers*, 116.

16. Halpern, *Naval History of World War I*, 345.

17. Barnett, *Swordbearers*, 114.

18. Barnett, *Swordbearers*, 114–115.

19. Barnett, *Swordbearers*, 115–116.

20. James C. George, *History of Warships from Ancient Times to the Twenty-First Century* (Annapolis: Naval Institute Press, 1998), 155.

21. George, *History of Warships*, 155.

22. Rebecca Stefoff, *Submarines* (Tarrytown, New York: Marshall Cavendish, 2006), 29.

23. George, *History of Warships*, 155.

24. Cynthia Owen Philip, *Robert Fulton: A Biography* (New York: Franklin Watts, 1985), 96–101.

25. T.L. Francis, *Submarines, Leviathans of the Deep* (New York: Metrobooks, 1997), 16–17.

26. George, *Warships*, 155–156.

27. Francis, *Submarines*, 22.

28. Lincoln P. Paine, *Warships of the world to 1900* (New York: Houghton Mifflin Harcourt, 2000), 26–27.

29. John Poluhowich, *Argonaut: the submarine legacy of Simon Lake* (College Station, Texas: Texas A & M University Press, 1999), 54–57.

Chapter 5: Armageddon

1. "It has now been conclusively proved that the assassination was funded by and undertaken in behalf of a secret Serbian society known as 'Union or Death' and popularly called 'The Black Hand,' which provided the bombs and pistols. The

mastermind of the plot to kill Franz Ferdinand was a mysterious, restless individual nicknamed Apis (Bee), the chief of Serbian military intelligence." From: http://www.law.uga.edu/academics/profiles/dwilkes_more/other_5tyrannicide.ht ml See also: http://net.lib.byu.edu/estu/wwi/comment/blk-hand.html about the Black Hand.

2. Lawrence LaFore, *The Long Fuse* (New York: J.B. Lippincott Company, 1973), 215.

3. Peter Gay and R.K. Webb, *Modern Europe Since 1815* (New York: Harper & Row Publishers, 1973), 938–939.

4. Ibid.

5. John Bach McMaster, *United States in the World War* (New York: Appleton and Co., 1918), 25.

6. *New York Times*, August 2, 1914, 3.

7. C. Seymour, ed., *The Intimate Papers of Colonel House* (Boston: Houghton Mifflin, 1926), vol. 1, 284.

8. Seymour, *Colonel House*, 285.

9. John Keegan, *August, 1914: Opening Moves,* Ballantine's Illustrated History of the Violent Century, Campaign Book No. 19 (New York: Ballantine Books, 1972), 14–22.

10. Allan Mazur, *Global Social Problems* (Lanham, Maryland: Rowman & Littlefild Publishers, Inc., 2007), 61.

11. Edwyn A. Gray, *The Killing Time* (New York: Charles Scribner's Sons, 1972), 46–52.

12. Priscilla Mary Roberts, "The Battle of the Falklands," in *World War One*, edited by Spencer Tucker (ABC-CLIO 2005), 660–663.

13. Julian S. Corbett, *Naval Operations,* vol. 1 (London: Longman Green and Co., 1920), 342–350.

14. Grace P. Hayes, *World War I: A Compact History* (New York: Hawthorn Books Inc., 1972), 102–105.

15. *World War One*, edited by Spencer Tucker (ABC-CLIO 2005), 444.

16. Gray, *Killing Time*, 64–65

17. Thomas Bailey and Paul Ryan, *The Lusitania Disaster* (New York: The Free Press, 1975), 56–58.

18. "*Falaba* Unarmed, Lord Mersey Is Told," *New York Times*, May 21, 1915.

19. Bailey, *Lusitania Disaster*, 56–58

20. *New York Times*, May 1, 1915, 1.

21. Bailey, *Lusitania Disaster*, 61.

22. *New York Times*, May 3, 1915, 1.

23. Bailey, *Lusitania Disaster*, 62.

Chapter 6: A "Lauriat Crossing"
1. Bernard, *Cock Sparrow*, 147–148.

2. "The Loss of La Bourgogne," *The New York Times*, July 13, 1898.

3. "Only forty-three passengers out of 550 aboard La Bourgogne were rescued; and only one of nearly 300 women who had taken passage on the vessel at New York was among the survivors. In a reversal of traditional French gallantry, never satisfactorily explained, women and children were sacrificed first, while of the complement of 164 of the steamer's crew, 120 managed to save themselves." Eberhard P. Deutsch, "Angele Marie Langles," *American Bar Association Journal*, vol. 48 (March 1962): 218.
4. Lauriat, *Lusitania's Last Voyage*, 4.
5. Lauriat, *Lusitania's Last Voyage*, 3.
6. Lauriat, *Lusitania's Last Voyage*, 5.
7. Lauriat, *Lusitania's Last Voyage*, 69.
8. Chidsey, *Day They Sank*, 59.
9. *New York Times*, May 10, 1915, 5.
10. Hickey, *Seven Days*, 87.
11. Ibid.
12. Hickey, *Seven Days*, 125.
13. Hickey, *Seven Days*, 115.
14. Hickey, *Seven Days*, 105.
15. Viscountess Rhondda (Lady Mackworth), "Recalling a Tragedy" *Living Age* (June 16, 1925): 636.
16. *New York Times*, May 10, 1915, 2.
17. Preston, *Epic Tragedy*, 133.
18. Hickey, *Seven Days*, 89.
19. Hickey, *Seven Days*, 93.
20. Rhondda, "Recalling," 636.
21. *New York Times*, June 24, 1933, 13.
22. Bailey and Ryan, *Lusitania Disaster*, 65.
23. Charles Herbert Lightoller, *Titanic and Other Ships*, A Project Gutenberg of Australia eBook, eBook No.: 0301011.txt, 2003.
24. Ibid.
25. Hickey, *Seven Days*, 128–129.
26. Morton, *Long Wake*, 100–101.
27. Morton, *Long Wake*, 101–102.
28. Lord, *Night Lives On*, 144–145.
29. Bailey, *Lusitania Disaster*, 131.
30. Bernard, *Cock Sparrow*, 149.
31. *New York Times*, May 10, 1915, 2.
32. Preston, *Epic Tragedy*, 129.
33. Hoehling, *Last Voyage*, 74.
34. Pope, "... And Then the Water," 98–99.
35. Morton, *Long Wake*, 101.
36. *New York Times*, May 9, 1915, 2.
37. Lauriat, *Lusitania's Last Voyage*, 13–14.

38. *National Geographic Video: The Last Voyage of the Lusitania* (1994).
39. Hickey, *Seven Days*, 157.
40. Hoehling, *Last Voyage*, 74.
41. Bernard, *Cock Sparrow*, 148–149.
42. "Boston Woman on Wedding Trip," *New York Times*, May 8, 1915.
43. Preston, *Epic Tragedy*, 95.
44. Lord, *Night Lives On*, 49.
45. *The Plain Dealer* (Cleveland), May 9, 1915, 2.
46. "Friends Hope and Despair," *New York Times*, May 9, 1915.
47. Preston, *Epic Tragedy*, 103–104.
48. Chidsey, *Day They Sank*, 56.
49. Hickey, *Seven Days*, 155.
50. Bernard, *Cock Sparrow*, 149.
51. Bailey, *Lusitania Disaster*, 136.
52. Bailey, *Lusitania Disaster*, 138–139.
53. Hoehling, *Last Voyage*, 87.
54. Rhondda, "Recalling," 636.
55. Lauriat, *Lusitania's Last Voyage*, 4.

Chapter 7: Old Head of Kinsale
1. Hickey, *Seven Days*, 160.
2. Hickey, *Seven Days*, 173.
3. Hickey, *Seven Days*, 161.
4. Lauriat, *Lusitania's Last Voyage*, 70.
5. Lauriat, *Lusitania's Last Voyage*, 70–71.
6. Ibid.
7. Hickey, *Seven Days*, 161.
8. Bernard, *Cock Sparrow*, 152.
9. Hickey, *Seven Days*, 170.
10. Hoehling, *Last Voyage*, 92.
11. Hoehling, *Last Voyage*, 93.
12. Bailey, *Lusitania Disaster*, 117–118.
13. Gordon Williamson, *U-boats of the Kaiser's Navy*, Osprey Publishing, 2002, p.10.
14. After serving as a gunnery officer, Tirpitz was ordered in 1877 to visit the *Torpedo-Fabrik von Robert Whitehead* at the Austrian naval center in Fiume. "When he returned to Germany, he was placed in charge of torpedo development for the German Navy." Robert K. Massie, *Dreadnought: Britain, Germany and the Coming of the Great War* (New York: Random House, 1991), 167.
15. Lowell Thomas, *Raiders of the Deep* (Annapolis: Naval Institute Press, 1928), 91.
16. Thomas, *Raiders*, 83.
17. Thomas, *Raiders*, 83–84.

18. Thomas, *Raiders*, 85–86.
19. Thomas, *Raiders*, 88–89.
20. Hickey, *Seven Days*, 103.
21. Hoehling, *Last Voyage*, 80.
22. Hickey, *Seven Days*, 143–146.
23. Hoehling, *Last Voyage*, 84.
24. Chidsey, *Day They Sank*, 65.
25. Pope, ". . . And Then the Water," 99.
26. *Shipping Casualties (Loss of the Steamship "Lusitania"), Proceedings in Camera at the Formal Investigation into the Circumstances Attending the Foundering of the British Steamship "Lusitania," Command 381* (London: HMSO, 1919), 3. Hereafter called *"Mersey Proceedings in Camera."*
27. Morton, *Long Wake*, 103.
28. David Dean, *Architecture of the 1930s: Recalling the English Scene* (Rizzoli, 1983), 116.
29. Bernard, *Cock Sparrow*, 152–154.
30. Preston, *Epic Tragedy*, 183.
31. Lauriat, *Lusitania's Last Voyage*, 71.
32. Lauriat, *Lusitania's Last Voyage*, 72.
33. Morton, *Long Wake*, 103.
34. Thomas A. Bailey, *Essays Diplomatic and Undiplomatic of Thomas A. Bailey*, edited by Alexander Deconde and Armin Rappaport (New York: Appleton-Century-Crofts, 1969) 191, *f* 4.
35. Bailey, *Essays Diplomatic*, 191–192, *f* 5.
36. Hoehling, *Last Voyage*, 103.

Chapter 8: Eighteen Lethal Minutes

1. Morton in his 1968 book, *The Long Wake,* states that he received an acknowledgement from the bridge, but according to his testimony before the Wreck Commissioner, he ran from his post before getting an acknowledgment in order to find his brother.
2. Hoehling, *Last Voyage*, 103.
3. Preston, *Epic Tragedy*, 198.
4. Hickey, *Seven Days*, 182.
5. Howard Cox, *The Global Cigarette* (Oxford University Press, 2000), 100.
6. Preston, *Epic Disaster*, 196.
7. *New York Times*, May 10, 1915.
8. *Plain Dealer* (Cleveland), May 9, 1915, 3.
9. Layton, *Lusitania*, 193.
10. "Most Women Calm in the Face of Death," *New York Times*, May 10, 1915.
11. Hoehling, *Last Voyage*, 104.
12. Morton, *Long Wake*, 103.
13. Morton, *Long Wake*, 105.

14. Hickey, *Seven Days*, 185.

15. *Shipping Casualties (Loss of the Steamship "Lusitania"), Proceedings on a Formal Investigation into Loss of the Steamship "Lusitania"* (London: HMSO, 1915), 41. Hereafter referred to as *"Mersey Proceedings."* Duncan testified that the interval between the two explosions was "about a minute or a couple of minutes." Many other survivors stated that the second explosion took place a split second or a few seconds after the initial report. While not doubting the sincerity of Duncan, the present author believes the two explosions took place seconds apart.

16. *New York Times*, May 10, 1915, 3.

17. "Saw Helpless Scores Swept To Their Doom," *New York Times*, May 9, 1915.

18. "Saw Helpless Scores," *New York Times*, May 9, 1915.

19. Preston, *Epic Disaster*, 203.

20. *New York Times*, May 10, 1915, 3.

21. Pope, ". . . And Then the Water," 99.

22. Hickey, *Seven Days*, 193.

23. Hoehling, *Last Voyage*, 132.

24. Hoehling, *Last Voyage*, 113.

25. Lauriat, *Lusitania's Last Voyage*, 8.

26. *Times* (London), May 10, 1915, 10.

27. *Plain Dealer* (Cleveland), May 9, 1915, 3.

28. *Plain Dealer* (Cleveland), May 10, 1915, 2.

29. Preston, *Epic Tragedy*, 210.

30. *Plain Dealer* (Cleveland), May 10, 1915, 2

31. Bernard, *Cock Sparrow*, 155–157.

32. Preston, *Epic Disaster*, 211–12.

33. *New York Times*, May 10, 1915, 2.

34. Hoehling, *Last Voyage*, 110.

35. "Saw Helpless Scores," *New York Times*, May 9, 1915.

36. "Testimony of William Thomas Turner," day 1, *Mersey Proceedings*.

37. Hickey, *Seven Days*, 195–197.

38. Hickey, *Seven Days*, 196.

39. Snyder, *Military History*, 26–27.

40. Preston, *Epic Tragedy*, 213.

41. Preston, *Epic Tragedy*, 213.

42. *Mersey Proceedings*, 40.

43. "Testimony of William Thomas Turner," day 1, *Mersey Proceedings*.

44. Hoehling, *Last Voyage*, 125.

45. Hoehling, *Last Voyage*, 126.

46. Lauriat, *Lusitania's Last Voyage*, 73.

47. Preston, *Epic Disaster*, 214.

48. Layton, *Lusitania*, 198.

49. Hoehling, *Last Voyage*, 111.
50. Hickey, *Seven Days*, 205.
51. Hoehling, *Last Voyage*, 134–135.
52. Hoehling, *Last Voyage*, 133–134.
53. *New York Times*, May 9, 1915, 2.
54. Hickey, *Seven Days*, 8 207–208.
55. Hoehling, *Last Voyage*, 133.
56. Hoehling, *Last Voyage*, 147.
57. Lauriat, *Lusitania's Last Voyage*, 74–75.
58. Lauriat, *Lusitania's Last Voyage*, 10–11.
59. Lauriat, *Lusitania's Last Voyage*, 78.
60. Lauriat, *Lusitania's Last Voyage*, 76–77.
61. Hoehling, *Last Voyage*, 128.
62. Hoehling, *Last Voyage*, 138.
63. Hoehling, *Last Voyage*, 148.
64. Colin Simpson, "Lusitania," *Life Magazine*, vol. 73, no. 15 (October 13, 1972): 76.
65. *Times* (London), May 10, 1915, 2.
66. *New York Times*, May 10, 1915, 2.
67. *New York Times*, May 10, 1915, 2.
68. Henry James, *Henry James on Culture* (University of Nebraska Press, 1999), 160.
69. *Times* (London), May 10, 1915, 10; "Used His Revolver," *New York Times*, June 2, 1915.
70. *Plain Dealer* (Cleveland), May 9, 1915, 3.
71. Morton, *Long Wake*, 106–107.
72. Preston, *Epic Tragedy*, 228.
73. "Were Saved By Lifebelts," *New York Times*, May 9, 1915.
74. Hoehling, *Last Voyage*, 112–113.
75. Hoehling, *Last Voyage*, 112–113.
76. Pope, ". . . And Then the Water," 100.
77. *Times* (London), May 10, 1915; "Testimony of James Baker," day 3, *Mersey Proceedings*.
78. Hickey, *Seven Days*, 223.
79. Rhondda, "Recalling," 636–637.
80. Hickey, *Seven Days*, 193.
81. Preston, *Epic Disaster*, 226.
82. Hickey, *Seven Days*.
83. Hickey, *Seven Days*.
84. Lauriat, *Lusitania's Last Voyage*, 81–84.
85. *New York Times*, May 10, 1915, 3.
86. Bernard, *Cock Sparrow*, 159–160.
87. Rhondda, "Recalling," 637–638.

88 Colin Simpson, The Lusitania (New York: Ballantine Books, 1974), 148.
89. *National Geographic Video: The Last Voyage of the Lusitania* (1994).

Chapter 9: The Struggle in the Water
1. Lauriat, *Lusitania's Last Voyage*, 86–87.
2. Wesley Frost, *German Submarine Warfare* (New York: D. Appleton and Co., 1918), 199–200.
3. "Most Women Calm in the Face of Death," *New York Times*, May 10, 1915.
4. Lauriat, *Lusitania's Last Voyage*, 21.
5. Lauriat, *Lusitania's Last Voyage*, 86.
6. Preston, *Epic Tragedy*, 244–245.
7. Morton, *Long Wake*, 108–109.
8. *New York Times*, May 10, 1915, 3.
9. Hoehling, *Last Voyage*, 167–168.
10. Pope, ". . . And Then the Water," 100.
11. Pope, ". . . And Then the Water," 100–101.
12. Pope, ". . . And Then the Water," 101.
13. Hickey, *Seven Days*, 244.
14. Preston, *Epic Tragedy*, 247–249.
15. Rhondda, "Recalling," 638.
16. Rhondda, "Recalling," 638.
17. Rhondda, "Recalling," 639.
18. Hoehling, *Last Voyage*, 169–170.
19. *New York Times*, May 20, 1915, 2.
20. Hickey, *Seven Days*, 243.
21. Hoehling, *Last Voyage*, 184.
22. Hoehling, *Last Voyage*, 168–169.
23. Hoehling, *Last Voyage*, 173–174.
24. Preston, *Epic Tragedy*, 256.
25. Preston, *Epic Tragedy*, 245.
26. Preston, *Epic Tragedy*, 251.
27. Hickey, *Seven Days*, 239–241.
28. Hoehling, *Last Voyage*, 168.
29. Preston, *Epic Tragedy*, 249.
30. Preston, *Epic Tragedy*, 254.
31. Lauriat, *Lusitania's Last Voyage*, 87–88.
32. Lauriat, *Lusitania's Last Voyage*, 88.
33. Lauriat, *Lusitania's Last Voyage*, 29–31.
34. "Survivors Describe Acts of Heroism," *New York Times*, May 10, 1915.
35. Preston, *Epic Tragedy*, 251.
36. Hoehling, *Last Voyage*, 185–186.
37. Snyder, *Military History*, 42.
38. Droste, *Documents on the War of the Nations*, 167.

39. Bernard, *Cock Sparrow*, 162–163.

40. Hoehling, *Last Voyage*, 186.

41. Preston, *Epic Tragedy*, 261.

42. "Lusitania Heroine Is Girl of Fourteen," *New York Times*, May 10, 1915.

43. *New York Times*, May 20, 1915, 2.

44. Lauriat, *Lusitania's Last*, 88–89.

45. Pope, ". . . And Then the Water," 102.

46. Preston, *Epic Tragedy*, 265.

47. Morton, *Long Wake*, 109.

48. Frost, *Submarine Warfare*, 187.

49. Frost, *Submarine Warfare*, 188–91.

50. *National Geographic Video: The Last Voyage of the Lusitania* (1994).

51. Frost, *Submarine Warfare*, 229.

52. Frost, *Submarine Warfare*, 207.

Chapter 10: The World Reacts

1. James W. Garner, "Treatment of Enemy Aliens," *The American Journal of International Law*, vol. 12 (1918): 38–41.

2. "Anti-German Riots," *Information Quarterly*, vol. 1 (July 1915).

3. Clive Emsley and Barbara Weinberger, *Policing Western Europe* (Greenwood Publishing Group, 1991), 106.

4. "Anti-German Riots," *Information Quarterly*, vol. 1 (July 1915).

5. Garner, "Enemy Aliens," 38–41.

6. Garner, "Enemy Aliens," 38–41.

7. Clive Emsley and Barbara Weinberger, *Policing Western Europe* (Greenwood Publishing Group, 1991), 106.

8. Garner, "Enemy Aliens," 38–41; Vivian Bickford-Smith, E. Van Heyningen and Nigel Worden, *Cape Town in the Twentieth Century* (New Africa Books, 1999), 57.

9. "Wild Scenes in Cape Town: Many Buildings Set on Fire," *The Argus* (Melbourne), May 15, 1915.

10. *Times* (London), May 13, 1915, 10.

11. Garner, "Enemy Aliens," 38–41.

12. Snyder, *Military History*, 8 51–52.

13. *Times* (London), May 10, 1915, 5.

14. *Times* (London), May 10, 1915, 9.

15. Armin Rappaport, *The British Press and Wilsonian Neutrality* (Stanford University Press, 1951), 34.

16. Snyder, *Military History*, 53.

17. Snyder, *Military History*, 53.

18. Snyder, *Military History*, 53.

19. William Tantum and C.L. Droste, *The Lusitania Case* (London: Patrick Stephens, 1972), 109.

20. Bailey, *Lusitania Disaster*, 181.

21. Bailey, *Lusitania Disaster*, 181.

22. Bailey, *Lusitania Disaster*, 181.

23. Bailey, *Lusitania Disaster*, 181–182.

24. Bailey, *Lusitania Disaster*, 181–182.

25. Bailey, *Lusitania Disaster*, 181–182.

26. Bailey, *Lusitania Disaster*, 183.

27. "Propaganda," *Encyclopedia Britannica*, vol. 32, 12th ed. (New York: The Encyclopedia Britannica Company, Inc., 1922). See page 184 for an informative discussion of German censorship during World War I by Dr. Theodor Wolff, editor of the *Berliner Tageblatt*.

28. "Germany Sends Regret, and 'Sympathy,' But Says the Blame Rests With England," *New York Times*, May 11, 1915.

29. "Foreign Views on the *Lusitania* Tragedy" *Literary Digest*, vol. 50 (May 22, 1915): 1206.

30. Lauriat, *Lusitania's Last Voyage*, 101–113.

31. "Foreign Views," *Literary Digest*, vol. 50, 1206.

32. Martin Gilbert, *The First World War: A Complete History* (New York: Macmillan, 2004), 157–158.

33. Tantum, *Lusitania Case*, 87–90.

34. McMaster, *U.S. in the World War*, 91.

35. George Abel Schreiner, *The Iron Ration* (New York: Harper & Bros., 1918), 313–315.

36. McMaster, *U.S. in the World War*, 90.

37. "Cunard Office Here Besieged for News," *New York Times*, May 8, 1915.

38. "Shocks the President: Washington Deeply Stirred By Disaster and Fears a Crisis," *New York Times*, May 8, 1915.

39. John Milton Cooper, *Pivotal decades: the United States, 1900–1920* (New York: W.W. Norton and Co., 1990), 232.

40. "Lusitania Sunk By Submarine . . . ," *New York Times*, May 8, 1915.

41. Robert Lansing, *War Memoirs* (Indianapolis: Bobbs-Merrill Company, 1935), 27.

42. *Nation*, "The Outlaw German Government," (May 13, 1915): 527.

43. Tantum, *Lusitania Case*, 147–148.

44. *Literary Digest*, "American Response to Germany's Challenge," (May 22, 1915): 1198.

45. "War By Assasination," *New York Times*, May 8, 1915, 14.

46. Tantum, *Lusitania Case*, 143.

47. Tantum, *Lusitania Case*, 146–147.

48. Tantum, *Lusitania Case*, 144–146.

49. *Akron Beacon Journal*, May 10, 1915, 4.

50. "National Indignation and National Self-Control," *The Independent* (May 17, 1915): 267.

51. *Plain Dealer* (Cleveland), May 8, 1915, 8.

52. John Milton Cooper, *The warrior and the priest: Woodrow Wilson and Theodore Roosevelt* (Cambridge: Harvard University Press, 1983), 288.

53. Tantum, *Lusitania Case*, 20–21.

54. United States Must Act At Once on Lusitania, Says Colonel Roosevelt," *New York Times*, May 10, 1915.

55. "Two Ex-Presidents' Views," *New York Times Current History: The European War*, vol. 3. (New York: The New York Times Co., 1917), 446.

56. Tantum, *Lusitania Case*, 113.

57. Senator Thomas's Views," *New York Times*, May 9, 1915.

58. Tantum, *Lusitania Case*, 113.

59. Utterance of National Leaders," *Literary Digest*, (May 22, 1915), 1201–1202.

60. Tantum, *Lusitania Case*, 113.

61. Tantum, *Lusitania Case*, 112.

62. Tantum, *Lusitania Case*, 113.

63. Tantum, *Lusitania Case*, 113.

64. "Utterance," *Literary Digest*, 1202.

65. Tantum, *Lusitania Case*, 113.

66. "Utterance," *Literary Digest*, 1202

67. *New York Times*, May 10, 1915, 6.

68. *New York Times*, May 10, 1915, 6.

69. *New York Times*, May 10, 1915, 6.

70. Tantum, *Lusitania Case*, 69.

71. Tantum, *Lusitania Case*, 69.

72. Tantum, *Lusitania Case*, 63–64.

73. Tantum, *Lusitania Case*, 67.

74. Tantum, *Lusitania Case*, 63–64.

75. Tantum, *Lusitania Case*, 86–87.

76. "Voice of the Clergy on the *Lusitania* Case," *Literary Digest* (May 22, 1915): 1218.

77. "Lusitania's End Arouses Pastors," *New York Times*, May 10, 1915.

78. Tantum, *Lusitania Case*, 92.

79. Tantum, *Lusitania Case*, 10.

80. Tantum, *Lusitania Case*, 7–8.

81. Tantum, *Lusitania Case*, 9–10.

82. Tantum, *Lusitania Case*, 15–18.

83. Tantum, *Lusitania Case*, 101–103.

84. Tantum, *Lusitania Case*, 84–85.

Chapter 11: The Formal Hearings
1. Bailey, *Lusitania Disaster*, 191.

2. Bailey, *Lusitania Disaster*, 191.

3. Tantum, *Lusitania Case*, 180–181.

4. Tantum, *Lusitania Case*, 180–181.

5. Thomas, *Raiders*, 95–97.

6. Tantum, *Lusitania Case*, 181–182.

7. *New York Times*, May 11, 1915, 2.

8. *New York Times*, May 11, 1915, 1.

9. Layton, *Lusitania*, 205.

10. Bailey, *Lusitania Disaster*, 200–201.

11. Bailey, *Lusitania Disaster*, 200.

12. *Mersey Proceedings*, 5.

13. *Mersey Proceedings*, 6

14. *Mersey Proceedings*, 76.

15. *Mersey Proceedings in Camera*, 3.

16. *Mersey Proceedings in Camera*, 5.

17. *Mersey Report*, 4.

18. *Mersey Report*, 5.

19. *Mersey Report*, 8.

20. *Mersey Report*, 6.

21. *Mersey Report*, 9.

22. *Mersey Report*, 9.

23. *New York Times*, November 21, 1915, 1–2.

24. *New York Times*, May 10, 1915, 2.

25. United States District Court (New York: Southern District), Julius Marshall Mayer, *The "Lusitania."* Opinion of court, United States District court, Southern District of New York, Issues 122–133, American Association for International Conciliation, no. 132 (1918), 605.

26. Bailey, *Lusitania Disaster*, 273.

27. United States District Court, *The "Lusitania,"* 611.

28. *In the Matter of the Petition of the Cunard Steamship Co. Ltd. As Owners of the S.S. Lusitania for Limitations of its Liability: Evidence Taken Under the Foreign Tribunal Act 1856 before R.V. Wynne, Esq. the Commissioner in London*, 306–312. Hereafter referred to as *Wynne Hearings*.

29. *Wynne Hearings*, 312–314.

30. *Wynne Hearings*, 314.

31. *Wynne Hearings*, 317.

32. *Wynne Hearings*, 106.

33. *Wynne Hearings*, 108.

34. *Wynne Hearings*, 110–116.

35. *Wynne Hearings*, 115.

36. *Wynne Hearings*, 40–41.

37. *Wynne Hearings*, 40.

38. *Wynne Hearings*, 42–43.

39. "Finds *Lusitania* the Victim of An Act of Piracy," *New York Times*, August

26, 1918.

40. *The Petition of the Cunard Steamship Company Ltd. As Owners of the Steamship Lusitania for Limitation of its Liability Decision*, 2–3. Hereafter referred as *Mayer Decision*.

41. *Mayer Decision*, 3–4.

42. *Mayer Decision*, 3.

43. *Mayer Decision*, 4.

44. *Mayer Decision*, 12.

45. *Mayer Decision*, 35.

46. *Mayer Decision*, 48.

Chapter 12: Charges and Counter-Charges

1. Johann Heinrich Graf von Bernstorff, *My Three Years In America* (New York: Charles Scribner's Sons, 1920), 139.

2. Bernstorff, *My Three Years*, 138.

3. Bailey, *Lusitania Disaster*, 117–118.

4. Winston Churchill, *The World Crisis: 1915*, (New York: Charles Scribner's Sons, 1923), 348.

5. Tantum, *Lusitania Case*, 33–34.

6. Simpson, *Lusitania*, 15.

7. *New York Times*, September 9, 1915, 1.

8. *New York Times*, September 10, 1915, 1.

9. Bailey, *Lusitania Disaster*, 13.

10. Snyder, *Military History*, 72–73.

11. *New York Times*, May 10, 1915, 1.

12. Bailey, *Lusitania Disaster*, 17–19.

13. A.A. Hoehling, letter to *Life*, November 3, 1972, 35.

14. Martin Bown, letter to the author; Dr. Robert Ballard, letter to the author.

15. Colin Simpson, "Lusitania," *Life Magazine*, vol. 73, no. 15 (October 13, 1972): 66.

16. Simpson, *Lusitania*, 99–100.

17. *The Quarterly Militia List of the Dominion of Canada* (Ottawa: Queen's Printer, 1915), 282; Canadian Expeditionary Force, 60th *Infantry Battalion and Reinforcing Draft* (Ottawa: Minister of Militia and Defence, 1915).

18. Bailey, *Lusitania Disaster*, 113–115.

19. Dudley Field Malone, letter to *Nation*, January 3, 1923, 15.

20. James Gerard, *My Four Years in Germany* (New York: Grossett & Dunlap Publishers, 1917), 169.

21. Gerard, *My Four Years*, 167

22. Gerard, *My Four Years*, 166–167. According to Gerard this gentleman beat his chest while uttering these angry words.

23. Gerard, *My Four Years*, 166–167.

24. Malone, letter to *Nation*, 15.

25. Tantum, *Lusitania Case*, 60.

26. Ballard, *Exploring the Lusitania*, 190.

27. Tantum, *Lusitania Case*, 29–30.

28. *National Geographic Video: The Last Voyage of the Lusitania* (1994).

29. Simpson, *Lusitania*, 138.

30. Simpson, *Lusitania*, 119–120.

31. *Secrets of the Unknown: The Lusitania* (Oak Forest, Ill.: MPI Home Video, 1989).

32. *Mersey Proceedings in Camera*, 3.

33. Ballard, *Exploring the Lusitania*, 194.

34. Ballard, *Exploring the Lusitania*, 194.

35. Tantum, *Lusitania Case*, 10.

36. Bertram Hayes, *Hull Down* (New York: Macmillan Co., 1925), 171.

37. Bailey, *Lusitania Disaster*, 142.

38. Patrick O'Sullivan, *The Lusitania: Unravelling the Mysteries* (New York: Sheridan House, 1998), 181.

39. *New York Times*, May 8, 1915, 3.

40. Hickey, *Seven Days*, 221.

Chapter 13: Strict Accountability

1. Tantum, *Lusitania Case*, 115.

2. Gerard, *My Four Years*, 169.

3. Seymour, *Colonel House*, 43.

4. William Jennings Bryan and Mary Bryan, *The Memoirs of William Jennings Bryan* (New York: Haskell House Publishers, Ltd., 1925), 412–413.

5. Bryan, *Memoirs*, 412–413.

6. Bryan, *Memoirs*, 396–397.

7. *New York Times*, May 11, 1915, 1.

8. *New York Times*, May 12, 1915.

9. Henry Steele Commager, *Documents of American History* (New York: Appleton-Century-Crofts, 1961), 103.

10. Commager, *Documents*, 103.

11. Commager, *Documents*, 103.

12. Commager, *Documents*, 103.

13. Commager, *Documents*, 103.

14. Commager, *Documents*, 103.

15. Commager, *Documents*, 103.

16. Commager, *Documents*, 103.

17. Commager, *Documents*, 105.

18. Woodrow Wilson, *President Wilson's State Papers and Addresses*, (New York: George H. Doran Co. 1917) 239–243.

19. Bryan, *Memoirs*, 380.

20. Bryan, *Memoirs*, 380.

21. Bryan, *Memoirs*, 378.
22. Bryan, *Memoirs*, 404.
23. *New York Times*, June 1, 1915.
24. *New York Times*, June 1, 1915.
25. *New York Times*, June 1, 1915.
26. *New York Times*, June 1, 1915.
27. *New York Times*, June 1, 1915.
28. *New York Times*, June 1, 1915.
29. David F. Houston, *Eight Years with Wilson's Cabinet*, vol. 1 (Garden City, N.Y.: Doubleday, Page and Co., 1936) 136. Houston served as Wilson's secretary of Agriculture.
30. "London Scoffs at Von Jagow's Reply," *New York Times*, June 1, 1915.
31. Spencer C. Tucker and Priscilla Mary Roberts, editors, *World War One* (ABC-CLIO, 2005), 380.
32. Arthur S. Link, *Wilson: the Struggle for Neutrality, 1914–1915* (Princeton: Princeton University Press, 1960), 422.
33. John Milton Cooper, *Woodrow Wilson: A Biography* (New York: Random House, 2009), 292.
34. Link, *Wilson*, 423.
35. Cooper, *Woodrow Wilson*, 293.
36. John Milton Cooper, *Reconsidering Woodrow Wilson* (Woodrow Wilson Center Press & Johns Hopkins University Press, 2008), 14.
37. Bailey, *Lusitania Disaster*, 259–260.
38. Seymour, *Colonel House*, 2–3.
39. McMaster, *United States in the World War*, 117.
40. Gerard, *My Four Years*, 176.
41. Bailey, *Lusitania Disaster*, 263–265.

Chapter 14: Towards War
1. "Earlier Effort to Wreck Arabic," *New York Times*, August 20, 1915.
2. *Akron Beacon Journal*, August 19, 1915.
3. "Theater People Numerous on Ship," *New York Times*, August 20, 1915.
4. *Akron Beacon Journal*, August 19, 1915.
5. *Akron Beacon Journal*, August 19, 1915.
6. *New York Times*, August 20, 1915.
7. William Finch, "The Captain's Story of Going Down With the *Arabic*," *Current Opinion* (October, 1915): 287.
8. *New York Times*, August 21, 1915.
9. Finch, "The Captain's Story," 288; see also Finch's sworn testimony in American Society of International Law, "Part IV, Submarine Warfare," *American Journal of International Law*, Proceedings, no. 64–67, 208.
10. *New York Times*, August 20, 1915.
11. *Times* (London), August 21, 1915.

12. Alfred Still, "The Story of the *Arabic* By One of the Survivors," *Outlook* (September 15, 1915): 123.

13. *New York Times*, August 21, 1915, 2.

14. Finch, "The Captain's Story," 288.

15. *New York Times*, August 20, 1915, 1.

16. "Earlier Effort to Wreck Arabic," *New York Times*, August 20, 1915.

17. *New York Times*, August 21, 1915, 1.

18. *Akron Beacon Journal*, August 20, 1915, 1.

19. *New York Times*, August 20, 1915, 1–2.

20. *New York Times*, August 20, 1915, 1–2.

21. "Tells of Cruisers in Rescue Work," *New York Times*, August 21, 1915.

22. "Bruguieres Swept Apart By Wreckage," *New York Times*, August 21, 1915.

23. "Captain Finch Tells of Narrow Escape," *New York Times*, August 21, 1915.

24. "Captain Finch Tells of Narrow Escape," *New York Times*, August 21, 1915.

25. "The Cost and the Loss," *New York Times*, August 24, 1915.

26. *Plain Dealer* (Cleveland), August 20, 1915, 8.

27. Lansing, *War Memoirs*, 43.

28. Burton J. Hendrick, *The Life and Letters of Walter H. Paige* (Garden City, New York: Doubleday Page and Company, 1922), 27.

29. Gerard, *My Four Years*, 177.

30. "The *Arabic* Horror," *The Outlook*, vol. 111, (Outlook Co., 1915), 24.

31. Cooper, *Woodrow Wilson*, 300.

32. Lansing, *War Memoirs*, 224.

33. Commager, *Documents of American History*, 112.

34. Lansing, *War Memoirs*, 224.

35. Barbara Tuckman, *The Zimmerman Telegram* (New York: Viking Press, 1958), 146.

36. Tuckman, *Zimmerman Telegram*, 185.

37. *Plain Dealer* (Cleveland), March 2, 1917, 8.

38. Commager, *Documents of American History*, 128–132.

39. Churchill, *World Crisis*, 349.

Chapter 15: Afterward

1. "Captain Turner Last to Leave *Ivernia*," *New York Times*, January 28, 1917.

2. "Britain Decorates Turner," *New York Times*, January 12, 1918; "*Lusitania's* Captain Quits," *New York Times*, November 11, 1919.

3. "Captain Turner Dies," *New York Times*, June 24, 1933.

4. Bailey, *Lusitania Disaster*, 160–161.

5. Edwyn Gray, *The Killing Time* (New York: Charles Scribner's Sons, 1972), 261.

6. Robert M. Grant, *U Boats Destroyed: The Effect of Anti-Submarine Warfare 1914–1918* (London: G.P. Putnam's Sons, 1964), 51.

7. Gray, *Killing Time*, 268.

8. John D. Craig, "Deep-Sea Diving Has By-Products," *The Rotarian* (March 1938): 18–21.

9. Kenneth Macleish, "Was There A Gun?" *Sports Illustrated* (December 24, 1962): 45.

10. O'Sullivan, *Unravelling the Mysteries*, 12.

11. Macleish, "Was There A Gun?" 45.

12. Macleish, "Was There A Gun?" 45.

13. Macleish, "Was There A Gun?" 45.

14. Macleish, "Was There A Gun?" 45.

15. Macleish, "Was There A Gun?" 46–47.

16. Preston, *Epic Tragedy*, 375.

17. Ballard, *Exploring the Lusitania*, 14–15.

18. Lord, *Night Lives On*, 238–239.

19. Ballard, *Exploring the Lusitania*, 10.

20. Ballard, *Exploring the Lusitania*, 14.

21. Ballard, *Exploring the Lusitania*, 144.

22. Robert Ballard, "Riddle of the *Lusitania*," *National Geographic,* vol. 185 (April, 1994): 79.

23. Ballard, *Exploring the Lusitania*, 148.

24. Ballard, "Riddle of the *Lusitania*," 79.

25. Ballard, *Exploring the Lusitania*, 148.

26. Ballard, *Exploring the Lusitania*, 148.

27. Ballard, *Exploring the Lusitania*, 148.

28. Ballard, *Exploring the Lusitania*, 148.

29. Ballard, *Exploring the Lusitania*, 152.

30. Ballard, *Exploring the Lusitania*, 194.

31. A coal dust explosion had not been ruled out by the German Navy or a 1915 study conducted by a torpedo laboratory in Kiel. See Preston, *Epic Tragedy*, 313, 376.

32. M.G. Wood, D.I. Smith and M.R. Hayns, "Sinking of the *Lusitania*: Reviewing the Evidence," *Science & Justice*, vol. 43, no. 3 (2002): 181.

33. Ballard, *Exploring the Lusitania*, 195.

34. O'Sullivan, *Unravelling the Mysteries*, 135–137.

SELECTED SOURCES

American Heritage, "...And Then the Water Closed Over Me," Theodate Pope's letter to her mother, April, 1975, pp 98–101.

Bailey, Thomas, "The sinking of the *Lusitania*," *American Historical Review*. October, 1935, pp 54–73.

Bailey, Thomas, and Ryan, Paul, *Hitler vs. Roosevelt* (The Free Press, New York, 1979).

Bailey, Thomas, and Ryan, Paul, *The Lusitania Disaster* (The Free Press, New York, 1975).

Baker, Ray, *Woodrow Wilson Life and Letters* (Double Day, Doran & Co. Garden City, 1935).

Ballard, Robert, and Dunmore, Spencer, *Exploring the Lusitania* (Madison Press Books, Toronto, 1995).

Ballard, Robert, letter to the author.

Ballard, Robert, "Riddle of the *Lusitania*," *National Geographic*, April 1994, pp 68–85.

Barrnett, Correlli, *The Swordbearers* (William Morrow and Company, New York, 1964).

Berghahn, V.R., *Germany and the Approach of War 1914* (St. Martins' Press, New York, 1973).

Bernard, Oliver, *Cocksparrow* (Jonathan Cap, London, 1936).

Bernstorff, Count J. von, *Memoirs* (Random House, New York, 1936).

——————-*My Three Years in America* (Charles Scribner's Sons, New York, 1920).

Bowen, Martin, letter to the author.

235

Brinnin, John Malcolm, *The Sway of the Grand Saloon* (Delacorte Press, New York, 1972).

Bryan, William Jennings, and Bryan, Mary, *The Memoirs of William Jennings Bryan* (Haskel House Publishers, Ltd., 1925).

Butler, Daniel Allen, *Age of Cunard*, ProStar Publications, 2004).

Canadian Expeditionary Force 60th Battalion (And Reinforcing Draft)

Champney, F. *Art and Glory: The Story of Elbert Hubbard* (Kent State University Press, Kent, 1983).

Chicago Tribune.

Chidsey, Donald, *The Day They Sank the Lusitania* (Award Books, New York, 1967).

Churchill, Winston, *The World Crisis* (Charles Scribner's Sons, New York, 1923, 6 Vol.).

Commage, Henry Steele, *Documents of American History* (Appleton-Century-Crafts, New York, 1967).

Corbett, Julian S., *Naval Operations* (Longman Green Co., London, 1920).

Current Opinion, "Are We On the Verge of a War With Germany," June 1925, pp 379–385.

Dorste, C.L. And Tantum, William, *The Lusitania Case* (Patrick Stephenson, London, 1972).

Finch, William, "The Captain's Story of Going Down With the *Arabic*," *Current Opinion*, October, 1915, pp 287–288.

Francis, Timothy L., *Submarines: Leviathons of the Deep* (Metrobooks, New York, 1997).

Gay, Peter, and Webb., R. K., *Modern Europe Since 1815* (Harper & Row Publishers, New York, 1973).

George, James, *History of Warships From Ancient Times to the Twenty-first Century* (Naval Institute Press, Annapolis, 1998).

Gerard, James, *My Four Years In Germany* (Grosset & Dunlap Publishers, New York, 1917).

Grant, Kay, *Samuel Cunard: Pioneer of the Atlantic Steamship* (Abeland-Schuman, London, 1967).

Grant, Robert, *U Boats Destroyed: The Effect of Anti-Submarine Warfare 1914–1918* (Putnam, London, 1964)

Gray, Edwyn, *The Killing Time* (Charles Scribner's Sons, New York, 1972).

Handin, Oscar, "A Liner, A U-boat, and History," *American Heritage*, June, 1955, pp 40–45.

Harper's Weekly, "Across the Atlantic in 5 Days 54 Minutes," September 28, 1907, p. 14–17.

Hayes, Bertam, *Hull Down* (McMillan Co., New York, 1925).

Hayes, Grace, *World War I: A Compact History* (Hawthorn Books Inc., New York, 1972).

Hendrick, Burton J., *The Life and Letters of Walter H. Paige* (Doubleday and Company, Garden City, 1922).

Hickey, Des, and Smith, Gus, *Seven Days to Disaster* (G.P. Putman's Sons, New York, 1981).

Hoehling, A.A. and Hoehling, Mary, *The Last Voyage of the Lusitania* (Henry Holt and Company, New York, 1956).

Hoehling, A.A., letter to *Life*, November 3, 1972, p. 35.

Houston, David F., *Eight Years With Wilson's Cabinet*, 2 Volumes (Double-day, Page, and Company, Garden City, 1926).

In the Matter of the Petition of the Cunard Steamship Co., Ltd. As Owners of the S.S. Lusitania for Limitation of Liability: Evidence Taken Under the Foreign Tribunal Act 1856 Before R.V. Wayne Esq. The Commissioner in London.

The Independent, "National Indignation and National Self-Control", May 17, 1915, p. 267.

Keegan, John, *August 1914 Opening Moves* (Ballentine's Illustrated History of the Violent Century, New York, 1971).

Kenworthy, Joseph, *The Freedom of the Seas* (Horace Livicht, New York, 1929).

La Fore, Lawrence, *The Long Fuse* (J.B. Lippincott Company, New York, 1971).

Lansing, Robert, *War Memoirs* (The Bobbs-Merrill Company, New York, 1936).

The Last Voyage of the Lusitania (National Geographic video, 1994).

Lauriat, Charles, *The Lusitania's Last Voyage* (Houghton Mifflin Company, Boston, 1915).

Link, Arthur S., *Wilson: The Struggle for Neutrality, 1914–1915* (Princeton University Press, Princeton, 1960).

Literary Digest

"The Blow to the Arts and Letters," May 22, 1915, pp 1214–1217.

"Foreign Views on the *Lusitania* Tragedy," May 22, 1915, pp 1201–1202.

"Utterance of National Leaders," May 2, 1915, pp 1218–1219.

"Voice of the Clergy on the *Lusitania* Case," May 22, 1915, pp 1218–1219.

Lord, Walter, *The Night Lives On* (William Morrow and Company, Inc. New York, 1986).

MacLeish, Kenneth, "Was There a Gun?" *Sports Illustrated*, December 24, 1962.

Maddocks, Melvin, *The Great Liners* (Time-Life Books, Inc., Alexandria, 1978).

Malone, Dudley Field, letter to *Nation*, January 3, 1923, pp 15–16.

Maxtone-Graham, John, *The Only Way to Cross* (The McMillain Company, New York, 1972).

Morton, Leslie, *The Long Wake* (Outledge & Kegan Paul, London, 1968).

Nation, "Outlaw German Government," May 13, 1915, p 527.

New York Times

O'Sullivan, Patrick, *The Lusitania: Unravelling the Mysteries* (Sheridan House, New York, 1998).

The Petition of the Cunard Steamship Company, Ltd. As Owners of the Steamship Lusitania for Limitation of the Liability Decision.

The Plain Dealer (Cleveland)

Preston, Diana, *Lusitania: An Epic Tragedy* (Walker and Company, New York, 2002).

The Quarterly Militia List of the Dominion of Canada/Corrected to 1st of April, 1915.

Rhondda, Viscountess (Lady Mackworth), "Recalling a Tragedy," *Living Age*, June 16, 1923, pp 635–640.

Scientific American

"Coal Consumption on the *Lusitania*," May 9, 1908, p 326.

"The Four Day Boat," October 19, 1907, p 270.

"The New Turbine Liner *Lusitania*, September 14, 1907, pp 181–190.

"Steam Trials of the *Lusitania*, August 24, 1907, p 130.

"The 25 Knot Turbine Liner *Lusitania*, August 10, 1907, p 96.

"Unsolved Problems in the Design and Propulsion of Ships II," August, 1907, Supplimentary, pp 122–124.

Secrets of the Unknown: The Sinking of the Lusitania (Video, 1987).

Seymour, Charles, *The Intimate Papers of Colonel House*, 4 Volumes (Houghton Mifflin Company, Boston and New York, 1926).

Shipping Casualties (Loss of the Steamship "Lusitania"), Proceeding in Camera at the Formal Investigation into the Circumstances Attending the Foundering of the British Steamship "Lusitania," Command 381, London HMSO, 1915

Shipping Casualties (Loss of the Steamship "Lusitania"), Proceeding on a Formal Investigation into Loss of Steamship "Lusitania," London, HMSO, 1915.

Shipping Casualties (Loss of Steamship "Lusitania") Report of the Formal Investigation into the Circumstances Attending The Foundering of the British Steamship "Lusitania," HMSO, 1915.

Simpson, Colin, "A Great Liner with Too Many Secrets," *Life*, October 13, 1972, pp 58-80.

Simpson, Colin, *The Lusitania* (Ballantine Books, New York, 1972).

Snyder, Louis C., *The Military History of the Lusitania* (Franklin Watts Inc., New York, 1965).

Still, Alfred, "The Story of the *Arabic* By One of the Survivors," *Outlook*, September 15, 1915, pp 122–124

Thomas, Lowell, *Raiders of the Deep* (Naval Institute Press, Annapolis, 1928).

Times (London).

Tuckman, Barbara, *The Zimmerman Telegram* (The Viking Press, New York, 1958).

Villard, D.G., "The True Story of the *Lusitania*," *American Mercury*, May, 1935, pp 41–51.

Wall, Robert, *Ocean Liners* (E.P. Dutton, New York, 1977).

Warren, Mark P., *Cunard Turbine-Driven Quadruple Screw Atlantic Liner "Lusitania"* (Patrick Stephens, Wellborough, 1986).